COMMUNICATING
HEALTH AND
ILLNESS

COMMUNICATING HEALTH AND ILLNESS

RICHARD GWYN

SAGE Publications
London • Thousand Oaks • New Delhi

SAGE Publications Ltd
6 Bonhill Street
London EC2A 4PU

SAGE Publications Inc
2455 Teller Road
Thousand Oaks, California 91320

SAGE Publications India Pvt Ltd
32, M-Block Market
Greater Kailash - I
New Delhi 110 048

British Library Cataloguing in Publication data

A catalogue record for this book is available from
the British Library

ISBN 0 7619 6474 6
ISBN 0 7619 6475 4 (pbk)

Library of Congress Control Number available

Typeset by SIVA Math Setters, Chennai, India
Printed and bound in Great Britain by Athenaeum Press,
Gateshead

For my parents

Contents

Acknowledgements

This book has evolved through the first three years of teaching a module in Health Communication to final year undergraduates at Cardiff University. The responses and positive feedback from students has been a source of encouragement, while any difficulties they might have had with some of the material has likewise been of benefit in the development of this book. They have, by and large, been a pleasure to teach.

Several sections of the book have been previously published elsewhere and I would like to acknowledge the publishers of *Social Science and Medicine, Health, and Narrative Inquiry* and two edited books: *Researching and Applying Metaphor* (Cambridge University Press) and *Narrative Based Medicine* (BMJ Books) for material reproduced in chapters 3, 4, 5 and 6.

Grateful acknowledgement is also made to copyright holders for the reproduction of material from *The Western Mail, The Daily Mirror, The Daily Mail, George* magazine and the BBC. Every effort has been made to obtain permission from copyright holders: if there are any errors or omissions please inform the publisher, so that subsequent editions can be adjusted accordingly.

Thanks are also due to Julia Hall, who first asked me to write the book, and to Seth Edwards and Rosie Maynard at Sage for their advice, encouragement, and professionalism.

The many people, either themselves ill or else who speak of the illness or loss of loved ones within these pages deserve special particular acknowledgement. I hope that I have not done a disservice to their words and emotions, and thank them for taking part in the work that has made this book possible.

I am particularly grateful to colleagues and friends at Cardiff University for reading early versions, or parts of, the book, notably Justine Coupland, Adam Jaworski, Srikant Sarangi, Nik Coupland and Joanna Thornborrow. I also offer thanks to Derek Edwards, Deborah Lupton and unknown readers for helpful comments about my work. Especial acknowledgement and thanks are due to Glyn Elwyn, medical colleague and co-author on two of the papers from which I have drawn in this book.

Finally, as ever, my thanks to Rose, Sioned and Rhiannon, for putting up with it all.

Richard Gwyn
Cardiff

KEY TO TRANSCRIPTION SYMBOLS

[simultaneous or overlapping utterances

=   contiguous utterances

[   ]   1) unclear utterances (estimation of utterance given inside brackets): if no words can be discerned, estimated number of syllables is given; if number of syllables cannot be discerned, the word 'unclear' is written inside the brackets
2) descriptions of non-verbal activity or noise e.g. [laughing]

(.)   pause of less than one second

(3.0)   length of longer pauses (in seconds)

?   functional question

!   animated utterance

italics   emphasis

'   '   in longer narrative passages involving reported speech inverted commas are occasionally used to establish provenance of an utterance

Introduction

This book sets out to introduce a range of themes in the field of health communication that are linked by a common approach, which gives centrality to the notion of 'discourse'. Discourse is used here both in its broad sense, as a way of thinking about and representing some aspect of reality (as in 'discourse of war', 'discourse of medicine or 'discourse of globalization'), as well as the specific manner in which language, texts and images are produced and reproduced in order to achieve particular communicative or ideological ends.

The field to which this study applies falls within what has become known as 'health communication'. Working on the premise that talk is a form of activity, and that spoken, written and visual discourses help constitute the world in which we describe ourselves and others, I have decided to focus on a half-dozen themes that are fundamental to an understanding of communication about health and illness. And while I am not concerned in this instance with examining specific health promotion schemes and strategies, nor in delivering a textbook in communication skills for health care providers, readers whose major concern is in either of those fields may well find material of interest within these pages.

Readers with a basic grounding in discourse analysis and sociolinguistics will, it is granted, find their way into this book more easily than others, but I have not felt confined to a 'sociolinguistic' approach (perhaps a sociolinguistic approach need not in any case be 'confining'), and have elected to follow as fully interdisciplinary an approach as I was competent to undertake. There are, in the topics tackled in the book, obvious historical connections with the sociology of health and illness, with social and cultural anthropology and with social psychology (as well as with 'discursive psychology') and a further predisposition towards the mytho-poetic dimensions of narrative analysis encountered in semiotic and cultural theory.

Although my principal methodological tools are discourse and narrative analysis, I have not considered methodology as a 'thing apart'. I am critical of the social scientific ritual of delimiting 'methodology' as some kind of sacrosanct orthodoxy – like its 'models', methodology too is a tool, not an end in itself. Method, it seems to me, should be implicit in acts of description and analysis rather than cocooned within its own ideological space.

Studying individuals' accounts of illness is a major preoccupation of this study, but is not carried out with the intention of establishing rigid explanatory models of illness. As Potter and Wetherell have observed, a discourse analytic approach to data prefers to avoid cognitive reductionism, or treatments of language deriving from explanatory models or other 'cognitive furniture such as attitudes, beliefs, goals or wants' (1987: 157). Although we must be aware that lay models of illness causation exist, there is a danger in conceiving of them as necessarily structured or delineated in the same way as, say, biomedical models are (Helman, 1984: 86–91). Nor is it my intention to impose consensus in the use of discursive repertoires to show that Group A will always employ a certain account of illness and Group B another. Interpretation along the lines of a metanarrative is not the concern of the present book, any more than the imposition of any inflexible model of representation. On the contrary, it might be said that the judicious and illustrative use and abandonment of all pertinent models is a feature of the approach I have taken; and I am inclined to agree with Jameson, who suggests that in academic discourse we 'steal the pieces that interest or fascinate us and ... carry off our fragmentary booty to our intellectual caves' (1987: viii). Eisenberg, who formulated the distinction between *disease* and *illness* as follows: 'Patients suffer "illnesses"; doctors diagnose and treat "diseases"' (1977: 9), warns of the dangers in adhering to models:

> Models are ways of constructing reality, ways of imposing meaning on the chaos of the phenomenal world ... [O]nce in place, models act to generate their own verification by excluding phenomena outside the frame of reference the user employs. Models are indispensable but hazardous because they can be mistaken for reality itself rather than as but one way of organizing that reality. (Eisenberg, 1977: 18)

A book, moreover, is not simply a manual that attempts to attract and preserve essential features of a topic of study: a book is a process, both for the author and for the reader. Within this process it is feasible, in fact it has become essential, in the cultural climate of postmodernity, to reflect upon the role of the author. Is a completed book necessarily a clear-cut and neatly ordered exposition of facts and perspectives, or does it reflect the ardours of composition by retaining elements of self-reflexivity and uncertainty once deemed unsuitable for academic discourse? Clifford, has, I think, answered this question, by referring to his own work as 'manifestly unfinished'. He also indicates that a degree of self-location is 'possible and valuable, particularly when it points beyond the individual toward ongoing webs of relationship' (1997: 12). This might well involve a more partisan engagement with the 'data', and a reflexivity on the details of its 'collection' (a metaphor that recalls the activities of lepidopterists) rather than the assumption that the 'facts' have simply been plucked like fruit, straight from nature (Paget, 1995). One of the benefits (or faults, if you happen to be a logical positivist) of this approach should be to breathe a certain immediacy into the text, to avoid the torpor, in Geertz's phrase, of the 'author-evacuated text' (1988: 141). Essentially a book, even an academic book, should be a source of enjoyment as well as of instruction. While there is much to admire in scholarly discourse, including the parsimonious adherence to empiricism that characterizes much work in the social sciences, it is worth reminding ourselves, as Clifford does, that academic writers are merely working within an evolving set of conventions. To what extent these conventions remain unquestioned, or at least normative (and thereby risk becoming stagnant and unproductive) must, to a large degree, define (or restrict) the vitality and resourcefulness of new and emerging areas of study. There should perhaps be a greater willingness, in Clifford's phrase, to make 'visible the borders of academic work' (1997: 12).

A bias towards narrative characterizes much of this book. Narrative, as a theme, makes an appearance in Chapter 2 although from the list of contents it is not scheduled until Chapter 6. It raises its head again in Chapters 4 and 5. This is because it has become apparent to me that even within the discourse of medicine, narrative is not simply an expository or descriptive facility, but the most convincing resource with which to make rhetorical acts. The book purports to be about 'discourse' (and therefore rhetoric) but in fact ends up as being very much about narrative also, perhaps because of a subjective inclination towards storytelling, but also because, as Bruner (1990) has argued, it seems that human languages have an in-built programming that disposes them towards narrativization, perhaps even influencing the way that human grammars have evolved. Illustrating theoretical issues with stories from the world of lived experience is a well established pedagogical custom, and the ways in which both patients and health care professionals use narrative to elucidate or illustrate goes far beyond the 'merely' communicative purpose of language as an exchange of functional messages. In fact Halliday's famous distinction between the 'interpersonal' and the 'ideational' functions of language (1978: 2) as a means, respectively, of both action and of reflection, seems to find its synthesis in narrative, which is, to pursue the analogy with anthropology, both 'good to eat' and 'good to think with'.

In Chapter 1, attention is paid to culturally validated notions of the healthy body and of 'being ill', ideas which since the 1970s have been considerably influenced by the work of Foucault, an influence so pervasive, suggests Frank (1996: 59), 'as to render specific citation superfluous'. The 'medicalization' of illness experience has caused a change in Western societies whereby people tend to consider almost every aspect of their health and their bodies as being subject to the 'medical gaze'. What seem to be recent innovations, such as the World Health Organization's criteria for good health, have been reformulated in the public consciousness as 'perfect health', an ideal towards which millions strive through undertaking 'body projects', raising expectations of the body, its potential and its powers of recuperation beyond all reasonable bounds. A summary of the concept of 'discourse' and of distinct approaches to its analysis closes this chapter.

Chapter 2 reviews the findings of a range of sociological studies into lay representations of health and illness. While broadly subscribing to a social constructionist approach to the subject, the modernist texts provided by the medical sociology of the 1970s and 1980s are seen as promoting a version of participants' views as though they were finished products representing the 'health beliefs' of a delineated category of people. Wider concerns of 'doing ethnography' and 'writing' appear to be taken as 'given', through adherence to a particular style of 'doing research'. Postmodern texts on lay perspectives, by contrast, are seen to focus more on individuals as subtle weavers of stories who are caught up in the multiple realities of their lives, and concerned with problems of meaning in a precariously reified universe. The chapter concludes with an extract from an ethnographic interview with an elderly couple in which attributions are made regarding the development of an incident of illness, as well as the role of 'the doctor', this last issue being the topic of Chapter 3. Here I discuss the kind of talk that goes on in the clinic between patients and health professionals; how power is negotiated, how asymmetry is established and sustained, and how decisions are (or can be) made. This is the most substantial chapter in terms of length, reflecting the centrality of the carer–patient (and predominantly the doctor–patient) relationship in published research on medical discourse.

Chapter 4 continues with the theme of the doctor's role in society, but looks at it through the camera lens and in newsprint, examining the way that the health professional is imaged and represented in Western culture. Using examples from cinema, TV 'docusoap' and radio show, we will consider both the role of doctor and other aspects of medical discourse in the media, especially the 'health scares' portrayed in the early years of HIV/AIDS in Australia and Britain, concluding with a study of a particular health scare in 1990s Britain – the 'outbreak' of 'killer bug' disease.

Chapters 5 and 6 are closely linked, Chapter 5 considering the metaphoric nature of talk about illness, both from a medical and a lay position, especially with regard to metaphors of embodiment. Here the classic metaphors of war and invasion are seen to dominate almost all writings on metaphor in a medical context, though there has recently arisen a culture of resistance to this metaphor, notably in the wake of Susan Sontag's well-known studies (1991). I will examine ways too in which a broader treatment of metaphor invites the study of non-linguistic metaphor, especially of a certain kind of 'active' metaphor or symbolic action, which can provide a redemptive quality in an individual's quest for health and a better quality of life. Finally, in Chapter 6, I turn to an area which has been implicit in the entire study, that of narrative reconstruction and the narrative bias of medical discourse, this last topic resonating with recent work in the field of 'narrative based medicine'. It will by now have become apparent that the conceptualization of 'discourse' preferred in this book favours a narrative perspective, centred on an ethnographic approach to language and culture.

While on the one hand, the book deals with an unfinished series of encounters between people, on the other it proposes that there are certain fundamental patterns which we can observe and usefully analyse in applying a knowledge of interactive strategies, narrative and metaphor, and the ways in which representations about health and illness are made throughout society. While a lot is being said (and has already been said) about the 'medicalization' of contemporary society, very little, it seems, is actually being done to limit or resist the rhetorical sway of multinational pharmaceutical companies who plunder and then exclusively patent the herbal medicines of indigenous peoples, or the extension of the 'medical gaze' into areas of behavioural, social and familial life in quite unprecedented ways, creating new pathologies and epidemics. Although this book will not change any of these things, it aims at least to provoke interest and concern in students from a variety of disciplines; and to encourage them to respond critically to the adoption and pursuit of normative discourses on health, illness and the practice of medicine.

The Body, Disease and Discourse   1

Illness is constructed, reproduced and perpetuated through language. We get to know about our own illnesses through the language of doctors and nurses, friends and relatives, and we often recycle the words picked up from our consultations in the doctor's surgery into conversation, sprinkling our stories of sickness with epithets that give the impression of a grander knowledge of medical science. When we open the newspapers or switch on the television or radio, we encounter an increasing variety of articles and programmes offering information, advice and warnings about every conceivable dimension of health and care of the body.

This concern with health issues is not new, but has never before been so omnipresent. We are saturated with health issues. We live in an era obsessed with health and fitness, in which 'perfect health' is seen to have its corollary in 'total fitness'. Advertisements, television programmes and films discharge a constant stream of images and models upon which we style our bodies and appearance. Advertising, for the main part, still relies on the human body to sell products. Beautiful, flawless models hawk healthy produce from billboards and TV screens. In these advertisements, a perfectly healthy body implies a kind of immortality in the moment, a defiance of death (cf. Bauman, 1992) or else flight from the insufferable workaday present into a state of perpetual happiness (or its correlative in 'real' time, the holiday). The current era, it has been said, is dedicated to the *body project* (Turner, 1984; Featherstone, 1991; Lasch, 1991; Shilling, 1993) in which millions of people throughout the affluent world strive to acquire toned muscles, to discard unwanted fat, to style their bodies just as they might style their hair; with new breasts, new buttocks, new noses – and all this external remodelling is quite apart from the steady and persistent growth in the market for internal organs of every kind. An illusory ideal of 'perfect health' is more and more being regarded as the norm, the undisputed prerogative of an unmarked version of humanity; and any hint of waywardness or defect, variance from established norms of weight or shape, deformity or disfiguration, is perceived as a type of deviance, indicating a marked and a lesser humanity.

Alongside the proliferation of discourses of health and illness are new terms which a generation ago either did not exist or else were entirely unknown to most people, such as PMT, ME and HIV, not to mention ADHD (Attention Deficit Hyperactive Disorder) and PTS (post-traumatic stress), terms which are now normal currency. These and other acronyms reflect a sense of the ever-growing territory claimed by the medicalization of language. For some earlier writers, such as the medical anthropologist Friedson (1970), a consequence of this ever-encroaching medicalization are that socioculturally induced complaints and syndromes were being wrongly redefined as 'illness'. This is an idea pursued at greater length by Showalter (1997), who argues that certain contemporary afflictions, ranging from chronic fatigue syndrome to alien abduction, are specific manifestations of a widespread cultural hysteria.

Medical terms are scattered throughout our conversations, and a much wider knowledge of terminology is discernible in everyday discourse than existed even a generation ago. One of the effects of this medicalization of language is to legitimize positions on topics about which even so-called experts actually know very little. In addition, there often appears to be little in the familiar world which is not either directly damaging to health or else suspected of containing carcinogenic agents. Recent debates in Britain on issues surrounding BSE-infected cattle and GMO (Genetically Modified Organisms) in food have emphasized most clearly the paradox that basic 'life-giving' foodstuffs such as bread might contain the ingredients for long term, and possibly irreversible, damage to human health.

In this chapter, then, I will consider the impact of medicalization on contemporary lives by examining various discourses on the body and embodiment, before moving on to discuss accounts dealing with the essentially external or 'exogenous' provenance of disease. It will be seen that along with the 'reification of the body', there has arisen a concomitant reification of disease and of medicine. The chapter concludes by considering the term 'discourse', its permutations in academic texts, and the importance to the current study of a discourse analytic perspective.

THE QUEST FOR TOTAL HEALTH

Health is by no means the 'natural' state of human beings, even if it is the preferred one. What might be considered a reasonable expectation – relative freedom from disease – is quite a different thing from the kind of 'total health' on offer from the thousands of outlets now selling ways to keep fit and stay young-looking. The World Health Organization's definition of health as unimpaired mental, physical and social well-being is little more than a dream to most of the human race. The more illnesses that are 'wiped out', the more versatile and virulent their successors. The costs of running the medical machine, with its emphasis on sophisticated equipment and ever more refined means of electronic surveillance, are astronomical. The metaphorical conceptualization of 'the war against disease' (Guggenbühl-Craig, 1980) is, in the eyes of the medical establishment, a perfectly appropriate one. For the researchers and medical practitioners involved the 'war' is a reality:

During the last century and a half, the vanguard of medical science has experienced one triumph after another. Disease, its fiendish adversary, twists and turns, writhing under the blows of the healers' swords, attempting to avoid its total eradication. On the other hand, doctors are busier than ever. Medical costs are rocketing ... Each new technique, each new machine demands more money: weapons are expensive, and wars are costly undertakings: 'What does that matter?' we ask. 'The important thing is to win!' We wait with bated breath for the long-promised victory. (Guggenbühl-Craig, 1980: 7)

Since the early 1970s there has been a growing awareness of, and opposition to this medicalization of society, reflected in the passage I have just quoted. Critics such as Zola (1972) described what they perceived to be a cultural crisis in modern medicine, of health care systems which were expensive, over-bureaucratized, inequitable and ineffective (Lupton, 1994a: 8). Illich (1976) argued that modern medicine was both physically and socially harmful due to the impact of professional control, leading to dependence upon medicine as a panacea, obscuring the political conditions which caused ill health and removing autonomy from individuals to control their own health.

In the dialectics of contemporary public health, much is made of the 'responsibility' of the individual for his or her health, but what does this actually mean? According to Lupton (1994a: 32), disciplinary power is maintained through a range of screening procedures, fitness tests and through health education campaigns which set out to invoke guilt and anxiety in those who do not follow a prescribed behaviour. The rhetoric of public health obscures its disciplinary agenda since health is presented as a universal right and a fundamental good. Campaigns aimed at encouraging individuals to change their behaviour, and to minimize risk taking, are therefore regarded as wholly benevolent.

THE SOCIALLY CONSTRUCTED BODY

My argument in this chapter arises out of the confluence of two mutually supportive types of discourse: *discourses of the body* and *discourses of medicine*. It is often difficult to consider either of these topics, the body and medicine, without reference to the other, since our contemporary view of the body has become thoroughly medicalized. Medicalization is a term originating from the constant exposure of human bodies to the 'medical gaze', a phenomenon described by Foucault (1973), which now appears to radically underscore perspectives on the human body, so that no newspaper is without its almost daily quota of articles and advice columns on health care, quite apart from the substantial literature in specialist 'health and fitness' magazines, websites and TV programmes.

With this in mind, it is worth examining the role of the body in the contemporary world, and the conflicting and uncertain nature of discourses surrounding it. In respect of this, Shilling, a leading theorist of the body, has written:

We now have the means to exert an unprecedented degree of control over bodies, yet we are also living in an age which has thrown into radical doubt our knowledge of what bodies are and how we should control them. (Shilling, 1993: 3)

A considerable burden of blame for the uncertainty or doubt with which many individuals regard their own bodies can be laid on the medicalization of society. A notable device by which a medicalized view of the body is reflected in cultural representation is the 'body as machine' metaphor. This presents the body as 'radically other to the self' (Shilling, 1993: 37). People are encouraged in government health promotion schemes and health product advertising to care for their bodies as they would care for pieces of machinery. A clear illustration of this is in the way the media cover the details of injuries to sports personalities and other famous people. In sport, especially, the body is regarded as a complex machine whose performance can be enhanced, and which can be repaired, just like any other machine. The injuries of sportsmen and women are frequently presented to us in the newspapers either photographically or in diagrammatic form so as to provoke easily understandable comparisons with pieces of machinery; incidentally, this creates totally unrealistic expectations of the recuperative powers of the body.

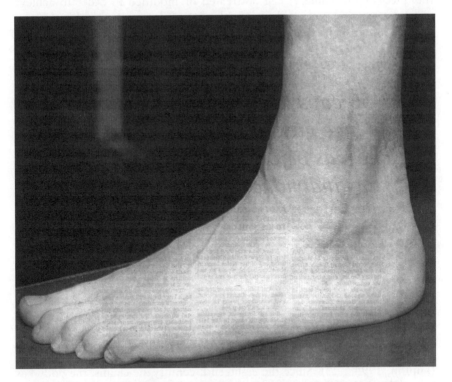

FIGURE 1.1   *Welcome back:* The left foot and lower leg of Welsh rugby player Ieuan Evans following surgery to ankle after suffering 'horrendous injury' (*Westen Mail,* 18 February, 1995; courtesy of the BBC)

The *body as machine* metaphor was nicely demonstrated in an American political magazine before the US presidential elections in 1996, in which the various physical 'flaws' of the two candidates were displayed in the form of line drawings of Clinton and Dole, followed by a brief summary of their comparative health status and vices. The two candidates are depicted in a walking posture, Dole head-on, and Clinton in profile. Both men are smiling, and clad only in underwear. Particular physical frailties are signalled with marker lines and circles, and captions are attached, summarizing that debility and its treatment. Apart from the detailed knowledge that the magazine claims to have of the two contestants' personal medical status (for example that Dole clutches a gauze-covered wooden crutch by night or that Clinton's blood pressure is 126/70) there is a use of technical language which encourages a reading of the text in a way that endorses the 'body as machine' metaphor. We are told, for instance, that Dole 'suffers from diverticulosis and benign polyp' (treated by a high-fibre diet and Metamucil), while Clinton has occasional bouts of gastro-oesophageal reflux, which he treats with Prilosec. The inclusion of the specialist medical terms as well as the brand name of medicines in their treatment provides a setting within which each 'malfunction' has a specific treatment or remedy. The effect of this is to promote an understanding of the body in which component parts (i.e. pieces of machinery) can be treated or modified in order to achieve adherence to a normative ideal, namely that of the unblemished body.

Both Shilling (1993) and Frank (1991, 1995), claim there are two major contemporary viewpoints on the body, exemplified by the post-structuralism of Foucault and his followers (indicating that bodies are controlled by *discourses*); and by the symbolic interactionist stance of Goffman. Shilling claims the differences between the two positions are not as great as might at first appear. This is because both theorists hold to a view of the body as being central to the lives of embodied subjects, while at the same time suggesting that the body's significance is dependent on social 'structures' which exist independently of those individuals (1993: 71). While not wishing to become entrenched in theories of the body, which provide the input for at least one specialist journal, *Body and Society*, and at the risk of neglecting other pertinent, but largely derivative theories, such as that provided by Turner (1984), I will briefly discuss the ideas of Foucault and Goffman, both of which seem to be to be central to a social constructionist understanding of health discourse and health communication studies.

FOUCAULT, THE BODY AND POWER

For Foucault, and for the many scholars he has influenced, the body is 'the ultimate site of political and ideological control, surveillance and regulation' (Lupton, 1994a: 23). Since the eighteenth century, he claims, the body has been subjected to a unique disciplinary power. It is through controls over the body and its behaviours that state apparatuses such as medicine, schools, psychiatry and the law have been able to define and delimit individuals'

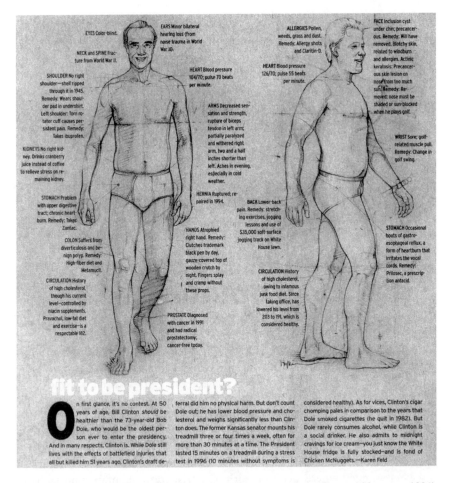

FIGURE 1.2   *Fit to be President?* (Clinton/Dole Illustration from 'George' Magazine, 1996)

activities, punishing those who violate the established boundaries and maintaining the productivity and political usefulness of bodies.

The Foucauldian approach to the body is characterized, first, by a substantive preoccupation with those institutions which govern the body and, secondly, by an epistemological view of the body as produced by and existing in discourse. Bodies which were once controlled by direct repression are, in contemporary societies, controlled by stimulation. Thus the body in consumer culture is coerced into a normative discourse ('Get undressed – but be slim, good-looking, tanned', as Foucault reminds us). Bodies, for Foucault, are 'highly malleable phenomena which can be invested with various and changing forms of power' (Shilling, 1993: 79).

Foucault regarded human history as falling into broadly defined epochs which are characterized by dominant discourses. These tracts of historical/discursive time he termed 'epistemes'. According to the medical sociologist Armstrong, the current episteme, of which we are a part, in which human anatomy is still regarded very much as it has been since the publication of *Gray's Anatomy* in 1858, will one day close, perhaps rendering the knowledge of *Gray's Anatomy* as redundant as an eighteenth-century doctor's discussion of 'humours' entering the body would be to a contemporary physician educated to believe in invasive bacteria.

Why, Armstrong asks, did people in the eighteenth century and earlier not perceive that disease could be isolated in organs and in body tissues? Why did they fail to realize that death comes from disease within the body rather than as a visitation from uncontrollable external forces? He answers as follows: 'What is today obvious was then unknown because in the past the world was not seen according to *Gray's Anatomy*' (Armstrong, 1987: 64). Because we cannot see or measure the 'humours' which were said to inhabit the body, must we dismiss them as mistaken? Or, following Foucault, can we simply accept that they represent a different and incommensurable vision of the body and of reality?

The activity of power in the doctor–patient relationship is treated in the broader context of its historical development in Armstrong's analysis. In this way he invokes several of the themes familiar from the work of Foucault. In *Discipline and Punish* (1977) Foucault writes that in the pre-modern era the sovereignty of kings demanded that power be overt, that (for example) a threat to the body of the king be punished with a display of raw and brutal power, the marking of one body by another (brandings, floggings, hangings) symbolizing the power of the sovereign over his subjects. Displays of power were evident wherever the sovereign passed, and castles, fortresses and regal ceremonies were ubiquitous manifestations of that power. At the end of the eighteenth century a new symbolic power emerged, which Foucault calls disciplinary power. This was symbolized precisely by the *panopticon*, a device designed by Jeremy Bentham to supervise and observe in the prison, but applicable too in the barracks, the school, the workhouse, the hospital – anywhere indeed where a central authority wished to maintain control from a central position, gazing outward, while the subject, unseeing, could only contemplate his or her own incarceration. Disciplinary power in this mode was based on the principle of total observation. Foucault refers to the *inversion of visibility* because previously the subjects had gazed upon the person, the majesty, of the king and on his symbolic strength, and now the gaze was directed from the guard to the person imprisoned. By the very nature of the panopticon, the guard was unseen, faceless. And the guard, of course, was himself monitored and under surveillance.

For Armstrong the *stethoscope* is a symbol of power in 'capillary' (a term used by Foucault to identify the individual or minimal) form. Apart from being of obvious practical use it is, claims Armstrong, a 'self-conscious emblem to mark out the figure of the doctor' (1987: 70).

> The prisoner in the Panopticon and the patient at the end of the stethoscope, both remain silent as the techniques of surveillance sweep over them. They know they have been monitored but they remain unaware of what has been seen or heard. (Armstrong, 1987: 70)

While there have been specific criticisms (Shilling, 1993: 80) that Foucault fails to engage with the body as a focus of investigation (rather than merely a topic of discussion) there is no questioning the extent of Foucault's influence in both the sociology of health and illness and in discourse studies concerned with the body, health and medicine over the past 30 years. Studies of a broader theoretical nature by both Bourdieu (1984) on the concept of 'taste' and Baudrillard (1988) on the theme of 'consumption' have contributed to the diverse theoretical perspectives on the body taken by more recent writers (see for example, Frank, 1991; Featherstone, 1991) but these writers have only added to, rather than replaced, Foucault's theories of power and subordination in relation to body-consciousness and the medical gaze.

GOFFMAN AND THE PRESENTATION OF SELF

According to Goffman (1959), individuals are constantly staging performances whose aim is to enhance their own interests and minimize loss of 'face'. Central to this notion of the *presentation of self* is the maintenance of a positive and convincing self-image. In recent years modern societies have gradually put in place many criteria for an ideal body, manifested most openly in the idea of the *commodified body*, and supported by industries which provide specifically for body care, dieting and keeping fit.

Goffman's discussion of the body is motivated by three principal ideas:

1 The body is material property of individuals which individuals control and monitor in order to interact.
2 Individuals present and manage their bodies in accordance with shared vocabularies of body idiom that are not individually controlled but hierarchically set and symbolically charged.
3 The body mediates the relationship between self-identity and social identity: consequently, the social meanings attached to the expression of bodily display are an extremely important factor in an individual's sense of self, and in his or her feelings of inner worth. (cf. Shilling, 1993: 82–3)

Much of Goffman's work relates to the healthy body, and the ways in which people devise and maintain strategies for carrying out interactions with each other. In particular he is concerned with the presentation of self in everyday life (1959), and the remarkable competence that individuals show in managing the expressions, movements and gestures involved in communicative interactions. According to Goffman, both *face work* (the maintenance of positive 'face' in social interaction) and body work (not only the appropriate use of 'body language', gesture and eye contact but also, for example, the way that certain men often appear to 'steer' their women everywhere they go) are crucial to the successful negotiation of encounters and the establishing and maintaining of social roles.

Without doubt the most relevant area of research that Goffman carried out in relation to the *pathologized* body was his work on *Stigma* (1968). He examines the distinction between the image that people have of themselves (their 'virtual social identity') and the way that other people see them (their 'actual social identity'). People with stigmas (attributes which have been labelled as deeply discrediting) confront problems in social interaction with 'normals' (Goffman's term) which can have particularly damaging consequences for their self-identity. If stigmatized individuals try to 'pass' as 'normal' they risk encountering a discrepancy between their own perceived virtual identity and their actual social identity. Such people are likely to become regarded, and to regard themselves, as somehow 'tainted' (Goffman, 1968: 12). Goffman's analysis is especially relevant in relation to the problems of the disabled and the chronically disfigured, because of the extra work these people need to do in order to be fully included as members of society, but it also raises questions as to the real divergence between people's 'virtual' and their 'actual' social identity. It might be, for example, that some elderly people feel that the distinction between these two identities is a spurious one; work by Featherstone and Hepworth (1991) has raised the notion of the 'mask of ageing', according to which the process of ageing provides a mask which shields the outside world from an individual's essential, and perpetually youthful, self.

Shilling criticizes Goffman for a failure to engage with the interactive dimensions of body management, and by assuming that categorizations of stigma can somehow exist prior to social encounters. This is a lacuna which the later Goffman acknowledged and addressed (1983) and need not concern us here. Shilling also criticizes Goffman, as he does Foucault, for turning the mind into the classificatory arbiter of bodies and therefore the 'site in which the meaning of the body is inscribed' (1993: 88). According to Shilling, neither of these writers does justice to the body as an active and reactive phenomenon. Locating the study of the body in the discourses about it or the representations and categorizations of it, means that the body remains always a thing apart, an 'item for discussion, but absent as an object of investigation' (1993: 99). Quite how (if at all) the body *can* be approached other than through discourse, representation and categorization remains open to question, and it could be argued that Shilling's criticisms of Goffman and Foucault apply equally to his own work. One author, however, of whom this criticism could not be made is Frank (1991, 1995).

FRANK'S IDEAL TYPICAL BODIES

Frank examines the relationship between the body and human action largely through mapping a typology of what he calls 'body types' onto sorts of action, or in Frank's terms, the kinds of choices that these particular 'body-selves' act out (1995: 40). Essentially this model consists of four 'ideal typical bodies', the *disciplined* body, the *mirroring* body, the *dominating* body, and the *communicative* body. Frank describes this typology of bodies as a 'metanarrative', that is, according to the criteria of postmodernism, an overriding structure under whose rubric individual narratives are made to make sense. This is a provocative stance for a theorist such as Frank to take, especially since he seems ill at ease with the adequacy of models of this sort. As he himself says: 'Ideal types are puppets: theoretical constructions designed to describe some empirical *tendency*. Actual body-selves represent distinctive mixtures of ideal types' (1995: 29). However, if we consider these body types, or body-selves, as categorial frames rather than as a means of simplistically labelling individual behaviours, they serve a useful purpose. 'Ideal types', he writes, 'provide a reflexive medium, a language, for talking about what is particular in real bodies' (ibid.). It is important to bear in mind Frank's caveat that no actual body fits a particular ideal consistently over time; more typically, individuals present an admixture of two, three or even all four ideal types.

The *disciplined* body, according to Frank, is concerned with patterns of self-regimentation. It has to be in control of events. This taking of control is at odds with the apparently *contingent* or random nature of illness. Thus the disciplined body is thrown into crisis by the loss of control which illness often brings with it. It responds by following a rigorous and ordered thera-peutic regimen in which, claims Frank, 'the body seeks to compensate for contingencies it cannot accept' (1995: 41). An effect of adopting this approach is to 'objectify' the body, to turn the body into an 'it' along the lines of the 'body as machine'. Moreover, a 'self' dissociated from its body is unlikely to seek out and associate with others similar to itself, so Frank describes the disciplined body as *monadic*, that is, as regarding itself as autonomous and alone. Individuals dominated by this body-self are unlikely to tell stories about themselves; rather, their stories concern their pursuit of the regimen. They are particular about getting the details of the regimen just right, and of managing their illness in accordance with the instructions of their doctor or therapist. Frank suggests that, despite being an unpleasant way to live, many people follow this type to some degree, cutting themselves off from others, as well as dissociating from a body that has become an 'it', needing to restore control and relinquish desire. The allegorical model for the disciplined body type is the monastic order, in which a regimented and ascetic lifestyle provides a means towards salvation.

By contrast, the *mirroring* body is defined through acts of *consumption* (1995: 43). The body is *enhanced* by consumption. Medicine, like food and clothing, services the mirroring body and helps it to become what it wants to be: more stylish and healthier. This narcissistic self-conception is primar-ily visual: 'the body sees an image, idealizes it, and seeks to become the image of that image. The mirroring body thus attempts to make itself exactly what the popular phrase calls "the picture of health"' (1995: 44). While the mirroring body is also monadic, it differs from the disciplined body in its concern with *appearance* rather than performance. Over-whelmingly, the images that the mirroring body selects for itself are drawn from popular culture, where image is paramount. Frank cites a line attri-buted to pop singer Michael Jackson, who, on hearing that Jacqueline Kennedy Onassis might have to undergo chemotherapy for non-Hodgkin's lymphoma said: 'She's too much of a legend to risk her hair falling out' (1995: 45). Whether apocryphal or not, the story nicely illustrates the idea that for the mirroring body 'the reality of death is less real than the image of baldness' (ibid.). Unsurprisingly, the allegorical model for the mirroring self is the department store.

The characterizing feature of the *dominating* body is *force*. Frank claims that there is a cultural resistance to talk about the ill as being dominating; nor do people wish to self-present as such, especially in written accounts. Most contemporary accounts of the sick and dying emphasize the heroic and courageous aspects of the struggle against disease, and many make mention of the sick person's serenity or selflessness. Carole Andersen's story (1994) of her husband's leukaemia, cited by Frank, gives another perspective entirely. She tells of her husband's anger and vindictiveness, the emotional abuse and possessiveness that he expressed in his dying years, at least until the final few months. Whereas the monadic position of the disciplined body reflects its fear of contingency back onto itself through a merciless adherence to the regimen, the dominating body, which forms *dyadic* relationships, expresses rage towards other people. If Carole's husband could not control his illness, Frank tells us, he could at least control Carole. It was only when his death became a certainty, and he once again, paradoxically, felt 'in control', that her husband reverted to being the person he had been before his illness began. Society, Frank warns us, does not want to hear illness stories such as this, in which abusive force stands in for either positive struggle or benign acceptance, and for which a state of war is the prevalent allegorical model.

Unlike the preceding three body types, the *communicative* body is an *idealized* type, rather than a temporary home for an essentially fragmented and fleeting body-self. As with the other three, no actual body fits this ideal for long: its difference lies in its acceptance of contingency as a fundamental characteristic of living. It is dyadic, but in this case the body realizes its ethical obligation to others, which manifests as alignment towards and solidarity with their suffering. It too has, or rather *is* a story, but the communicative body *communes* with others, inviting them to recognize themselves in it. This is exemplified by Frank's quotation from Anatole Broyard (1992), who wanted, he said, 'to be a good story' for his physician. This remark stands in contrast to a patient who might say 'I want you to listen to my story.' 'The remark occurs', Frank tells us, 'as Broyard talks about the ill person's need to personify his illness and to "own" it, rather than allow it to be the anonymous disease that medicine depicts' (1995: 50). The communicative body's acceptance of contingency and its dyadic concern with the other can be likened to Schweitzer's (1990) joint emphases on the inevitability of suffering and the productive desire to join with other bodies (ibid.).

According to Frank, the four body types are neither mutually exclusive nor exhaustive: each of us, he writes, is 'not one type or the other, but a shifting foreground and background of types. The value of the types is to describe the extreme moments of these shifts, thus providing some parameters for hearing the body in story' (1995: 51). In this way, suggests Frank, we can use the ideal types not as constricting frames in which to categorize individual voices, but as the means to become better listeners, and better communicators.

These ideal body types are of considerable interest to this book because they are concerned, overwhelmingly, with sick, or *pathologized* bodies, and because the way that the pathologized body responds to, and interacts with, others is through discourse, particularly through narrative. Frank relates each of his body types to examples of specific narratives, and he suggests that it is by way of narratives that these body-selves most pertinently express themselves. For the ill, more acutely than for the healthy, choice of narrative determines the way that the self is regarded and treated in society. This consideration lies behind the inclusion of an extended narrative extract in Chapter 2, where I am concerned with locating more general 'lay' representation within a specific instance of storytelling. For Frank, the patient narrative gives expression to a predominant body type at any given moment, even if this is not the one which 'fits' that patient/speaker *consistently*, and thus his model helps locate and identify the patient/speaker from within a cacophony of available voices.

While Frank regards self-identity as being forged through the available ideal body types, and Goffman identifies stigma as a key facet in identity-making, Parsons (1951) in his sick-role theory asserted that although the ill are not deemed responsible for *being* ill (though there are clearly cases when this has been brought into question) they *are* responsible for how they conduct themselves and manage the outward signs of their illness. They have to legitimize their illness by adhering to certain constraints and behaviours that are consistent with 'being ill', at the risk of being accused of lying or malingering. There is an ambiguity at play here: to what extent should individuals conceal their illnesses, and to what degree must they assert 'control' over them? At stake are issues of life insurance and employability as well as those of stigma and identity. Goffman coined the term 'passing' to describe the ways in which a spoiled identity was kept from public view. Frank, by contrast, investigates the notion of *reverse passing*, in which, for example, members of cancer support groups, people with HIV/AIDS or members of Alcoholics Anonymous wear lapel badges to outwardly mark their membership of these groups. Frank considers this a distinctively postmodern phenomenon, akin to 'coming out'. Such behaviour is, he says, a means of doing something about the apparent contingency or randomness of being ill or in remission from illness. This refusal to become a 'victim' of 'random' illness constitutes a kind of meta-control. Similarly, turning illness into story is a means of establishing meta-control, though, as Frank insists, 'meta-control is only one reason for storytelling' (1995: 32).

HEALTH BELIEFS AND HEALTH ACCOUNTS

Health *beliefs* are culturally located and culture-specific. We fabricate and endorse beliefs about health and illness continually through discourse, out of the stories we tell one another and the stories we hear from those around us. These beliefs vary enormously from culture to culture and from era to era. For example, in the seventeenth century water (especially hot water) was considered to be injurious to the body, making it vulnerable and susceptible to disease. Similarly, air was thought to be potentially harmful to sick people, as it contained various humours or 'miasmas' from the soil and standing water (Porter, 1997: 10). Although such beliefs have a place in health psychology, and have been studied at length in medical anthropology, our concern in this study will be more with health *accounts*.

Illness and health constitute an ideological field. People do not simply 'have' a state of health – they construct and repackage it continually in their accounts (Radley and Billig, 1996). Being ill involves demands on the healthy. You cannot simply 'be ill' – you have to adopt a 'sick role' (Parsons, 1951). Moreover there is a paradoxical attitude towards illness in Western culture – illness was for centuries associated with sin, and there is still, especially in the Protestant tradition, a strong tendency to associate feelings of guilt with being ill, or regarding it as a form of 'weakness' (R. Williams, 1990). Nowadays this is particularly true of illnesses which have been associated with 'deviant' or socially unacceptable behaviours, such as HIV/AIDS, or which are deemed to be 'marginal' (perhaps because offering less immediately visible symptoms, like depression). Other illnesses, and addictions, like alcoholism, are considered by many to have arisen through the 'fault' of the patient. Such beliefs about a whole range of conditions have spawned a literature of accusation and denial regarding cancer, initiated by Groddeck (1950) and pursued by LeShan (1977), both of whom suggested that cancer is, to a large degree, the result of individuals' psychosocial fears and inherent lack of the 'will to life', claims attacked, most notably, by Sontag (1991).

Debates such as these are highly emotive and might well distract us from an incipient movement in medicine, endorsed by the World Health Organization, which encourages a broader and more tolerant definition of what constitutes 'illness'; namely, anything that adversely affects an individual's physical, mental or emotional health. But what is common to all representations of illness is their existence first and foremost as *accounts*, and so we should consider the study of health and illness beliefs not as defined or presumed objects lying within the mind but as an 'activity', the activity of accounting for oneself and one's relationship to health, or the lack of it.

'EXOGENOUS' ILLNESS

In lay, as opposed to professional discourses, good health is often represented as being *intrinsic* to the individual, as residing within (Herzlich, 1973; Helman, 1984). It can be contrasted with illness, which is an assault upon health from the *outside*, precipitated by such external factors as pollution, an unhealthy way of life, and the pressures of city dwelling. This dualism is identified in Herzlich's (1973) work as *endogenous* (intrinsic to the person) versus *exogenous* (exterior to the person). Thus when we talk of 'catching a bug', or of there 'being a virus around', our understanding of illness at large is of an 'it' that strikes the individual from outside, making him or her ill. This kind of dualistic framework (health = inner; illness = outer) is familiar from a wide range of anthropological studies in many societies (Helman, 1984; Good, 1994) and forms the empirical basis for witchcraft accusations; that is, the individual will not be sick *unless someone is making them sick*. In contemporary societies in which explanations based upon witchcraft are not taken very seriously, the onus of explanation for illness falls to science. Science is supposed to provide an explanatory framework to account for why people become ill. Science, as medicine, provides most people with a model of 'why things are going wrong' when we are in ill health. In contemporary society the explanations of illness given by science satisfy most of the people most of the time, just as, in other societies, and at other times, an explanation of illness based on witchcraft or sorcery would have been acceptable. 'Illness' says Herzlich 'may be ... of magical origin, caused by the action of another man or a sorcerer. Or it may be of religious origin, produced by a god or a spirit. The essential point here is the absence of any clearly defined differences between medicine, magic and religion. The practices associated with all three are interlinked, just as systems of values and representations are interlinked' (1973: 5).

The blurring of distinctions between these forces of medicine, magic and religion is exemplified for me in David Lan's play *Desire* (1990), which is set in Zimbabwe shortly after the civil war. In the play, Rosemary becomes sick with an unknown and incurable ailing disease. She loses interest in living and rejects both her family and husband in turn. During an invocation ceremony held by the women of the village, she becomes possessed by the spirit of her dead girl friend, a guerrilla fighter named Freedom who was killed during the latter stages of the war. Speaking through Rosemary, Freedom tells the villagers that Rosemary will not be well until the person who betrayed her admits to what he did. The village women, especially Rosemary's younger sister, demand that the culprit own up to his betrayal of Freedom. It transpires that Freedom's own father, Wireless, betrayed her whereabouts in order to save himself from a beating, or worse, at the hands of the soldiers, and Rosemary's husband, Jericho, made no attempt to protect her once the soldiers were on her trail. The men make their respective confessions and Rosemary is delivered of the sense of betrayal that she must carry on Freedom's behalf, and of the illness through which it is expressed.

To develop this line of enquiry about the juxtaposition of beliefs surrounding illness causation and cure, as well as the *reification* of illness, I will paraphrase a story contained in an essay by the French anthropologist Lévi-Strauss (1967), originally taken from the work of Boas (1930). The events in the story take place at the turn of the twentieth century.

Quesalid, a Kwakiutl Indian from the Vancouver region of Canada, was cynical of the healing powers of shamans, and set out to apprentice himself to a group of sorcerers, driven, we are told, partly by curiosity, and partly by a desire to discredit them. He soon discovered that a trick was widely used by the sorcerers of the north-west coast. The shaman would hide a small tuft of down in the corner of his mouth, and after performing a series of intimate and purposeful manoeuvres on the body of the patient, would bite his own tongue or make his gums bleed and spit out the blood-soaked piece of down, presenting it to the patient and onlookers as the 'foreign body extracted as a result of his sucking and manipulations'.

Although Quesalid's suspicions regarding the probity of shamans had been confirmed, he was himself no longer free. As an initiate, he was called upon to heal, and he did so with remarkable success, justifying this to himself in psychological terms: the sick became well because they believed in the efficacy of his 'cures'. However, when Quesalid travels to a neighbouring area, and finds himself among the Koskimo Indians, he is amazed to discover that the shamans there do not practise the technique of the 'bloody worm', or concealed down; instead they 'merely spit a little saliva into their hands, and they dare to claim that "this is the sickness"'. Intrigued, Quesalid obtains permission to try out his own technique on a patient for whom the method of the Koskimo shamans had proved unsuccessful. He cures her. At this point Quesalid is made to think long and hard:

> Though he had few illusions about his own technique, he has now found one which is more false, more mystifying, and more dishonest than his own. *For at least he gives his clients something. He presents them with their sickness in a visible and tangible form*, while his foreign colleagues show nothing at all and only claim to have captured the sickness. Moreover Quesalid's method gets results, while the other is futile.

The Koskimo shamans are shamed by the success of their visitor. They are also confused: how has Quesalid produced, in material form, the illness that they had always thought to be of a spiritual nature? They invite Quesalid to a secret meeting in a cave and there they explain to him their system of belief regarding illness, its invisibility and consequent impossibility of capture. Why, when Quesalid operates, does the sickness stick to his hand like glue? Quesalid does not reply, bound by a vow of silence to his profession. He maintains his silence even when 'the Koskimo shamans send him their allegedly virgin daughters to try to seduce him and discover his secret'.

On returning to his village Quesalid discovers that the most distinguished shaman of a neighbouring clan, disturbed by rumours of Quesalid's prowess as a healer, has invited all his colleagues to compete with him in the healing of a selected number of patients. Quesalid goes along and observes the older shaman. Like the Koskimo, this shaman does not display the illness as an object in his hand; instead he claims that the invisible sickness has 'gone into' one of his ritual artefacts, a rattle or a bark head-ring. During the course of the healing session, certain cases are deemed hopeless by the shaman. Quesalid's turn comes, and, as before, he heals the hopeless cases with his technique of the bloody worm.

The older man is devastated. Mocked by the villagers and shamed by his public humiliation, he begs Quesalid to explain what it was that stuck to his palm during the healing session the night before. Was it the 'true sickness or was it only made up?' Despite impassioned pleas from the shaman (and his daughter), Quesalid remains silent. That night the shaman leaves the village, taking his entire family with him, heartsick and broken. A year later he returns, 'but both he and his daughter had gone mad'. Shortly thereafter, he dies. Quesalid continues his life as a shaman and healer, but his attitude as cynic gives way to a more generous acceptance of the practical requirements of his profession: 'at the end of the narrative ... he carries on his craft conscientiously, takes pride in his achievements, and warmly defends the technique of the bloody down against all rival schools. He seems to have completely lost sight of the fallaciousness of the technique which he had so disparaged at the beginning' (adapted from Lévi-Strauss, 1967: 175–8).

What relevance does this story hold for us today? I think that the way that illness is perceived in the story to be something visible and tangible (Quesalid's bloody worm), has its counterpart in the way many people conceive of germs and malevolent entities residing in the body, a type of reification that facilitates understanding of germ theory and of the 'disease process'. Moreover, the narrative within which Quesalid's activities as a shaman are presented provides a classical example of how 'storied' the events of our lives become in the telling of them. In other words, we make sense of the past events of our lives as if they were driven by a consistency and logic of their own, however fragmented and *contingent* (to use Frank's term) they may have appeared at the time of their occurrence. It is as though 'the past' possessed its own inevitable narrative impetus whose arrival point could only ever be 'the present'. This is a theme to which I return in Chapter 2, and which I will examine in greater detail in Chapter 6. However, the *topic* of the narrative is most evidently the issue of illness reification and the disease process.

GERMS, REIFICATION AND THE DISEASE PROCESS

The metaphor of the body as a vehicle to be cleaned of malevolent external influences often demands a degree of euphemization. Expulsion of germs from the urinary tract and from the bowels is considered by Helman (1978) in his study of folk beliefs in a London suburb. He treats expulsion as one of three ways to deal with the invasive *it* in its guise as a 'Germ' (the upper case being used by Helman himself throughout his study, as if to emphasize, figuratively, the objectified status of Germs, Viruses and Bugs), the other two being starvation (as in the folk saying 'feed a cold, starve a fever') and killing the germ *in situ*, by means of antibiotics. Expulsion calls for quantities of fluids to liquefy the Germ so that it can be 'washed out of the system'. Helman's data – gathered from his own general practice and from interviews and random recordings of district nurses and surgery receptionists in conversation with patients – provides a fascinating insight into conceptions among patients as to the nature of Bugs, Germs and Viruses. The folk model most commonly employed by Helman's patients is that of the Germ, and it is apparent that the exogenous attribution of the cause of a cough, for example, to the invasive germ (or the *it*) accounts for the prescription of 'about six million gallons of relatively useless coloured water every year in Britain'. It is Helman's hypothesis (now outdated, but no less relevant) that 'a major reason for this is that cough medicine, in the terms of the widespread Fevers/Colds/Chills folk model, can be seen as something that will expel or "wash out" or dilute the external entity causing the feverish cough; that is, a Germ' (1978: 129).

A universal means of ridding oneself of a germ, according to Helman, is the practice of diluting it and flushing it out 'usually via the orifices through which it entered the body'. Expressions used by Helman's informants include 'getting it off your chest'; 'coughing up the muck'; 'getting it out of your system'; 'to flush it out of your system'. With regard to expulsion of the germ through the skin, induced by sweating, a range of expressions bear witness to the fact that the germ is indeed leaving the body: 'The aim of the treatment ... is to "sweat it out" or "sweat it off". Various fluids and other remedies are used for this purpose, including hot drinks ... aspirins and other patent anti-pyretics, which are always ingested with large amounts of fluid. The appearance of a skin rash is also welcomed, as the Germ is now, according to Helman's respondents, "showing itself" and is "on its way out of the body"' (1978: 121).

Blaxter (1983) cites women in Aberdeen who refer to a particular type of representation of 'disease as some malevolent entity residing outside the person, lying in wait to attack ... "My family wis never bothered wi' their chest ... it wis always their throat. It always went for their throat, not their chest"'. Blaxter continues: '"It went into" was a common phrase, suggesting a process over which there was no control, one disease changing irrevocably into another: "I got a chill and it went into bronchitis"' (1983: 61).

One clinician who wrote to me while I was researching this subject believes that the tendency towards exogeny is particularly associated with older people:

> certain concepts of disease ... have certainly come to my notice much more frequently from the old than from the young. I have heard it said with great frequency, 'it's in my head doctor' (or my back or my stomach). One has to parry that by saying 'What's in your head?' ... Could it be a pain or a noise or a smell of garlic? When you press the issue, you so frequently get an indefinite answer but what they mean is that the *disease process* is in the head but it is something detached from themselves; an external affliction which speaks volumes about the Victorian attitude to illness.

Here the 'disease process' is isolated as the referent, and this seems a useful category to hold with: it is the disease process that is being reified rather than the disease itself, and this too lends itself to the notion of a mobile, invasive phenomenon. That the doctor in question associates the tendency towards exogeny with an older generation is also worthy of note. Patients who could be termed 'elderly' at the time of writing were born after the Victorian era proper, of course, but they would have been reared by parents and teachers thoroughly imbued with 'Victorian values'. This system of beliefs, in regard to health and illness, has its corollaries in many different cultures. As Lupton (1994a: 94) writes, 'Diseases ... are conceptualized as invading, alien objects, which must be removed before bodily integrity can be restored ... this conceptualization of disease is expressed in practices used to treat illness: people in many cultures use such measures as emetics, purgatives and sweat baths to remove sickness from the body'. Such practices were common among the Victorians, and, as the same GP explains, the focal point of their purging and scouring was frequently the bowels:

> The bowel and its contents provide a fruitful field for words used by my generation [the writer describes himself as 'elderly']. Our Victorian mothers were maniacal with their urge to purge themselves and their young and some of the words still creep into the vocabulary of the old. *Costive* for constipation or just *passing marbles* are terms which I hardly ever hear used by the young ... *having your bowels down* is a term which I frequently heard in old Breconshire people. *Scoured*, for diarrhoea, is a term which I heard frequently in the past among the old, but never hear now. (Humphreys, personal communication)

The attribution to illness itself of an 'otherness' can be paralleled in modern Western culture by a dissociation on the patient's part that is often expressed, or hinted at, in that particular person's use of language. This pursues the Western cultural distinction between mind and body prevalent since Descartes in the seventeeth century. The term used for conceiving the body as 'other' to the self is *reification*. One of the impressions gained from Helman's study and other accounts is that the reification of the disease process in an identifiable physical form has its correlative in the objectification of a particular type of treatment or medicine. In other words, the reified illness can only be expelled by a concrete 'it' – a potion or medicine, hence the continuing consumption of vast quantities of 'relatively useless coloured water'. This notion of exorcizing an essentially invasive and harmful substance (the germ) from the body by ingestion of another (beneficial) substance lies at the heart of Helman's folk model of medical beliefs, and appears to be widespread. It is also a belief which underpins the overprescription of antibiotics, the easy availability and extreme popularity of Western pharmaceuticals in 'developing' countries, and of exotic and herbal remedies in the industrialized West.

THE 'ITNESS' OF MEDICINES

Van der Geest and Whyte (1989) in 'The charm of medicines: metaphors and metonyms', propose that it is the very concreteness of medicines, their *itness*, that directly relates to people's understanding of, and attempts to deal with, illness. Moreover, they suggest that through examining processes of metaphor and metonymy we might achieve a better grasp of individuals' subjective experience of illness.

In everyday life one of the most perceptible accomplishments of metaphor is in transforming the inchoate into the concrete. Applied to the experience of illness this means that the person who feels pain, for example, must somehow communicate an essentially inchoate sensation in order to gain any kind of recognition by others of their condition. By using metaphor, the individual is able to make the complaint specific, even palpable:

> Images from the tangible world of nature and physics are applied to the elusive experiences of nausea ('a wave') and pain ('a vise'). Illness assumes an appearance of concreteness which makes it accessible for communication and therapeutic action. (1989: 354)

Van der Geest and Whyte's argument, backed up with examples from anthropological data, is that concrete and material images of health and illness are an essential prerequisite for establishing a belief in the efficacy of medicines. They refer to the *charm* of medicines, and argue that the 'key to their charm is in their concreteness; in them healing is objectified ... Medicines are commodities which pass from one context of meaning to another. As substances they are "good to think with"' (1989: 345).

> The body and the heart ('ticker'), in particular, are referred to as an engine that may break down, not run well, become worn out, and need to be checked. Terms like 'fuel,' 'battery,' and 'spare part' are frequently used to describe health problems. The plumber's model of the body, with its pipes, pressure, circulation, flushing, and draining, is apt for many of us. (1989: 355)

Essentially then, 'if the problem is physical, then the remedy should be physical. Medicines appear the perfect answer to the problem' (ibid.). It may even be that the concreteness of the treatment creates the precondition that the illness be reified. Hence the treatment invokes the conception of illness as an *it* as clearly as that conception calls for the appropriate treatment. How then are we to read the metaphoric account of illness and treatment as presented in this form? Van der Geest and Whyte provide an example taken from the world of social science, that of 'data collection'. They say that we may not recognize the expression as a metaphor, that the movement from inchoate to concrete has become absorbed through our familiarity with the term and rendered 'dead' as a metaphor. However, the idea that one might conceive of 'collecting' knowledge, conversations, visual impressions and kinship systems in the same manner as one collects stamps or butterflies, and that such an idea is not regarded as in the least bit strange, suggests that the metaphor has 'completed its journey from elusiveness to the world of substance and has settled there. It has become a native in that new world and no one knows where it has come from, where it belongs. It has disguised its status as metaphor and passes for real, for literal truth' (1989: 357). Citing the work of Lakoff and Johnson (1980) and their insistence that metaphors set many of the conditions for our construction of reality (e.g. 'time is money'), Van der Geest and Whyte suggest that the most effective metaphors are the most invisible, or forgotten ones. Thus, in terms of our understanding of health and illness: 'The concretization that has taken place in our thinking about feeling ill can be seen as a metaphor in the process of losing its figurative character and becoming plain truth, even science' (ibid.).

The *metonymic* association is also scrutinized in Van der Geest and Whyte's paper, particularly that pertaining to doctors and medicine. Medicines, they argue, are able to represent an entire cultural context, one that is far removed from the individual patient's 'here and now'. Approbation of the exotic, of the unknown, may, through some mysterious process, lead to healing or relief of pain, when the local and familiar remedies fail:

> Hand in hand with the near universality of ethnocentrism goes a widespread belief in cultures throughout the world that extraordinary knowledge can be found elsewhere, usually far away. Supernatural (or rather supercultural) capacities lie outside the domain of the familiar. An exotic provenance of medicines, therefore, is easily seen as a promise that these are indeed superior. (1989: 360)

So it is that in the West we purchase quantities of Siberian and Korean ginseng, suitably packaged with insignia and images suggestive of the 'Wisdom of the East', while in the Philippines the Chinese community prefer the variety that grows in Wisconsin. A further example of the objectification of a particular cultural context in order to promote a sense of good health (and reliability) comes from a Philippine television advertisement:

> Pictures show a 'Swedish doctor' taking the drug [Alvedon], while an announcer explains that Alvedon is the product of 'the same Swedish technology' that produced the Volvo. This is followed by pictures of the tennis champion Björn Borg, and the Nobel prize ceremony in Stockholm. (1989: 360)

Van der Geest and Whyte argue that the objectification and *commodification* of medicines fulfils and promotes a need to conceptualize the disease process as an extraneous 'it' that can be treated only by another concrete 'it'. It is this concreteness of medicines which separates them from other forms of treatment, and makes them, in a sense, more readily comprehensible. Moreover, this concreteness symbolizes the triumph of the biomedical model of healing, since pharmaceuticals refer (metonymically) not only to doctors, but to the power and potential of advanced technology: pharmaceuticals predicate a graspable world of healing for the sufferer, giving the imagined 'itness' of the disease the countering 'itness' of the medicine, and vice versa (1989: 361).

By ingesting beneficial medicine the disease process is negated and the condition is removed. 'It' (the medicine) has removed *it* (the illness). The dualistic model that is apparently so marked a feature of human patterns of representation and cognition serves to provide us with an elementary lesson: as is borne out by Quesalid's excursions into shamanistic practices, the easier it is to conceive of the objectified reality of one's condition, the easier it is to be convinced of the concrete means of its removal. The fact that the 'concrete means' is a metaphor appears to make no difference to the 'cure'. What links these concepts together – the 'it' of disease and its removal through some kind of metaphorical process – is discourse, and it is through discourses that such representations become objectified in language, are talked about, reproduced and turned into commonsense knowledge about events in the world.

THE ENIGMA OF 'DISCOURSE'

'Discourse' as used in this book refers to both (a) a generic style of representation, that is, constrained ways of thinking and talking within a given sociocultural orbit, as well as (b) the more specific meaning of spoken or written discourse, the particular means by which individuals express themselves in language (for a concise introductory discussion of the term 'discourse' see Mills, 1997). The first of these meanings is the one used predominantly by cultural and literary theorists; the second is used by linguists and social/discursive psychologists. Since in this book I will be examining texts, or discourse from the perspective of a cultural studies agenda as well as using discourse analysis, it is appropriate that I define in what sense(s) I intend to use the term, and how it is used in the adjacent academic disciplines.

These two uses of the word 'discourse' can be regarded as embracing a macro meaning and a micro meaning. The 'macro', or broader sense derives directly from the use made by Foucault. Discourse is the most important concept in Foucault's work and it is centrally concerned with, although irreducible to, language. According to Foucault, discourse can be seen as sets of 'deep principles' incorporating specific 'grids of meaning' which underpin, generate and establish relations between all that can be seen, thought and said (Dreyfus and Rabinow, 1982). Following this definition, it makes sense to talk of a 'discourse of conservatism', a 'discourse of advertising' or a 'discourse of medicine'. Foucauldian discourse analyis or 'French discourse analysis' (G. Williams, 1999) is an attempt to render meaningful entire modes of representation in culture – so that, as we have seen, Foucault studied institutions such as hospitals, mental asylums, prisons and sexual practices across history as specific 'discourses'. Moreover, discourses are, according to Foucault, 'practices that systematically form the objects of which they speak' (1972: 49) providing a clear link with the more extreme linguistic determinism of Whorf. In other words, following the relativist/Whorfian paradigm, realities are at least in part constituted by the descriptions and representations (i.e. the discourses) we make of them.

Discourse in the 'micro' or 'local' sense emphasizes specific textual (spoken, written, visual or multimodal) practices and regularly isolates extracts of text for in-depth analysis. There are, however, differences in opinion as to the methodology that should be employed in the analysis of spoken and written language. At least three related but distinct methods, or paradigms, are relevant to this book, and they have emerged from separate academic traditions: I do not, however, intend to trace the genealogy of each tradition here (see, for example, Potter, 1996; Mills, 1997; Sarangi and Roberts, 1999b). While these disciplines are never entirely clear-cut, there are certain defining features which help to distinguish them one from the other.

The first of these is conversation analysis (CA), which arose from the ethnomethodology of Garfinkel, Sacks and Schegloff. The second is critical discourse analysis (CDA), whose roots are in critical linguistics. The third is ethnographic discourse analysis, whose aims and concerns are almost indistinguishable from interactional sociolinguistics, except that, as might be expected, there is a greater attention to ethnographic background. The latter two methodologies draw on the ethnography of communication and conversation analysis, and some analysts are also influenced by the work of critical discourse analysis (Scollon, 2000: 142; Sarangi and Roberts, 1999b: 30).

Conversation Analysis

Conversation analysis (CA) evolved in the USA out of the ethnomethodology of Garfinkel and Sacks, beginning with the seminal work of Sacks, Schegloff and Jefferson (1974) on turn-taking in conversation and expressed most effectively in the retrospectively collected lecture notes of Harvey Sacks (1992) following his death in 1975 (see also Silverman, 1998). Conversation analysts are overwhelmingly concerned with asking the question, *Why that now?* (Schegloff and Sacks, 1973) about utterances in interaction. CA expressly considers talk as a kind of social action, rather than as representative of an attempt at communicating ideas and principles 'fixed in the mind'. As Edwards has summarized: 'CA avoids attempting to explain talk in terms of the mental states that precede it, generate it or result from it' (1997: 85). An emphasis on *indexicality* and *reflexivity* urges analysts always to question the context of the interaction, but, importantly, without going beyond the text in order to furnish or 'explain' utterances – i.e. the context should be allowed to 'speak for itself'. While indexicality determines that an utterance's meaning will not be satisfactorily understood without a knowledge of the occasion on which the utterance is used (Potter, 1996: 43), reflexivity enables analysts to consider not only the actions being described or the reports being made, but also what is being done (rather than said) in that description or report. Furthermore, true to its origins as a systematic social science, CA focuses in great detail on the *sequences* that occur in interaction. Little or (preferably) no attempt is made to contextualize the events being analysed in terms of the age, social class or cultural background of the participants. Following the initial teachings of Sacks, CA works 'from the bottom up', relying entirely, or almost entirely, on participants' perspectives, as expressed in the text under scrutiny. In the UK sociologists such as Silverman (1987, 1997) and Heath (1992) have made compelling use of CA in their analyses of medical and counselling talk.

Since the late 1980s there has arisen a school of *discursive psychologists* based mainly at Loughborough University in the UK, whose adherents now practise a markedly anti-cognitivist type of analysis which is in many respects indistinguishable from conversational analysis but which is still referred to (confusingly) by some of its practitioners as discourse analysis (see, for example, Edwards and Potter, 1992; Potter, 1996; Edwards, 1997). It is appropriate to regard this group as psychologists reacting against the cognitivist tradition within their discipline, particularly the belief within cognitivism that language is intrinsic to and reflective of fixed 'states of the mind', as well as against what they regard as the dogmatic orthodoxies of experimental psychology (see especially Edwards, 1997).

Critical Discourse Analysis

Critical discourse analysis (CDA) emerged from (and to an extent is a reaction against) a linguistics-based (non-critical) discourse analysis, whose practitioners analyse grammatical structure and choice of lexis (vocabulary) in order to make inferences about meaning above the level of the sentence (see e.g. Stubbs, 1983; Brown and Yule, 1983). However, according to the self-declared *critical* linguists who emerged at the end of the 1970s (including Kress, Fowler, Hodge and Fairclough), the earlier, linguistic-based variety of discourse analysis lacked any sort of developed social orientation, was not concerned with issues of power, and was not interested in locating itself reflexively in the wider historical context of social change. These new scholars were particularly concerned with the formulation and expression of power relations in discourse, and several of their publications attest to this (Fowler et al., 1979; Kress, 1989; Fairclough, 1989; Hodge and Kress, 1993).

Methodologically, CDA was influenced by the systemic functional grammar of Halliday (1978, 1985), which, in the work of Fairclough especially (1989, 1992, 1995) was fused with a theoretical grounding in the works of Foucault and Bourdieu. CDA offers a politically inflected mode of analysis, adding to Foucault by constantly referring to actual textual practice (Mills, 1997: 157), and by exploring in detail the way that texts refer back to each other, the practice of *intertextuality* (see e.g. Fairclough, 1989). By examining discursive practices in this way, CDA hopes to mark out and challenge the *normative* parameters by which society is governed, and to question the basis upon which we judge social realities. Practitioners of CDA make frequent reference to the context in which an interaction is taking place, and use such 'background information' to enforce their arguments, which, predominantly, concern exposing and undermining the power structures in which they perceive all social interaction to be embedded.

Ethnographic Discourse Analysis/Interactional Sociolinguistics

Practitioners of ethnographic discourse analysis believe that studies of talk need to be embedded within an ethnographic project. A feature of this project, like the cultural anthropology in which it originates, is the 'making strange' of phenomena that are either taken for granted or else regarded as commonsensical. As Sarangi and Roberts have noted: 'Both "making strange" and issues of context focus the ... ethnographer on the explicating of actual local practices and their relationships to wider social orders' (1999b: 28). Early work in the ethnography of communication (Gumperz and Hymes, 1972) followed by studies in cross-cultural and contextually located practices (Bauman and Sherzer, 1989; Duranti and Goodwin, 1992) set out the paradigms for research; and work in medical settings, including Mishler (1984), Coupland N. et al. (1991), Coupland J. et al. (1994), DiGiacomo (1992), Fisher (1995) and Ainsworth-Vaughn (1998) has had varying degrees of allegiance to this tradition. Unlike conversation analysts, whose practitioners find their evidence exclusively in the data provided by the discourse itself – and like critical discourse analysts – ethnographic discourse analysts search beyond the local discourse context, using field notes, self-reflexive commentaries, and observation from other sources such as media accounts to fill out their analyses. *Interactional sociolinguistics* also has its roots in the work of Gumperz and Hymes, but generally lacks a detailed ethnographic commentary. Sociolinguists in this tradition are often more concerned with Speech Act Theory (Austin, 1962), politeness strategies (Brown and Levinson, 1987), and the way that such issues from the field of *pragmatics* interact with sociolinguistic variables like gender and status (Sarangi and Roberts, 1999b: 32).

There are significant differences of methodology and evaluation among these various practices, especially between CA and CDA (for an informative and diverting review of some of these differences see Schegloff, 1997, 1998, 1999a, 1999b; Wetherell, 1998; Billig, 1999a, 1999b). A well known argument of conversation analysts is that critical discourse analysts 'skew' the reading of texts in order to fit in with their own political agendas (e.g. Potter, 1996), while conversation analysts' claims to be working entirely from a 'participant's perspective' can be questioned on the grounds that it is the researcher who makes the choice of which selections of text to study in the first place, implicitly providing a form of interpretation from 'outside the text'. However, without wishing to gloss over the differences between exponents of CDA, CA, ethnographic discourse analysis and interactional sociolinguistics, they are similar in that, unlike the 'macro' discourse analysis undertaken by cultural theorists, they concentrate their studies on explicitly presented pieces of predominantly spoken text, from which readers may or may not choose to draw wider sociocultural implications. By contrast some cultural theorists never show any of the data from which they are extrapolating.

While there may be inherent methodological problems in extracting macro significance from pieces of text, notably the question of how to produce a working method which does not undermine its own claims to truth (Wetherell and Potter, 1992: 101; Mills, 1997: 133), there remains room, I believe, for a more eclectic approach which makes selective use of more than one methodology without compromising what social scientists consider to be scientific rigour (cf. Wetherell, 1998: 405). Following Wetherell, I would argue that just as cultural anthropologists and ethnographers of communication have found an eclectic approach to be the most effective way out of methodological quandaries, so might critical discourse analysts and practitioners of CA. If one of the aims of research on communication in health and social care is to provide helpful material for the training and instruction of future generations of medical and nursing staff, this might involve employing a more ethnographically based discourse analytic approach and the use of texts (spoken, written and visual) as the central data source. Research would then be located within a specific site or domain, but there would be room for contextual information, detailed accounts of news media issues on the same or related topics, as well as comparison with other relevant ethnographic studies.

A key lesson of CA, and the strongest legacy of Sacks, is how talk can be used to provide rhetorical substance to an argument, as a way of 'doing', quite apart from the cognitive notion of words reflecting ideas and experience in the speaker's mind. Put another way, talk is more to do with action, with 'getting things done' than it is with information-giving. It is just such concerns which occupy Edwards (1997), whose work reminds us that much academic discussion of language and mind, notably within psychology, is guided by the erroneous presumption that we 'know' intuitively how people talk. Again and again in scholarly works, argues Edwards, we find examples of social scientists mapping talk onto alleged 'mental states' instead of studying the interactive and continuous construction of discourse. By synthesizing this approach with appropriate analyses along post-structuralist or Foucauldian lines (Wetherell, 1998: 388), we are able to explore the more fruitful paradigm that the micro discourses which people produce in everyday talk, rather than being mappings of particular 'mental states', *intrinsically reflect and are constitutive of* wider sociocultural discourses.

Is the underlying assumption, then, that we need only look at the particular in order to gain an understanding of the whole? Yes, and no. While any available text can be examined and analysed only in the context in which it arose, it is unquestionable that if the sociocultural conditions were not as they are, then the context for the production of that particular text would not be in place. In this sense discourse analysis is a *metonymic* process, that is, one in which the part (in this case a short extract of text) is seen to represent the whole (that, is the wider discourse, in the Foucauldian sense) and specific 'discursive' practices cannot fail to throw light on the wider cultural practices in which they are embedded. If this were not the case, there would be little point in studying them. Consequently, my use of the term 'discourse' in this book moves from the local and specific to the wider sociocultural meaning and at times encompasses both meanings at the same time. Usually the context should determine in which sense the term is meant to be read.

The language researcher is, or should be, essentially an ethnographer, shunting between cultural enclaves and reporting on the strangeness that he or she finds there, the better to recognize the strangeness of the familiar and known. The kind of ethnographic discourse analysis which finds support in these pages requires a degree of *reflexivity*, as well as participant observation 'among the artefacts of a defamiliarized cultural reality' which Clifford considers to be the characteristic attitude of ethnography (1988: 121). It is to be expected that an era of interdisciplinary reformulation and of 'blurred genres' (Geertz, 1988: 13) will emphasize the role of subjectivity within the writing process also. An example of such practice is to be found in the work of Zulaika, who believes that 'a successful ethnography must itself become a distancing device by pointing out the "otherness" of what people experience, the ethnographer included, within the boundaries of their own cultural constructions' (1988: 350). Similarly, Cameron et al. (1992: 5) comment on the language researcher as a 'socially located person':

> We inevitably bring our biographies and our subjectivities to every stage of the research process, and this influences the questions we ask and the ways in which we try to find answers. Our view is that the subjectivity of the observer should not be seen as a regrettable disturbance but as one element in the human interactions that comprise our object of study.

It seems important not only to retain an awareness of the researcher's own role in relation to the data that he or she has selected for analysis, but also, and equally importantly, to appreciate the *otherness* of the worlds that are being described. This sense of otherness is an integral element of the ethnographic process, especially if we regard illness as a kind of culture – possessing its own 'nationality', as Sontag (1991) has suggested. The effect of this dual responsibility (both to reflexivity and to otherness) is to render strange the commonplace, imbue with unexpected meaning the categorizations and descriptions of the seemingly mundane. This corresponds too with a belief that that research which is not self-reflexive and self-critical, which holds to a notion of ultimate truth-value, as if 'plucked like fruit right from nature', fails entirely to perceive itself as located within the unfolding social drama of daily existence, and as such is likely to reproduce the normative and restricting mechanisms of power and oppression.

CONCLUSION

The idea that the human body and its illnesses are the result of discursive processes as well as being biological realities is the underlying theme of this chapter. Contemporary societies are inundated with images and texts concerning health and health care, delivering a highly idealized notion of the body, and leading to the adoption of 'body projects' by a significant proportion of the population. In the meantime, theorists have developed various ways of studying the body and its illnesses, from the work of Foucault on discourses of the body and power, and the prevalence of the 'medical gaze', to the emphasis on self-presentation and commodification of the body propounded by Goffman. Frank's idea of four ideal typical bodies lends itself to a narrative perspective in which individuals deliver storied accounts of their illness experience and thereby, ideally, reclaim control over their bodies and illnesses, in a way, Frank suggests, that is consistent with Foucault's advocacy of resistance and initiative.

One area of interest to the larger aims of the book is the way in which the body, illness and medicines are reified in accounts across cultures. Exogenous concepts of illness all involve a belief in illness as an extraneous phenomenon which 'comes into' the body, and are thus compatible with most known folk models of illness as well as with germ theory. This phenomenon reflects an apparently universal preoccupation with the notion of a concrete reified medicine acting upon a specific reified condition in ways that have become absorbed into a cultural system as normative, and which are most evidently reproduced and perpetuated in discourse.

How 'discourse' might be the primary focus of a study of illness and the body raises methodological questions, one of which concerns what kind of discourse analysis best suits our purpose. Critical discourse analysis and conversation analysis both have advantages, but fundamentally disagree on issues such as the amount of contextualization that is 'given' in a commentary on a text, and whether the political views of analysts should be allowed to flavour their readings of text (although both are agreed that it is impossible to do analysis without 'assuming a position'). I have suggested that an ethnographic approach to discourse analysis might provide the best perspective on medical discourse and health communication, but am encouraged by the practices of both CDA and CA within the domain of health and social care.

'Lay' Talk about Health and Illness   2

Illness is a social phenomenon, defined through the interaction of the patient with his or her relatives, the doctor or health care worker, and society at large: consequently it is a behaviour that has to be learned. The knowledge of illness that the patient brings to bear on each fresh encounter with a health care professional is likely to have been gained from prior experience, stories from friends and relatives, information from television and other media (and increasingly from the internet), quite apart from folk knowledge of a more general kind. A 'lay' understanding of illness is therefore constituted from several different and often conflicting sources, but typically will include scientifically grounded knowledge mixed in with local 'folk models' of illness causation and cure.

This chapter will focus on the way that lay talk about illness is discursively organized, most specifically in terms of its narrative formulation. I will therefore examine the way that causes of illness and accounting for illness experience together provide explanatory models for the understanding of and management of, illness.

First I will review three seminal studies of lay accounts of illness, at the same time considering certain methodological issues which seem to me to be inextricably bound up with the kind of research described. These issues are further developed in a review of two post-structuralist studies, one relying on respondent accounts, the other reflecting a more theoretical perspective. I will then move on to the narrative analysis of an extract from a research interview with an elderly married couple, which will illustrate certain of the theoretical points covered in the reviewed material, as well as providing an example of how accounts given in the research interview are necessarily self-reflexive as well as descriptive. The data discussed in the extract also provides a platform for the study, in the following chapter, of the doctor–patient relationship.

LAY REPRESENTATIONS AS SOURCES OF KNOWLEDGE

There is something at once suspect about the modifier 'lay' in the description of anything. The word presupposes the existence of another 'official' or 'expert' version. Along with the knowledge that one's version of reality is not 'official' comes the implication that it is necessarily deficient.

As a prefix, 'lay' is most commonly used in relation to religious and medical terms. Medical science, like religious orthodoxy, excels at exclusion (Strong, 1979; Armstrong, 1983; Arney and Bergen, 1983): the hierarchical structuring of the health care system, along with the sequestering of medical knowledge as something exclusive and arcane, seem to dictate that information should be excluded from the very people who are most directly affected by that knowledge (Atkinson, 1981; Silverman, 1987). In a universe where knowledge is specialized, technically complicated, and only gained after years of arduous study, that knowledge is jealously guarded. Alternative models of knowledge are strenuously opposed, or ridiculed: we might consider, for example, the antipathy with which the discipline of psychiatry was regarded during the early part of this century (Jung, 1983: 129) and the suspicion with which the skills of acupuncture and homeopathy are regarded in many quarters of the medical establishment today (Lupton, 1994a: 126).

Lay representation of illness provides a problem area for medical science, especially since lay representations are often far older and more culturally embedded than the more recent representations provided by modern medicine, and have, within a local cultural context, become commonsensical. On this theme, we might refer to Moscovici's theory of social representations (Moscovici, 1984; Moscovici and Hewstone, 1983). This suggests that modes of thought (concerning health, for example), are not a limited or limiting framework that the individual applies to his or her body and personal experience; instead, individual modes of thought are directed by understandings and representations of health and illness in the wider society.

Moscovici portrays social representations as applying to causality in a singular and illuminating way: for example, he points out that right-wing thinking lays responsibility for success or failure in life at the feet of the individual, so, broadly speaking, if a person 'makes good' it is due to his or her own innate energy and initiative, and if they fail, it is because they are idle and unimaginative. We might consider unemployment as an example. Right-wingers frequently attribute unemployment to the individual's own behaviour, to his or her social attitude, to being 'too choosy' about what work he or she does, or simply to being lazy. Left-wingers ascribe unemployment to the inherent injustices of the capitalist system, to unjustified redundancies, to forces beyond the individual's control. In Moscovici's words: 'The first representation stresses the individual's responsibility and personal energy – social problems can only be solved by each individual. The second representation stresses social responsibility, denounces social injustice and advocates collective solutions for individual problems' (Moscovici, 1984: 49). Needless to say there is little trace of the latter attitude among the majority of the ascendant classes, and not much evidence of the former among the homeless and the underprivileged. Either set of arguments could be supported by lines such as 'It stands to reason' or 'It's plain common sense'. In fact it is precisely this contrary character of common sense which makes it such a pivotal element in argument, a fact acknowledged by Aristotle in his *Rhetoric* and employed in courtroom oratory in the present day (Billig, 1991: 21). Common sense is a commodity which can be called upon simultaneously by opposing parties to back up conflicting arguments.

This can only happen, according to Moscovici, because a social representation has been *objectified*: the representation has become incorporated into our consensual reality. These representations provide an alternative source of knowledge, one that is hard to pin down and harder to contradict. Essentially, for our purposes, the usefulness of the theory lies in the perception that commonsense talk and 'lay' understanding are often interwoven with, and dependent on, professional discourses.

Kleinman (1988: 121), on the other hand, refers to the *conflict* between two explanatory models of illness, the medical and the lay. Often the doctor may feel that a patient's beliefs about the nature of his or her illness are in conflict with the medical 'truth': how then might an understanding be reached that serves the best interests of the patient without dislodging the basis of trust and co-operation so essential to the successful doctor–patient interaction? How, too, might the doctor 'translate' some of the concepts and beliefs about health and illness that patients bring along to the clinic?

'DISEASE' AND 'ILLNESS'

Helman (1984: 86) regards the difference between medical and lay views of sickness as being encapsulated in the distinction between *disease* and *illness* (cf. Eisenberg, 1977: 9). 'Disease' represents the doctor's perspective because the biomedical version requires an understanding of pathology that is discrete and rational. Within this model, disease is delimited and categorical, an identifiable entity residing in the body of a host. Illness, by contrast, is 'the subjective response of the patient, and of those around him, to his being unwell' (Helman, 1984: 91). Furthermore, accounting for illness tends to correlate with the psychological, moral and social explanatory models of any given culture; so that the same objectively defined *disease* will not be experienced as the same *illness* by individuals in distinct societies. Specific afflictions such as *crise de foie* (malaise or torpor originating in the liver) in France, *susto* (a loss of soul) in Latin America, and *chronic fatigue syndrome* in post-industrialized societies, might be examples of culturally 'untranslatable' conditions. Helman is at pains to point out that lay theories of illness are part of a more general conceptual framework about the origins of misfortune at large (1984: 102). As such, a model of the causes of ill health will not be markedly different from a model of the causes of any other kind of misfortune.

In general, explanations for being in ill health which are deemed to reside within the individual patient are 'important in determining whether people take responsibility for their health or whether they see the origin, and curing, of illness as lying outside their control' (Helman, 1984: 106). In a study of young mothers in Cardiff it was shown that socioeconomic factors play a large part in whether or not individuals felt responsible for many areas of their lives, health included. Responsibility for one's own health was clearly linked with respondents' theories about illness causation. Women who were home-owners and had an upwardly mobile image of themselves were more likely to take a view that their diet and lifestyle contributed significantly to their state of health compared to respondents with lower social goals and expectations, whose attitude was more fatalistic and who were more inclined to attribute illness to 'germs', 'being run down', heredity, or the environment (Pill and Stott, 1982).

However, there is perhaps an inherent danger in insisting too rigidly on the distinction between the 'expert' and the 'lay' interpretations of disease/illness. As Atkinson (1995) has pointed out, the disease/illness dichotomy is a product of a particular cultural frame, brought about by the hegemonic control of bio-medicine. Under this rubric, 'expert' opinion holds a virtual monopoly on the biomedical 'truth' of *disease*; while the lay voice seeks to establish subjective meaning and understanding of *illness*. However, the cultural relativism of a medical anthropology such as Helman's encourages us to regard biomedicine as 'other', just as biomedicine regards alternative/complementary systems as 'folk', 'ethno-' 'quack' etc., thereby exposing the falsely dichotomous 'illness' and 'disease' as nothing more than descriptive labels devised to delineate crudely the two perspectives of the 'lay' and the 'biomedical'.

In the section which follows I will consider three studies of the lay representation of illness, drawn from the fields of medical sociology/social psychology. Individuals' responses to questions about health and illness are presented in each of these studies as constituting a kind of belief system, categorized mentally by respondents in such a way as to make sense of illness and health issues. In this emphasis the merging of *accounts* with the cognitive notion of *beliefs* means that these studies differ radically from a discursive approach, but they do provide us with examples within the sociology of health and illness, as well as a context for the kind of discursive work which we will be examining towards the end of this chapter, and in the remainder of the book.

THREE STUDIES OF LAY REPRESENTATIONS OF HEALTH AND ILLNESS

Herzlich (1973)

Herzlich's study, based on loosely structured interviews with 80 middle-class respondents from Paris and Normandy, investigates concepts of health and illness from the theoretical standpoint of social representations (cf. Moscovici, 1984). This perspective suggests that modes of thought concerning health are not a limited or limiting framework that the individual applies to his or her body and personal experience, but rather that individual modes of thought are directed by understandings and representations of health and illness in the wider society.

Health is perceived by Herzlich's interviewees as, most importantly, the *absence of illness*. This concept of health Herzlich refers to as *health in a vacuum*. Under this definition, one is unaware that one *has* good health until it becomes threatened. 'Health in a vacuum' is perceived as being somehow independent of the individual, and existing within its own chronology. Conversely, the concept of *having* good health, rather than *being* in good health (health in a vacuum), is regarded as an asset, a form of capital. Health is therefore 'the reserve of defence from which everyone draws the possibility of reaction against illness' (1973: 61). This Herzlich terms the *reserve of health*. One can possess more or less of this commodity, which is often regarded as hereditary, or as the consequence of a healthy childhood.

Equilibrium, the third of Herzlich's concepts of health, is dependent upon the particular circumstances and events in a person's life and represents a norm that 'goes beyond the purely physical, because it is a norm of life as well as a norm of the body' (1973: 62).

These three conceptions have been summarized by Radley as follows:

> 'Health-in-a-vacuum' is only a fact, an impersonal condition; the 'reserve of health' is a value, a stock that can be built up or depleted; 'equilibrium' is a norm, against which individuals compare themselves at different times and against other people. (Radley, 1994: 40–1)

An important consequence of these findings is that health cannot be viewed simply as the opposite of being ill, but that 'concepts of health … connect with other areas of life, giving it meaning in terms of feelings and capacities involving activities and other people' (1994: 41). *Illness*, as experienced by Herzlich's respondents, is bound up with their relationship to, and attachment to, their 'way of life' (1973: 27).

Herzlich's model, therefore, is one of the healthy individual at odds with the disease-bearing society. The individual, inherently healthy, is in a state of conflict with society. This is because his or her essentially unhealthy way of life (dictated by membership of society) causes, or can cause, illness. The symmetry of Herzlich's equation becomes evident when we observe that it is health which binds the individual to society. The sick individual, on the contrary, ceases to be a fully valid member of society.

As she did for health, Herzlich specifies three conceptions of illness. They are: (1) *Illness as destructive*; (2) *Illness as a liberator*; (3) *Illness as an 'occupation'*. It is in terms of one (or more) of these that the individual is able to express his or her relation to society when enduring illness.

Illness as Destructive People who are particularly active in society are prone to regard illness as destructive. Feelings of inadequacy, helplessness, of being shunned by others or of being a burden on family or friends predominate. Persons who consider themselves indispensable in their place of work are likely to consider taking time off for illness as unthinkable, whatever the state of their health. For such individuals illness is a form of deviance. The solitariness of the invalid is emphasized, the inactivity and loneliness; the notion that one cannot enter into a world of invalids because it 'is a world of irremediably solitary individuals' (1973: 108). Self-worth is devalued. One respondent speaks of being invaded by a lesser person since becoming ill, and of being 'psychologically, spiritually and physically deformed' (1973: 110). The individual can, at one extreme, react with total passivity and behave like an invalid to be cured, or, at the other, completely reject the illness and attempt to carry on with life as though nothing were the matter.

Illness as a Liberator Serious illness is likened to a love affair, or at the very least to freedom from the burdens of worry. It is seen as a way of being set free. It is also likened to a journey of the imagination, to the discovery of another world. Illness is an escape from reality. Workaday time has no meaning: time stands still. In this sense it resembles a holiday. Whereas in the representation of illness as destructive the individual is annihilated by exclusion from society, here the patient rediscovers possibilities of a new freedom which appears to be stimulated by a sense of power over others. There is, moreover, a 'religion of pity' for invalids and the patient can take advantage of surprising privileges and exercise an individuality and capriciousness which in a healthy person would be socially unacceptable. Illness too is regarded as character-building in a rather profound way. This follows a subscription to the belief in growth through suffering, which grants exceptional insights into one's own life and greater lucidity and awareness of questions relating to life and death.

Illness as an 'Occupation' This refers to the active and sustained fight against specific illness that for many individuals is a life's work. It comprises the following aspects: (a) the invalid maintains the normal social values associated with health: levels of activity, energy and willpower are just as relevant to the invalid as to the healthy person; (b) the invalid learns through the experience of illness, and through the process of struggle becomes a 'stronger' person; (c) the invalid is preoccupied with getting cured: illness is essentially both a stage and a behaviour by which a cure is achieved. Time is as 'real' as it is in a state of health; (d) adjustments are made by the chronically ill in order to create a 'new form of life' for oneself. This life may be limited, but has its compensations and may provide an introduction to new interests. In this representation: 'The invalid is therefore not defined by values and a personality basically different from those of a healthy person. Similarly, illness remains, like health, a socialized situation' (1973: 125).

Herzlich considers the notion of activity/inactivity to be of prime importance in the social representation of illness. Inactivity becomes the central image of the representation, splitting off the patient from the rest of society. Around this notion of activity/inactivity 'crystallizes the totality of meanings affecting the experience of illness, as these meanings are constituted in social life. Giving up activity becomes the sign of illness' (1973: 137).

The work of Herzlich requires attention because it sets out a number of perceptions of health and illness, and is used as a benchmark for later studies of its kind. It is a seminal work which influenced comparable research by Blaxter and Paterson (1982), Pill and Stott (1982), Cornwell (1984), R. Williams (1990) and Rogers (1991).

Blaxter (1983)

Blaxter's (1983) study concentrates data from the longer cross-generational investigation (Blaxter and Paterson, 1982) of the health beliefs of women brought up in poor social circumstances in Aberdeen. The preferred categories for the causes of disease were found to be infection, heredity, family susceptibility and harmful agents in the environment. The women tended to reject chance or natural degenerative explanations and Blaxter suggests that the women's models of disease were not very different from those of modern science and 'no less sophisticated' (1983: 59). The women were encouraged to talk about whatever was of interest to them regarding their health and illness beliefs. The data does not consist of answers to predetermined questions but of conversations of 1–2 hours' duration during which the women would tell stories about particular episodes involving illness. 'Every instance,' writes Blaxter, 'was then examined to see whether cause was explicitly or implicitly stated, and the causes for each disease were allotted to data-derived categories' (1983: 59).

Blaxter accepts the distinction between illness and disease described by Helman, in which diseases are named pathological entities that constitute the medical model of ill health, and illness refers to a subjective experiencing of symptoms. The women are said to regard disease as a 'thing, a noun which one usually "has" or "gets" or (if it is infectious) "catches"' whereas illness is viewed predominantly from a moral perspective: 'illness was weakness, "lying down to it", being functionally unfit, giving in to diseases' (1983: 60). Blaxter's main objective, though, lies not in the analysis of conceptual differences that may or may not pertain to disease and illness, but in evaluating 'the structure of the women's thinking and its similarity or difference when compared with the models of medical science' (ibid.). She makes interesting reference to the *reification* of disease and the use of either the definite or indefinite article in its description. She claims that the more familiar and common ailments are prefixed with the definite article marking them as familiar, 'almost friends: the cold, the flu, the chronic bronchitis, the mumps' (ibid.). Heart disease and cancer are notable exceptions to this pattern.

There was widespread agreement that 'germs' could be defeated by washing, boiling and disinfecting, but the introduction of a 'new' word like *virus* caused some degree of scepticism. As one of Blaxter's women says: 'You'd get a doctor come in and he'd say, "Oh, a virus". They've found a new word' (1983: 62). Interestingly, although 'germs' could be overpowered by vigilance and copious amounts of boiling water and carbolic soap, viruses were regarded as invasive agents of far greater and more insidious power. Certain people (and animals) were regarded as 'carriers' of disease, even though they themselves might not suffer from them; heredity was seen as a decisive element in the 'taking' of a disease, and there was a particular tendency to attribute certain categories of disease to hereditary or family 'weakness'. This family inheritance was viewed ambiguously, because although the exploration of familial patterns was worrying, it was at the same time a source of some degree of comfort, claims Blaxter, because it absolved one from taking any responsibility for one's own diseases.

Just as happiness was associated with the maintenance of good health, stress, overwork and worry were all considered causes of disease, especially of heart disease. However, it was apparent that women, despite offering stress-related explanations for diseases themselves, resented doctors trying to impose such explanations on them: 'such theories of cause and effect were acceptable only when they were based on the detailed knowledge which they themselves had of the interrelations between life events and symptoms' (1983: 64). Women were apt to pour scorn on a doctor who diagnosed 'nerves' as the cause of a physical symptom, especially if the diagnosis was accompanied by a prescription of sedative drugs: 'And a woman gets spots on her face and it's nerves! Now I've had spots on my face, but it's nae nerves. They hand them this Valium!' (Blaxter, 1983: 64).

There were very few diseases which were attributable solely to the ageing process, though there was a general acceptance that poor health was an inevitable component of old age. Although the women were in their late 40s or 50s they considered themselves, says Blaxter, older than their years. Blaxter attributes this attitude to the early childbearing common to members of the group and the difficult conditions of their lives. As one woman remarks: 'I'm getting on in years, so I'm not really bothered now. See, I'm 47.' Rheumatism, back pain and arthritis might be judged as 'wear and tear' or due to 'getting older', and according to another woman the cause of anaemia is that 'your blood deteriorates as you get older' (1983: 66).

In summary, Blaxter's women seem to regard the causes of disease as the interaction of a malign external catalyst with an inherent susceptibility to a particular disease. The women thought, claims Blaxter, 'in terms of causal agents, which required initial susceptibility to take effect, and also required precipitating factors'. Thus one woman says of cancer: 'Everyone's got it, but it needs something to set it off'. Such models, says Blaxter, are in fact 'very similar to those of advanced medical science' (1983: 67).

Blaxter concludes that folk models of disease are not oppositional to scientific medicine on the whole; this occurs only if we take a narrow and outdated view of modern medicine – that of single causes, the dichotomy of soma and psyche, a limited definition of heredity, and of disease and behaviour as discrete. A good understanding between doctor and patient depends upon trust and respect on the doctor's part for the veracity of these lay models of disease; and real communication depends upon establishing an equilibrium between the formal medical taxonomy and the informal folk knowledge of the group: 'Formal knowledge, with time, diffuses and becomes standard and traditional: conversely, some of the lay accumulated wisdom contains insights and clues which the medical profession can use, and systematise into formal knowledge' (1983: 69).

This neatly adds to the social representation theory of Moscovici by making the relationship between 'expert' and 'lay' knowledge a symbiotic one, rather than one in which the flow is simply from the professional domain into the public. Our next study (also, coincidentally, set in Aberdeen) considers some of the same issues of illness causality and representation. applied more specifically to an older group of respondents.

R. Williams (1990)

This study examines the ways in which elderly people respond to the onset of illness, ageing and eventual death. In his treatment of the illness theme, the author, like Pill and Stott (1982) and Blaxter (1983), acknowledges a debt to the pioneering work of Herzlich (1973). As with Blaxter's study, the distinction between illness and health was defined according to the capacity to work, to 'carry on normally'. Health was conceived of in a threefold manner, along similar lines to those of Herzlich. Most significant, according to Williams' respondents (1990: 31), were the strength to resist illness and the ability to function normally. The claim of 'being ill' was not a valid one unless it could be accompanied by the *proof* of visible effect or clinical testing. This resilience in the face of illness was accompanied by *pride* in functioning normally. *Strength* was a means to prevent illness, and strength mitigated illness when it did occur, providing the foundation for an essentially *moral* struggle:

> 'If you sit down to it, well you've had it really, you won't get up. At my age. Or even at 70. Some of them say they're old at 60, oh I canna get up, I have to sit in a chair, and this and this. And I tells them, I says, you should move about, I says, and get out.' (1990: 34)

Restrictions on activity are an aspect of being ill that presents a challenge to the individual, and succumbing to those restrictions is akin to 'giving in' to illness. The release from obligation that illness might bring, a release welcomed by a significant proportion of Herzlich's interviewees in Paris (see 'Illness as Liberator', above), was expressed by few people in the Aberdeen study, apart from as a kind of disengagement that Williams likens to daydreaming, a component of ageing with 'an uneasy mixture of voluntary and involuntary elements' (1990: 46). Williams actually terms this category *illness as disengagement*.

Just as strong mental purpose and physical activity are seen as preventing the individual from succumbing to illness, a lack of willpower or vigilance is regarded as contributory to the breakdown of resistance. The underlying assumption, that the person involved harbours a secret desire to become ill, or possesses hypochondriac tendencies, is only rarely advanced, but, says Williams, such assumptions 'form a threat and a moral sanction of disproportionate significance, and are the ultimate weapon for either keeping oneself in hand or for criticizing others' (1990: 51). Comparison with Herzlich's Parisian informants provokes reflection on the distinctive nature of the 'Protestant legacy' that Williams regards as integral to the Aberdonian consciousness:

> Aberdeen appears, in regard to illness, as a somewhat conservative society where boundaries are quite strongly marked. The tradition of dissent, and the ambivalence between the active and the contemplative life, which enables the French at times to see illness as a liberator, and personal autonomy and alternative styles of life as a legitimate response, is virtually absent. But at the same time older Aberdonians have a confidence in the health-giving character of their way of life which contrasts sharply with the metropolitan disillusion of Paris. (1990: 53–4)

Recourse to the doctor is subject to heavy qualifications in the minds of most older Aberdonians. Especially if the sick person is a man, a ritual drama will often take place in which a female member of the family phones the doctor despite the efforts of the sick person to stop her. The caller may even plead with the doctor to make it look as though he paid the visit 'as a casual afterthought while passing by' (1990: 161). Along similar lines, working-class respondents who have been hospitalized cite tales of rebellion (smuggled bottles of whisky; illicit strings of sausages) that reinforce the image of the doctor as the voice of authority against which must be pitted the inevitable disobedience of the wilful individual. (By contrast, Williams' middle-class respondents were more likely to interpret conflict with the doctor, not as patient delinquency, but as the doctor being wrong.) The role of the reluctant patient within this society is a creditworthy one, exhibiting characteristics of true grit, but it is also interesting in that the relationship with the doctor can be regarded as metonymic of the patient's relationship to medicine (cf. Herzlich and Pierret, 1987; Van der Geest and Whyte, 1989). So, although there may be a certain resistance to medical care, in the person of the doctor (which can be regarded as status-related among the working-class men in Williams' study), there exists also a more subtle identification of the figure of the doctor with the institution of medicine, which when challenged or subverted, can prove problematic for the patient. We examine such an instance later in this chapter.

PROCESS AND CONTEXT AS METHODOLOGICAL CONCERNS

The three studies reviewed in the preceding section followed a broadly uniform line of enquiry and employed remarkably similar methodologies. Each researcher selected informants from a definable social group or groups: 'middle-class Parisians'; 'working-class grandmothers' and 'elderly (middle- and working-class) Aberdonians'. Informants were invited to give their accounts of illness and of health, and sometimes to relate anecdotally their experiences with doctors and other health care workers. None of the studies employs discourse analysis as the primary means of investigating respondents' talk, but all of them provide quantities of transcribed material. This material is not presented in the texts in as detailed a manner as it would be by discourse analysts or sociolinguists, and the authors provide very little by way of ethnographic contextualization.

All three studies present an overview of the health beliefs of a closely delineated target group, and report on these views in a manner that tends towards generalization, that is, presenting the views of individuals as though they were speaking on behalf of a group. Inevitably, perhaps, through their presentation in short quotation formula, the views and beliefs of individuals are put forward as though they were fixed and irrevocable, thereby neglecting the importance of the *process* and *context* of their construction. By *process*, I mean that there is little or no reflection on the manner of the data gathering and no subjective appraisal of the researcher's role in the interviewing process. The 'observer's paradox' (Labov, 1972), whereby the researcher's presence is considered to markedly affect the production of 'data', is not even considered as a methodological issue, nor even as a factor influential upon the interpretation of data. It could be argued, of course, that it was not the intention of these authors to proceed in this way; and that such a method would indeed be an anachronism, since the deconstruction of the researcher's role within ethnography is a relatively recent notion. Nor are these comments intended to deny the importance of the studies, or detract from the originality and quality of the research: but without incorporating an account of the process of data gathering in their work it is difficult for researchers, in the words of Lupton (1994a: 162), 'to examine their own position of power and claims to truth in the research and writing process'. This accounting for one's own research processes has been termed *reflexivity* in post-structuralist writings. Fox (1993: 162) defines reflexivity as 'analysis which interrogates the process by which interpretation has been fabricated'. We will be returning to a consideration of reflexivity, and its special relevance to discourse analysis, at different stages in this book.

The implication of *context* is the second aspect of these kinds of study that I would like to question. As Radley observes:

> One of the main findings of the 'Health and Lifestyles Survey' (Blaxter, 1990) was that individuals give different sorts of explanations depending upon context. These might be different for illness and for health; different for health as a generalised concept and 'my own health', different for generalised 'illness' and for specific 'disease', depending upon the person's own experience. This conclusion bears upon the point made by Herzlich: that we think about health and illness both through shared representations and through their transformation in our own experience. (1994: 47)

Interestingly enough, Blaxter herself (1993) returned to her Scottish data in an attempt to show how people struggle to negotiate meanings in their accounts of illness. According to Radley: 'She contrasts this search for "experiential coherence" with the provision of "theoretical coherence" that might be expected if people were giving a logical account' (1994: 47). There is a clear connection between the quest for 'experiential coherence' and what Potter and Wetherell regard as the *discursive* processes by which individuals negotiate reality (Potter and Wetherell, 1987: 37–8). This experiential coherence necessarily contains contradictory strands, even conflicting versions of the same event as related by the same speaker, but the proposal that people do express seemingly contrary themes in their thinking, or that 'meaning is related to argumentative context' (Billig, 1991: 31), finds confirmation in Radley's belief that 'thinking is less a predictive or representational activity than it is a kind of inner argument, in which the pros and cons of different points of view are put forward and countered' (1994: 59). To illustrate these more discursive perspectives, I single out two studies that emphasize, first the *diversity* of representations of health and illness, and secondly the topic of *subjectivity*, or the postmodern notion that 'the subject is no more than an effect of power, constituted in discourses of power/knowledge' (Fox, 1993: 163).

POST-STRUCTURALISM, HEALTH AND ILLNESS

Rogers (1991)

Accounts is the term used by Rogers (1991) in her ethnographic study of lay beliefs about health and illness, subtitled *An Exploration of Diversity*. The term 'account' is preferred over 'representation', 'schema' or 'personal construct' 'because', the author says, 'it is simple and has explicitly story-like qualities' (1991: 2). Nor does the term connote an *explanation* as such, but more the 'knowledge and understanding base upon which an explanation can be formed'. An account is marked out as being neither 'personal' nor 'social' but as able to accommodate both individual and collective perspectives. Rogers seeks in her study to discover what range of accounts is available for 'the weaving of explanations about health and illness' (1991: 2).

Another stated aim of the study is to confront the assumption made by professionals in the fields of health and psychology that it is only experts who are capable of making sense of other people's lives and that 'ordinary people lack any reflexive self- or other- awareness' (1991: 4). Rogers draws upon a postmodern theory of explanation, which envisages the individual as living at one and the same time within multiple realities (cf. Berger and Luckmann, 1967; Potter and Wetherell, 1987). However, explains Rogers, this multiplicity of self is not to suggest a kind 'of personal or collective "schizophrenia"' (1991: 10), of surviving 'within a complete muddle of unmanageable confused and contradictory thoughts and selves' but rather to advance the idea of people as 'clever weavers of stories, whose supreme competence is that they can and do create order out of chaos, and moment to moment make sense of their world amid the cacophony' (ibid.). Such a conception meshes with the postmodernist argument that there are 'many potential worlds of meaning that can be imaginatively entered and celebrated, in ways which are constantly changing to give richness and value to human experience' (Mulkay, 1991: 27–8, cited in Rogers, 1991: 9).

In her review of anthropological and sociological approaches to health and illness Rogers turns her attention to the problems posed by the concept of *reification* in medical discourse. She represents Western biomedicine as a self-perpetuating ideology that will not tolerate epistemological scrutiny. Reification induces in people a way of seeing the world in a particular way, and she cites by way of example, the manner in which terms like *stress, anorexia, pre-menstrual tension* and *post-traumatic shock syndrome* have become ideological in their impact. One of the consequences of these processes of reification is that the medical establishment has authorized itself (by creating the definitions of these categories of illness) to be the sole provider of their treatment, and has derogated rival systems and alternative healers as charlatans and quacks (1991: 20).

The biomedical model of reality is perpetuated through a process of *legitimation*, the key concept in Berger and Luckmann's (1967) social constructionism. Legitimation, within the medical context, comprises four levels: the use of language (e.g. *patient*; *doctor*; *cure*), which continually bolsters a vision of the world 'as it really is'; lay explanations taking the form of proverb or cliché such as 'doctor knows best', and the commonsense precaution of 'the visit to the doctor'; explicit theories that 'explain' medical knowledge, such as germ theory, but which can apparently be overturned at a moment's notice by a 'new discovery' in medical science; and the process of 'internalization' of the symbolic sub-universe of medical knowledge whereby 'worldviews' are created, sustained and controlled by 'expert' legitimation (Rogers, 1991: 33).

Through legitimation, particular kinds of knowledge – specifically here, biomedical knowledge – are processed by individuals into a 'social and psychological construction of reality, available ... to all in the culture who have access to it, and consequently acting as a powerful frame within which people ... make sense of their world' (1991: 33). The correspondences of this theory with Moscovici's theory of social representations are apparent, even if Rogers' theory lacks detail of the actual means by which these kinds of knowledge are 'anchored' (Moscovici, 1984). In fact Rogers, like other observers (cf. Billig, 1988), regards Moscovici's formulations as contradictory and unprovable (even, she suggests, untestable): useful as 'helpful metaphors rather than a full-blooded theory' (Rogers, 1991: 66), a view with which the present author would concur.

Using a combination of interviews and 'Q methodology' (a classificatory system on a sliding scale in which participants themselves are reportedly in control of the classification process) Rogers' first study set out to 'identify and explain' some representations of health and illness. The selection procedure for participants poses problems in a study such as this, as Rogers explains:

> I did not select people to interview formally according to principles of representativeness or sampling. Rather I did my best to find people who were likely to draw upon diverse ideas, understanding and indeed whole worldviews, as different from each other (and my own) as possible. (1991: 135)

Nonetheless, of her 70 participants, 24 are health workers. She claims to have recruited 'about half' to ensure a spread of 'ordinary' viewpoints. The occupations of other respondents varied; they included: 'students, teachers, lecturers and researchers, administrators, an architect, a social worker, a factory worker, a cellarman, a fireman, a police officer and a retired army major' (1991: 138). A second study, relying more completely on the 'Q' system, recruited 100 persons in order to examine the factors of responsibility and blame in illness. Again there appear to be a disproportionately large number of people from academia, psychology, social work and health care (including six actively involved in alternative medicine). Even her token unemployed man is a psychology graduate. Despite her ideological concerns and previously stated belief in reflexivity as an integral part of the research process, she is inexact in writing about her participants, or rather her superficial 'exactness' only gives us the information that she considers necessary in order to fulfil her curious notion of 'diversity':

> I made strenuous efforts to include more 'working class' people than I had in the previous study, for example by seeking contacts via a local pub, a housing scheme for retired people, and in local shops. I also recruited a Hindu student, a woman with spina bifida, a psychotherapist, a woman who had had a mastectomy and another who had been operated on for a pituitary tumor. (1991: 178)

I have dwelled upon the problems inherent in selecting informants for a study of this kind because such considerations appear to be of particular importance to the researcher herself. However there does not seem to be any single answer to the correct way of selecting participants – short of disclaiming all pretence at representativeness of any kind. If the themes of the fragmented self and intertextuality so central to postmodernism are to be embraced in earnest, it certainly seems unnecessary to justify one's selection of candidates on the grounds of their diversity, while at the same time implicitly *denying* that diversity by emphasizing a particular facet of the individual's social persona (can a 'Hindu student' not be at the same time the habituée of the local pub *and* have had a mastectomy?). We might instead remark that the classification of these is formulated in order to stress a diversity (recalling the subtitle of Rogers' study) which simply – and simplistically – bolsters some kind of ideological 'researcher-view' on reality.

However, Rogers' findings are of great interest, and the cultural analysis with which she concludes her study provides a convincing account of eight of the predominant metaphors employed in respondents' accounts. These are: (1) *the body as machine* account, which, along with (2) *the body under siege*, most clearly 'reflect Moscovici and Hewstone's (1983) assertion that within Western culture, social representations are often popularized or "commonsense" versions of scientific, academic or professional theories, operating within everyday discourse' (1991: 209). The remaining accounts are: (3) *the inequality of access account*, which reflects the unfair distribution of the benefits of modern medicine; (4) *the cultural critique of medicine account*, which stresses the power/knowledge factor and the social construction of biomedical reality; (5) *the health promotion account*, which allocates collective and personal responsiblity for maintaining a healthy lifestyle; (6) *the robust individualism account*, concerned with the freedom to live one's life as one chooses; (7) *the 'God's power' account* and its antithesis, the (8) *willpower account*, stressing the individual's moral responsiblity to use 'willpower' to maintain good health (1991: 208–9).

In conclusion Rogers emphasizes the *'sympatricity'* [*sic*] of her reported accounts, that is, the tendency of accounts to co-exist with other, seemingly contradictory ones. This acknowledgement of 'diversity', and willingness to confront and accept 'sympatricity' lies at the centre of Rogers' work. She urges that her book be regarded as part of a postmodern movement towards emancipatory study; study that is the result of 'searching first here and then there to weave the story that, informed by the texts, is still my own' (1991: 227). She insists upon the principle of intertextuality: that the arguments of other texts should be borne in mind while pursuing the thread (to adopt her own metaphor) of any account.

Fox (1993)

In her study on illness and metaphor, Sontag (1991) asks the question: 'why can't illness just be illness?': 'illness is *not* a metaphor, and ... the most truthful way of regarding illness ... is one most purified of, most resistant to, metaphoric thinking' (1991: 3). Fox (1993) presents a postmodern social theory of health, in part as a reaction against Sontag's plea:

> illness cannot be *just* illness, for the simple reason that human culture is consti-
> tuted in language, that there is *nothing knowable outside language*, and that
> health and illness, being things which fundamentally concern humans, and
> hence need to be 'explained', enter into language and are constituted in lan-
> guage, regardless of whether or not they have some independent reality in
> nature. (1993: 6)

Fox sees the starting point of a postmodern social theory of health (he uses the abbreviation PSTH), as the 'politics of health-talk' or 'illness-talk' rather than the subjects 'health' and 'illness'. Although highly theoretical in outlook, Fox's work bears upon the present book with at least two of the five aims that he sets himself at the beginning of his work (1993: 19). The first of these is 'a concern with the constitution of subjectivity through discourse, knowledge and power. In place of the unitary, prior, essential subject, there is a fragmented subject, constituted in difference'. The second is 'a concern with intertextuality (the "play of texts" upon each other), and a reflexive-ness over the production of my own text'. There is, too, the conceptuali-zation, derived from Foucault (1973), of the body as a text to be read and surveyed:

> The body ... has become – along with its 'health' or 'illness' – a text to be read,
> written and rewritten by 'body-experts', be they doctors, beauticians, sports
> instructors or lovers. (1993: 20)

Perhaps most importantly, for Fox, we must forsake the possibility of 'know-ing the world' and certainly of knowing what 'really is "out there" in terms of any kind of grand design or metanarrative' (1993: 15). Apart from introducing a rich and frequently bewildering lexicon to the sociology of health and illness, Fox does provide a socially committed approach with such notions as *responsibility to otherness* (1993: 21), which suggests the continuous negotiation of discursive freedom in the ethical and political maze that constitutes the world of biomedical reality. In its oblique and self-consciously dislocated fashion, Fox's critique of 'modernist' approaches to representations of health and illness alerts the reader to the problems of 'authenticity' or 'authority' that the researcher might encounter:

> Biographical approaches which claim to present 'real' patients' or professionals' thoughts or feelings are to be treated with extreme caution, as are reports which use extracts of talk to 'prove' structural schemata generated to explain the patterning of health settings. (1993: 10)

Such a perspective appears to be broadly consistent with the discursive approach proposed in this book, while the principle that patient accounts represent 'states of mind' that can be 'objectively' reported and categorized only leads to the kinds of reductionist model that are at odds with a discursive methodology.

Fox aspires to provide a blueprint for a postmodern social theory of health, one in which the 'lay perspective' is reframed as an emancipatory participation in health care, and integral to the meaning-making process. He deconstructs the metanarrative of the biomedical worldview in order to promote and encourage a nurturing of responsibility and resistance in tones which at times sound neo-romantic or utopian, never more so than when he is writing of the *nomad subject* (1993: 104), a kind of guerrilla fighter for discursive freedom within the hostile terrain of biomedical reality. While it would probably not be fair to suggest Fox as compulsory reading for the staff of a casualty unit on a Saturday night, the practice and provision of health care can only be enriched by the constant re-examination of theoretical positions urged by Fox, and by considering the larger picture of embodiment, health and medicine in the postmodern world.

In the remainder of the chapter I will be considering an extract from a research interview, in which narrative analysis is used to uncover and foreground some of the issues raised by the studies in the first half of the chapter. Again, methodological concerns will be addressed in the course of the commentary and analysis, in which I hope to suggest that methodology is not a 'thing apart' from the practice of research and writing, but provides an element within a single, although fragmentary process.

NARRATIVE AND RITUAL CODE IN A MEDICAL ENCOUNTER

According to Young (1987), oral narrative, in contrast with written forms, 'plays on, out and through the continuities between realms, particularly between contiguous realms like the story and the conversation' (1987: 14). The story itself is constructed as a discursive process within conversation, or

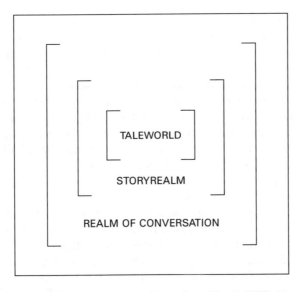

FIGURE 2.1   Narrative laminations (Young, 1989)

informal interview, and it is the story that directs attention to another realm of events not in the conversation, which she terms the 'Taleworld'. While opening onto the Taleworld, the story retains its own status as an enclave in conversation, a 'Storyrealm'. Thus, we learn, 'the terms "Taleworld" and "Storyrealm" discriminate these alternative ontological presentations of stories'. We, as listeners, have access to the Taleworld by way of the Storyrealm. Characters in the Taleworld 'are unaware of their realm as a tale. They enter into it as real, engaging, a realm to be experienced by its inhabitants as a reality' (ibid.). By contrast, the 'Storyrealm ... is part of the intersubjective world of sociality and communication, an enclave in conversation, one orienting to another realm, the Taleworld' (1987: 16).

According to Young's allegory, in the context of research interviews the enclave of the Storyrealm is approached through the questions I, the researcher, ask of the interviewee, who then provides access to the Taleworld, that is, their own experiential reality. I (as listener) shift between these realms: the more I am drawn into the Taleworld, the more invisible (ideally) becomes the Storyrealm; and the more I lose my sociality and engagement in the act of *holding an interview*. The transformations between the three realms of our conversation, the Storyrealm, and the Taleworld, can be conceptualized, following Goffman (1974: 82) as *narrative laminations* and are represented in Figure 2.1.

'In virtue of their frames,' writes Young, 'stories can be identified as a different order of event from the conversations in which they are enclaves, a Storyrealm. The Storyrealm, that region of narrative discourse within the realm of conversation, then directs attention to a third realm, the realm of the events the story is about, or Taleworld. Events in the Taleworld are framed by the story, itself framed by the conversation. A single event can, in this way, be multiply framed, so that as Goffman suggests, 'it becomes convenient to think of each transformation as adding a *layer* or *lamination* to the activity' (Young, 1987: 24). It is within this framework of multiple laminations, and of 'shifts between realms', that I am best able to re-enter and reconsider the multiple realities represented by the analysis of narrative discourse.

In the course of collecting illness narratives (Gwyn, 1997) I interviewed an elderly couple, whom I call Bruce and Sylvia Ryan. Bruce was the principal interviewee and had a long history of illness. He was a retired postal worker and World War II veteran, having spent three and a half years as a prisoner of war in Japanese camps between 1942 and 1945.

Before the interview I was introduced to the Ryans by my contact, who explained simply that I wished to ask them a few questions about illness and health care for my research, after which my contact left almost immediately. I was invited to sit on the sofa in the living room/kitchen area. While Sylvia made tea we chatted about the neighbourhood (I myself lived nearby) and I was asked about my own family – where I came from, whether I had children, etc. When Sylvia brought the tea over, she sat in a large armchair to my right. Bruce, meanwhile, was seated in an armchair directly in front of me: we therefore formed an irregular triangle, with a small microphone placed on the coffee table between myself and Sylvia, pointing towards Bruce. I directed most of the questions to Bruce, by looking at him and occasionally by using his name as I spoke, but Sylvia contributed freely. She often, especially later in the meeting, took an impatient attitude towards Bruce's frequently lengthy explanations, telling him good-naturedly to 'shut your mouth now', 'shut up now' or to 'answer the question not gabble on'. It was clear that Sylvia wanted to make a fuller contribution, and in the later part of the interview she did so.

There were occasions throughout the interview when a complete narrative was presented by one partner, only to have the other partner reopen it and add a new twist to the story, or provide further narrative detail. The example that we will examine follows this pattern, and as such constitutes what Young (1987: 175) considers joint storytelling within a conversation.

Strictly speaking, of course, the performance of Sylvia Ryan in the interview cannot be treated as though it were taking place within a 'conversation'. Although the boundaries between 'interview' and 'conversation' are at times barely perceivable in our talk, it is clear from several comments made by Sylvia Ryan that she is following the broad agenda of 'interview', even if in her speech behaviour she is the participant whose contributions are the most conversational in style, as illustrated by the kinds of 'interruption' that were quoted above. This leads me to locate the interaction (following Wolfson, 1976) within the frame described as 'conversational interview', or somewhere in the 'gap' that Mishler has identified as existing 'between research interviewing and naturally occurring conversation' (1986: 6). There is much in our talk that adheres more to the conventions of conversation than of interviews, one aspect of which is the floor-seeking behaviour sometimes evidenced by both the Ryans, which would be out of place in an 'interview' situation (Kress and Fowler, 1979: 63). As Young reminds us, 'utterances in conversation have been seen by analysts as moves in a game' in which participants 'monitor conversation for sequentially relevant next moves'. Such behaviour is 'floor-seeking, as if getting the floor were their intention in talk' (1987: 178). Floor-seeking occurs quite overtly then, when Sylvia demands of her husband to 'shut up' or not to 'gabble on', but also in more subtle ways throughout the interview, where she provides orientation for one of his stories, which she does frequently (as he does with her). On occasion too, she completes an utterance for him, as occurs when he talks of his feelings for doctors and army officers:

> [BR   =Bruce Ryan SR=Sylvia Ryan]
> BR   that's it (.) they're not above me they're not better than me (.) you're
>   the same as me mate you'll come to the same end in the long run so
>   why should you worry (.) I lost all (2.0) well=
> SR   =respect for authority=

This last example can hardly be classed as floor-seeking behaviour since Sylvia immediately relinquishes the floor for Bruce to continue with his story. She is extending conversational solidarity by supplying the term that she feels he is searching for, just as, a few seconds later she supplies the name of a politician who supported the cause of the ex-POWs in Parliament, a process of 'collaboratively constructed sentence-making' (Lerner, 1991).

The narratives that are jointly constructed between Bruce and Sylvia do not conform to any single pattern. They constitute an interweaving and sometimes mutually contradictory joint discourse, at times supportive, at times chiding, but generally directed towards the same narrative agenda and a shared explanatory model of illness. This involves relating all of Bruce's illnesses back to his period of incarceration in a POW camp.

Bruce Ryan was 75 at the time of the interview: a tall, lean, straight-backed man, with white hair, a dark complexion and an aquiline profile. He possessed evident self-respect combined with a mild propensity for self-deprecation, carried along by a strong sense of humour and a stated willing-ness to 'let things take their course'. Bruce was civil and forthright with me, and appeared to be relaxed throughout the course of the interview. The only exceptions to this were when he described aspects of his incarceration, or the consequences of it. His self-presentation was characterized by an over-riding tendency towards stoicism. At several points elsewhere in his inter-view he typifies the kind of older man studied by R. Williams (1990), whose accounts reinforce the image of the doctor as the voice of authority against the inevitable disobedience of the wilful individual. He also fits into Rogers' category of the 'robust individualist'.

An account is given seven minutes into the interview which relates events that occurred when Bruce was taken into hospital to have a kidney removed. Bruce has been describing his continuing treatment for skin cancer, when Sylvia (l. 112–13) introduces an incident that happened two years before:

> 108 BR   so from nineteen sixty eight when it started I've been=
>   [
> 109 SR   until now

```
110   BR    =going to Fieldend and I'm still going up to Fieldend and then
            every so
111         often ( . ) they break out and I've got to have radio therapy=
112   SR    =he had one each side of his back here [indicating]  ( . ) and then
113         two years ago he had a haemorrhage  ( . )
114   BR    oh aye=
115   SR    =and I phoned the doctor and he said oh sometimes it happens in
            men
116         his age but if it keeps recurring send for the locum well he came out
117         and he said ooh you look all right it's just an infection in the
            bladder=
118   RG    =yeah=
119   SR    =he gave me tablets to give him ( . ) no instructions ( . ) well when
120         it kept happening I phoned the infirmary and took him down to the
121         infirmary ( . ) and within a week he was in to have his kidneys
122         removed kidney removed ( . ) he had a tumor in this kidney [points]
123   BR    [chuckles]
```

Bruce's comments regarding his visits to Fieldend hospital provide a kind of orientation (Labov, 1972) to the incidents that Sylvia and he will shortly describe. The illness is presented as something that is ongoing. The remedial action of visits to the hospital (Fieldend) has taken place since 1968 – and still continues. This establishes a sense of sequentiality to the illness: the skin tumours reappear at intervals and are treated 'every so often'. Sylvia (l. 112) demonstrates where on his body he had the tumors. This contextualization – 'one each side of his back here' – is already familiar because Sylvia has twice indicated to me the actual damage caused to Bruce's face and neck by the cancer, first in line 93 – 'there you can see the mark' – and again half a minute later:

```
103   SR                    there's the one in your neck and then
104         [getting up and pointing] there and then there he had one there [to
105         researcher] one there one in the middle of his forehead [continues
106         demonstrating and indicating places sotto voce while BR speaks]
```

In fact, the demonstration is repeated later in the conversation, when I am encouraged to stand and examine Bruce's scars in close detail. Orientation to the narrative detail is therefore accomplished to some degree by permitting phenomenological access to the experiences being described. By inviting me to look at Bruce's scar tissue, Sylvia is granting me access, in Young's terminology, to the Storyrealm of described experience.

The contextualization, or orientation, now completed, Sylvia introduces the new topic, Bruce's haemorrhage (l. 113). Sylvia's utterance here constitutes an 'abstract' (Labov, 1972), by concisely stating what her story will be about. Its tellability is confirmed by Bruce's 'oh aye', since the corroborative tone of his brief utterance suggests Bruce's endorsement of the forthcoming narrative. The historical time – 'two years ago' – provides the conventional framing in chronological terms that many narrators favour. Further orientation of a more specific kind is then provided in lines 115–16, indicating what happened at the outset of the events about to be described.

The plot, or storyline, of the narrative then begins, with the arrival of the locum. However, rather than unfolding gradually, the ensuing mini-narrative provides an account of the entire sequence of events in brief (lines 116–22). The mini-narrative (or extended abstract) completed, Sylvia returns to the plot or storyline in order to provide details of the locum's visit:

[RG=Richard Gwyn]
124   RG   and the the locum that
                          [
125   SR   the *locum* came he took he was a Pakistani nothing
                                                        [
126   BR   he took me pulse [ironically]
127   SR   against them

When the locum arrives Sylvia finds it necessary to comment on his supposed racial origins, 'he was a Pakistani nothing against them' which again serves as a kind of orientation, but one which here draws on the assumption of a knowledge (why else mention it?) that I am expected to share regarding the nature of Pakistani doctors (or more generally, Pakistanis). The conventional disclaimer, 'nothing against them' (ll. 125–7) conforms to the type of discourse strategy that van Dijk has identified as employed to 'emphasize negatives in positive ways' (1987: 388). It also serves as what Potter (1996: 125) refers to as 'stake inoculation'. The 'Dilemma of Stake' states that anything a person says or does can be discounted as a product of stake or interest (Potter, 1996: 110). In this instance stake inoculation is used by Sylvia to counter the potential criticism that she has an 'axe to grind' or that her account of the incident is prejudiced by her depiction of the doctor as a 'Pakistani'. Sylvia (according to her) is not simply perpetrating stereotypes about the kind of behaviour one might expect from a Pakistani (doctor) because she has, in her words 'nothing against them'. Bruce's ironic interjection: 'he took me pulse' (l. 126) can, in the present context, be interpreted to indicate the doctor's lack of competence, especially when considered alongside other more salient events remarked upon later, notably the amount of blood that Bruce had already lost – 'it was *everywhere*' – (l. 164); – 'I showed the locum that when he came I left the toilet as it was he wasn't a bit interested' (ll. 165–6). Sylvia then continues the narrative in a manner that further suggests the lack of professionalism, if not the absurdity, of the doctor's actions:

127   SR   he took his pulse looked at him said have you got a pain
128   no oh come down to my car I'll give you tablets so he had a Sainsbury's
129   carrier bag on the back seat of his car he rummaged in it gave me two
130   strips of tablets I didn't know *how many* he had to take *when* he had to
131   take them and I was afraid to give them to him so I rung the infirmary
132   and when we took the tablets down he put them in the bin he said don't

133   give him *these* (3.0) they arranged for him to have *x-rays* on the
         Monday
134   (.) he saw the *specialist* on the Wednesday he had a *body* scan
         on the
135   Thursday (.) he was *in* on the Sunday and he had his kidney out
         on the
136   Tuesday (.)
137 RG good heavens (.) that was quick
138 BR [laughter]

The action proceeds with the taking of the pulse and, again, the *gaze*
('he ... looked at him', l. 127). However, it seems that this is not the all-
encompassing medical gaze of the professional that we are familiar with
from Foucault (1973), but rather a visual platform for what is about to be
said, and one that is recognizable from Bruce's own tendency to preface
important utterances with a reference to the establishment of visual contact.
Devices such as 'I looked at him and said' or 'He turned around and said'
are common features of discourse where the speaker is about to make a significant utterance (Edwards, 1998, personal correspondence). The question
which the doctor asks – 'have you got a pain?' (l. 127) – is answered in the
negative, which is apparently sufficient grounds for a diagnosis (further
evidence, in this context, of the doctor's alleged indifference) because the
next utterance by the doctor is an invitation to Sylvia to 'come down' (the
Ryans live on the fourth floor) to his car to collect some tablets. We are,
implicitly, being invited to ask of this doctor: why did he not bring what was
needed up to the flat himself? Why should the patient's elderly wife accompany him downstairs simply so that he saves himself making the journey
from his car to their flat twice?

Sylvia accompanies the doctor down to his car, where his lack of professionalism is highlighted in almost comic terms as he 'rummages' in a
'Sainsbury's carrier bag' (ll. 128–9). The appurtenances of power and dig-
nity so important to our perception of a 'doctor' are parodied in this back-
seat fumbling, as is the absence of the proper container for the tablets
(the doctor's unfolding bag belonging to the same symbolic category as the
stethoscope and the white coat). The doctor takes two strips of tablets from
his plastic bag (suggestive of both the distribution of sweets to children as
well as the street-corner transactions of drug-dealers) and gives them to
Sylvia, but without any instruction as to how many should be taken, or
when. Naturally, Sylvia is 'afraid to give them' to Bruce (l. 131). The clan-
destine ambience of her securing of the drugs makes her wonder what she
has been handed. There are, I think, three points to be made about the way
the doctor is presented in Sylvia's description.

We are made aware of *the discrepancies between this doctor's behaviour
and the privileged role assigned to doctors in our society*: 'the professional
doctor has a social monopoly of expertise and knowledge which is the very
basis of the professional claim to a privileged status in society' (Turner,
1987: 50); '[d]octors themselves are subject to the field of power that
constitutes institutionalized norms of behaviour as necessary and rational'

(Lupton, 1994a: 118). Normally, as we shall see in Chapter 3, the dialogue between doctor and patient reads like the script of a play in which the characters know their roles perfectly, and any deviation from the script is seen as 'exceptional' (Treichler et al., 1984: 175). Power is perceived as static and as residing in the practitioner, the voice of medical authority. The doctor is here seen to abuse this position utterly.

The metonymic relationship of 'doctor' with 'medicine'. The dispensing of pharmaceutical drugs during or after a medical consultation involves a particular and ordered procedure that constitutes a 'ritual order' (Goffman, 1967). We might recall that Van der Geest and Whyte discuss medicine as metonymically linked to the person of the doctor, in that the medicine is an 'extension of the doctor'. They cite Cockx's (1989) view that the placebo effect is the result of uniting patient and doctor through the symbolic transfer of medicine. In other words, 'the healing hand of the doctor reaches the patient through the medicines'. They continue: 'By the same token, the doctor's reassurance is presented to the patient in the form of a prescription ... Both prescription and medicine bridge the gap between patient and doctor. The confidence awakened in the patient by the doctor is recaptured in the concreteness of medicine or prescription, in the same way that a souvenir brings back feelings of the past' (1989: 359–60). Doctors are metonyms for 'medicine' – and as such the handing out of a strip of tablets from a Sainsbury's bag utterly corrupts the talismanic value of the medicine, by associating it with the profane commerciality of the bag from which it is so unceremoniously produced, as against the professionally neutral black of the traditional doctor's bag. A Sainsbury's carrier bag is, after all, the receptacle of the weekly groceries – the sausages and cat food and kitchen roll – and therefore diminishes the 'charm' value of medicine entirely, and via metonymy, discredits the doctor as a handler of common merchandise.

The breaking of a ritual code. The doctor's transgression of this traditional code of behaviour disrupts symbolic expectations and the attendant atmosphere of 'medical magic'. Because this doctor does not perform the rites properly he is invested with the status of an evil sorcerer or witch doctor and neither he nor his drugs are to be trusted, a mistrust which is shortly to be substantiated.

Sylvia rings her local hospital, Saint Cadi's Infirmary, five minutes' walk from their home. When the Ryans get to the hospital the doctor whom they see *throws away* the tablets they have been given (another symbolic action) and says *'don't give him these'* (ll. 132–3). This places the infirmary doctor in opposition to the locum, whose actions are supportive of, rather than harmful to, the Ryans. Sylvia then describes the fluent efficiency with which the infirmary deals with their case, and the Ryans are restored to the care of a system that follows the conventional and ritually approved procedures:

133 (3.0) they arranged for him to have *x-rays* on the Monday
134 (.) he saw the *specialist* on the Wednesday he had a *body* scan
on the

135 Thursday (.) he was *in* on the Sunday and he had his kidney out on the

136 Tuesday (.)

This swift repertoire of events confirms the opinion expressed several times in the course of the interview regarding the high quality and professional excellence of their local hospital. The rhythmic litany of the days of the week provides a satisfying sequentiality of almost biblical simplicity. It also serves as the immediate result of the preceding narrative, and in turn acts to introduce an evaluation of the events, of the kind that Labov terms a 'comparator' (Labov, 1972: 380) i.e., one which implicitly compares the actual outcome of events with *what might have happened*:

139 SR this skin cancer that he'd had before I think must have spread into one

140   of spread *into* the kidneys because it was right there where the kidney

141   the kidney is and it it must have gone into the kidney I think but they got

142   it all away (.) everything clear (.) they said if it hadn't have

143   spread to some of the blood vessels=

144 BR =they wouldn't have known about it=

145 SR =they wouldn't he wouldn't have known it was there=

146 BR =I wouldn't have known it was there I had no pain at all (.)

According to this explanation, the cancer *moved* from the outside of Bruce's body to the *inside* (the kidney) and was detectable only because it spread into some blood vessels also. If it had not spread into the blood vessels 'they [the medical staff at the infirmary] wouldn't ... have known it was there' (l. 145). It may well be that the Ryans' voicing of this is a reformulation of what medical staff at Saint Cadi's Infirmary have 'rehearsed' to them at the time described, in which case a script is being followed that has filtered into their model of understanding illness. The appearance of such a 'received' model in Sylvia's talk would correspond with Moscovici (1984) on the dissemination of scientific knowledge, and would also corroborate Blaxter's finding that her 'women's models of disease processes ... were in principle no different to those of advanced medical science' (1983: 59). Certainly in relation to cancer, representations that are expressed in lay terms have a clear correlation with medical belief, as Blaxter observes. An example from the same study (Gwyn, 1997) in which two women (BJ and HL) discuss the universal *potential* for cancer is worth reproducing here:

BJ we've all got a *spot* of cancer=

HL =well everybody's got it (.) and those who worries more (.) w worry *into* it

Bruce then presents *his* account of the incident already described by his wife, contextualizing the events of the evening against a background of routine domesticity. We hear of his repeated visits to the toilet, the call to the doctor, the blood 'all over the pan' in the bathroom (which convinced his wife to call the doctor in the first place), until Sylvia intercedes to provide some anecdotal detail omitted from her earlier narrative concerning the locum:

165 SR =I showed the the locum that when he came I left the toilet as it
          was he
166   wasn't a bit interested
          [
167 BR oh he said that *that* won't hurt he said you've got a bladder
          infection=
168 SR =he said *these* are nice *flats* int they are there any to rent? [laughs]
169   that's all he was interested in (.)

The locum is here shown not only to be unconcerned about the heavy loss of blood evidenced by the state of the toilet, but far worse, he actually remarks on the Ryans' home – '*these* are nice *flats*' – and voices his own domestic or familial interests – 'are there any to rent?' This invites us to make a judgement upon the character of the locum, as a doctor (if not as a 'Pakistani doctor'), who with his comment about the flats allows the professional gaze to wander, taking in his immediate environment – not in a pleasant or helpful but in an acquisitive and needy way: 'are there any to rent?' His gaze, moreover, is seen to be severely restricted (he does not 'see' the blood in the toilet) and again he is compared unfavourably with the staff of the Ryans' local hospital who 'moved like *that*' (l. 170):

170 BR but fair play to Saint Cadi's Infirmary they moved like *that* [clicks
          fingers]=

                                              [
171 SR   they were *marvellous*

which completes Bruce's evaluation of the cited events, and enables him to return, not to the present (Storyrealm) time, but to the time of the Taleworld, and to recount further events, not reproduced here, regarding his hospitalization.

'NARRATIVE LAMINATIONS' IN THE FRAMING OF A LAY ACCOUNT

My experience as listener and as participant in the interview with Bruce and Sylvia grants me access to details of Bruce's life viewed in hindsight. This unusual privilege entails certain responsibilities along with certain inherent ambiguities. I know, for instance, that the realities described are not possessed of a natural order, perceivable by the speakers and reported back to me as observable fact. I know that a transformation of experience is involved in the telling of stories, so that Bruce and Sylvia have attuned their versions of 'the facts' to their own sustaining fictions, and produced evolving versions, which at times coincide or overlap with Herzlich's concept of 'illness as occupation' and at times with Williams' notion of wilful individualism. I know too that the world I shared with the Ryans was an intersubjective one, one that provided different vistas on account of a single muted word here, a glance there, a perceived recalcitrance here or a movement of the hand there.

Properties of their lives, especially Bruce's, that pertain to the Taleworld rather than the Storyrealm, to use Young's terms, to lived experience rather than to the recounting of that experience in the front room of their home, are offered, glimpsed by me, and accommodated within the frame of 'interview', or, more generously, 'conversation'. There is a threefold structure apparent throughout our talk, which Goffman (1974: 82) represents as narrative laminations. We shift from the realm of conversation to the Storyrealm, the narrative process which opens into the deeper realm of the Taleworld. The Taleworld feeds the Storyrealm and the Storyrealm feeds the conversation. I, as interviewer/listener, am hearing these stories for the first time. I am, in a sense, reading time backwards (cf. Ricoeur, 1980: 180) in order to attend to the individual grains of meaning that together constitute Bruce's personal narrative: and by using the term 'personal' I am provoking the question of whether, in the social world, any mythology can be construed as 'personal' (and the particular instantiation of joint storytelling I have recounted seems to question it further). I would argue, however, that the evolution and continuous renewal of any mythology involves intertextual and collective processes, but its identity and sustenance through the telling of stories remains, I believe, 'personal'. This runs counter to the prevailing tenets of postmodernism, by which the results of such interviews merely represent a *subjectivity*, with the 'subject ... no more than an effect of power constituted in discourses of power/knowledge' (Fox, 1993: 163). My preferred interpretative role would be the one suggested by Rogers (1991), of a weaver stitching together diverse scripts or representations. And although I believe this process of synthesis or *bricolage* to be going on, it seems to be true also that Bruce's narrative, whatever its origins and influences, is uniquely his, since the experience that sustains it is his. As the neurologist Oliver Sacks writes:

> Each of us *is* a singular narrative, which is constructed continually and unconsciously by, through, and in us – through our perceptions, our feelings, our thoughts, our actions; and, not least, through our discourse, our spoken narrations. Biologically, physiologically, we are not so different from each other; historically, as narratives, we are each of us unique. (Sacks, 1985: 12)

A final word on methodology seems apt at this point. My task as a researcher in the above study was to examine how, through the use of narrative, individuals provide a sequencing of events in a way that enables them to make sense of their illness within the context of an informal interview; the recording and representation of a 'lay perspective'. That this process involves 'multiple realities' is unavoidable. There is, in the first instance, the realm of conversation that exists between myself and the other speakers: a tenuous reality this, because as well as having a 'conversation' we are also embarking upon an 'interview'. There is then the reality of the space and time of the events under description in the speaker's account – the reality which Young (1987) calls the Taleworld – as well as the 'here and now' of the interview (which Young terms the Storyrealm). The interview is a continuous process of slipping in and out of the world described, back into the act of description, back to the Taleworld, back to the Storyrealm, and so forth. If more than one interviewee is present then the account becomes one that involves a joint or multiple response, and this too involves divergent representations, or alternative versions of reality. For instance, when I listen to Bruce and Sylvia Ryan I might hear their account/s as a collaborative narration. I listen again, and I hear it as a type of competition.

Once completed, the interview becomes another reality: the tape. The tape requires resubstantiation into the 'reality' of a transcript (an interpretative process). The transcript becomes another 'field of discourse' that I show to people, publish, and speak about at conferences. It becomes the focus for an interpretative process that we might call the reality of 'research'. The reality of 'research' (subsumed under the reality known as 'academic discourse') is therefore connected to the events in the original speaker's described experience, or Taleworld, only through a lengthy and convoluted process of reformulation and recontextualization. So, in conclusion, I can only concur with Young (1987: x), when she writes: 'Reality is not properly an attribute of any realm but a relationship between the realm I inhabit and my descriptions of it'.

CONCLUSION

The distinction between the terms 'disease' and 'illness', while unsatisfactory because of the terms' interchangeability in most people's understanding, provides the basic premise for a *medical* as opposed to a *lay* model of ill health. The medical model requires an understanding of pathology that is discrete and rational. By contrast, lay theories of illness causation are seen to be a part of a more general framework about the origins of misfortune at large.

Several studies of lay representation of illness, drawn from the fields of medical sociology/social psychology, were considered in this chapter. Individuals' responses to questions about health and illness were presented in each of these studies as constituting a kind of belief system, categorized mentally by respondents in such a way as to make sense of illness and health issues. I suggest that individuals are likely to give different and perhaps conflicting accounts of illness and health according to the criteria of *process* and *context*, and that this variability constitutes a normal feature of discursive practice. I therefore considered a postmodernist position on lay representations, and the interplay of seemingly contradictory explanations in the accounts of speakers. Rogers, for instance, advances the notion of people as 'weavers of stories' who are caught up in the multiple realities of their lives, ever seeking to attribute meaning in a shifting and reified universe, while Fox insists upon the *intertextuality* of texts, the fragmentation of self, and an emancipatory development of the *nomad subject*, who, ideally, resists the discourses of health and health care altogether.

In the second half of the chapter, taken from an ethnographic interview with an elderly couple discussing an incident in the illness history of the husband, this 'play of texts' appears to be most acutely evidenced in the story of the doctor's visit, and the way in which the Ryans respond and react to its retelling. Their joint narrative exposes a piling on of narrative laminations that operate at least four major themes: (1) a lay account of illness causation, in which a cancer of the skin is said to 'spread into the kidneys'; (2) an evaluation of the role of doctor, in this instance the representation of a doctor who transgresses the traditional code of behaviour appropriate to his profession; (3) reinforcement of the authenticity of local values by the response of the trusted neighbourhood hospital in an emergency; (4) an assertion of Bruce Ryan's identity of stoic individualism, in keeping with his attitude towards the sick role. Other themes might be identified by other readings of the text, but these ones suffice to illustrate that it is possible, even within a fairly short narrative extract from an informal interview, to identify a rich diversity of representation in the Ryans' account. It is this diversity, and the way that discourse reproduces its own inner momentum in accounts such as these, that lends support to the discursive perspective on lay representations of health and illness, rather than the seeking out of texts simply in order to confirm or disconfirm previously held theories about 'lay health beliefs' or the 'states of mind' of speakers.

Power, Asymmetry and Decision Making in Medical Encounters 3

In studies of interviews with patients, stories are told and folk wisdom is passed on that owe their existence to the many and often contradictory voices to which people are exposed in the realms of illness and health care. In Chapter 2 we saw, from the account given by the Ryans as well as in the studies by Blaxter and Williams, that even when accounting for illness experience in everyday life people refer overwhelmingly to doctor–patient relations. The medicalization of experience, perpetrated by popular magazines, television documentaries and an array of media 'experts', also contributes to the manufacture of 'commonsense' knowledge about health issues. But by far the most influential and powerful influence is the voice belonging to biomedical expertise, and that is the voice that people will hear, in some form or other, in their doctors' surgeries. Were it not for doctor–patient consultations, and misunderstandings arising from them, there would be no need to discriminate between the terms of lay and specialized knowledge. In this chapter, therefore, we turn to the domain of medical professionals, and consider the discourse of medicine within the context of the clinic. We will examine the roles of health care professional and patient, consider issues regarding power, asymmetry and the conflicting 'voices' of biomedical expertise and everyday reality, and then focus on the notion of 'partnership' and shared decision making in the clinical consultation. On this last topic, we will consider an extensive extract from a consultation (Gwyn and Elwyn, 1999) in which a general practitioner attempts to reach a 'shared decision' with a patient.

DEFINING THE ROLES

Research into the field of medical discourse has taken many forms since the appearance of the first studies in the sociology of medicine. The work of Parsons is frequently cited as an embarkation point, his studies (1951, 1958) describing illness as a type of deviance which society, notably through the role of doctor as arbiter, seeks to overcome. Parsons' lasting impression on the sociology of medicine rests on his elaboration of the *sick role* which established a social category for illness beyond that of the personalized representation of defilement and contamination familiar to anthropologists

(Douglas, 1984). According to Parsons, a principal function of illness is that it 'incapacitates for the effective performance of social roles' (1951: 430) and that consequently it 'may be treated as one mode of response to social pressures, among other things, as one way of evading social responsibilities' (1951: 431). The evasion of responsibility (whether intentional or not) is accompanied by the imposition upon the patient of obligations: being ill becomes a social contract. One of the immediate consequences of this kind of formulation is that there hangs over the patient the potential accusation of malingering, so he or she is obliged to produce evidence and take action to prove that the malady is not contrived. This necessarily places the doctor in the role of a social arbiter, since it is the doctor who will determine the authenticity of the patient's complaint. If the patient concerned is shown to be recurrently reprobate in his or her claims to seek refuge from work in illness, s/he runs the risk of acquiring the reputation of a malingerer or a scrounger: 'both the sick role and that of the physician assume significance as mechanisms of social control, not only within the bounds of the common-sense definition of the traditional functions of the physician, but more broadly, including intimate relations to many phenomena which are not ordinarily thought to have any connection with health' (1951: 477). These 'intimate relations' to phenomena that serve as functions of social control have occupied the attention of many writers in the sociology of health and illness, as well as featuring in the work of discourse analysts and socio-linguists working within the field of medical discourse. The aspect of 'social control' most evident in the medical consultation is the exercise of physician power, and patients' apparent concurrence with it.

Many commentators in the 1980s saw the alleged asymmetry of the doctor–patient relationship as being expressed in a conflict of *voices* in the consulting room (Fisher and Todd, 1983; Frankel, 1983; Paget, 1983; Treichler et al., 1984; and particularly Mishler, 1984). These voices can be seen as a kind of dichotomous chorusing that arises as a consequence of the structure of the medical consultation itself. In the seminal work conducted by Byrne and Long (1976) six phases of the clinical encounter were enumerated, and became the standard upon which most following research was based:

1 relating to the patient;
2 discovering the reason for attendance;
3 conducting a verbal or physical examination or both;
4 consideration of the patient's condition;
5 detailing treatment of further investigation;
6 terminating.

It should be noted however (Ainsworth-Vaughn, 1998: 177) that the focus of all these phases is from the standpoint of the *physician's* activity rather than that of the patient. An updating of the model by ten Have (1989) avoids these limitations, emphasizing the specific genre of the consultation as warranting more attention to locally negotiated speech activities. Specifically, Heath (1992) argues that phases 4 and 5 often provide particular instances of asymmetry in the way that patients typically respond to the doctor's opinion of their condition, by 'making no response, or uttering downward-intoned *er* or *yeh*; doctor making recommended management, treatment, arrangements and the like' (1992: 241). However, there is, as Heath notes, an important element of consensus in the patient's accommodation of power asymmetry, and the interactive stakes between participants are further complicated by the effects of the 'new capitalism' in which, typically, hierarchies are reduced and terms such as 'empowerment' and 'shared decision making' have become common currency (Sarangi and Roberts, 1999b: 10). These developments have created tensions of their own, involving the 'renegotiation of old identities and formation of new ones' (ibid.). Many of the most representative struggles and contradictions of late modernity are to be encountered in medical institutions and in medical practice; and if medicine is in some measure a metaphor for society (Illich, 1976), then the doctor–patient encounter is the most acutely focused expression of medical discourse.

PROBLEMS AND PROBLEMS

It has for a long time been the specific aim of a number of social scientists involved in studying health care interactions to deconstruct the evident conflict of interests between patient and doctor, since the outstanding feature of most talk between doctors and their patients is said to be the unequal nature of the power relationship. This inequality of power is presented as a social fact, established, according to Treichler et al. (1984: 175) *a priori* by the participants in the typical consultation:

> Much like actors who have memorized and rehearsed their lines before a performance, participants are seen as bringing power with them to the health care encounter: differences in rights, duties, and obligations are known in advance.

One aspect of the difficulty in approaching problems that oscillate between the medical and the social in the doctor–patient interview is described by Treichler et al. as 'problems and *prob*lems', where the stress on the first syllable of the repeated word (spoken by an elderly black patient to a younger and unresponsive white male doctor) indicates that there are problems whose intensity and diversity do not warrant explanation within the confines of this specifically clinical encounter:

Physician:	Great. So *how* you doing today Joseph.
Patient:	Not too good doct//or
Physician:	Not too good. I see you kinda hangin' your head low there.
Patient:	Yeah.
Physician:	Must be somethin' up (.) or down I should say. Are you feelin' down?
Patient:	Yeah
Physician:	What are you feelin' down *about* (0.7)
Patient:	Stomach problems, back problems, *side* problems.

Physician: *Problems* problems
Patient: Problems and *problems*
Physician: Hum. What's:: we- what's goin' on with your stomach. Are you still uh-havin' pains in your stomach?

Although he comments on the patient's social presentation ('I see you kinda hangin' your head low there'), the doctor is focused on determining a clinical outcome, on 'dealing with' the patient within a biomedical perspective. He is singularly unprepared to cross the boundary between the clinical and the social, or even to understand the language of his patient in expressing strictly non-clinical concerns:

Physician: (O:kay) (3.2.) What do you think is uh – is goin' on here. Wadda you – wha' do you think has been happenin' with ya. Any ideas?
Patient: Lots a' worri*a*tion
Physician: Lots a' what?
Patient: Worriation (0.2)
Physician: Worriation? Lotta worryin' y' mean?=
Patient: =Yes
Physician: What've you been worried about.
Patient: Well I don't have no income anymore.

This extract is eloquently suggestive of the rift between the patient's highest expectations of the interview and the doctor's capacity to meet those expectations. The doctor, failing to understand the dialectal word 'worriation', 'corrects' it with a standard usage. This failure of communication at even a lexical level is reproduced in wider issues concerning the patient's loss of invalidity benefits and related '*problems*'. Treichler et al.'s paper also contains a lucid critique of the way the doctor prevents the patient from expressing his innermost concerns, which he (the patient) later reveals quite candidly to a medical student. The student, unlike the physician, is prepared to do rather more constructive listening, and elicits from the patient a history of disturbances (as well as details of current prescribed medication) which the physician, with his more directive approach, fails to elicit.

The doctor is, in contemporary Western society, one who provides a service, that of *health care*; the patient is, appropriately, *one who waits, suffers*, and is *treated*. We will see that a considerable amount of the existing research on medical discourse has been conducted specifically to analyse and to criticize the means, methods, dialectics and humaneness of the doctor–patient relationship, particularly in relation to the interactional asymmetry and the ceremonial nature (Strong, 1979) of the majority of such interviews. The language of the medical consultation is shown repeatedly to reflect the non-egalitarian nature of the doctor–patient relationship. Moreover, it has been suggested in Chapter 2 that illness (normally perceived as the *raison d'être* for such a consultation) is itself dependent upon such a relationship in order to achieve definition: the patient visits the doctor with an unspecified ailment, and returns home with a named disease. As Valabrega (1962: 25) writes: 'Illness is something which occurs between the patient and the person who is taking care of him.' One of the means by which this is realized is by the *naming* of disease: in the classificatory universe of the clinic you can only be cured of something that has a name.

But *naming* illnesses is only a small part of the practice of medicine – that of diagnosis – and to the lay person many of the names that doctors call diseases by are incomprehensible, although perhaps not as incomprehensible as they once were. Fifty years ago it was not even expected of the doctor to give an explanation of disease in lay terms: in fact a major review of its time, the Goodenough Report of 1944 on medical education, scarcely makes mention of the patient. In reviewing practices around the time of the Goodenough Report, Armstrong, in his *Political Anatomy of the Body*, writes:

> To be sure, the medical student had to be taught to diagnose disease in his patients, but the patient was viewed essentially as a passive object in which was contained interesting pathology. (1983: 102)

The doctor obtained information regarding the patient's condition through a physical examination and through a process of interrogation (ibid.). Nowadays, however, medical practice has extended its *gaze* and demands that the patient and doctor engage in a 'joint adventure' (Arney and Bergen, 1983), one that redefines the boundaries of their relationship. How those boundaries have traditionally been defined, and the organization of their redefinition, is of concern to a great many practitioners and researchers in the field of health communication.

Atkinson (1995: 36) has suggested that, as researchers, we give this relationship too much prominence, that we perhaps too readily regard the clinical interview as a synecdoche for all aspects of medical work and practice (see also Hak, 1999; Sarangi and Roberts, 1999b). More relevant, for Atkinson, are the 'ethnopoetics' of medical work and the question: *How is the clinical gaze shaped by language* (1995: 4). However, the doctor–patient or, more fashionably, the 'provider–patient' relationship remains the pivotal one in many people's experience of illness and its management, and is therefore of particular interest to discourse analysts as constituting the core data for their work.

COMMUNICATION AND ASYMMETRY IN THE MEDICAL ENCOUNTER

In over two-thirds of medical encounters recorded by Beckman and Frankel (1984), physicians intruded on patients' initial utterances and redirected talk towards specific concerns. On average physicians interrupted within 18 seconds of the encounter's start. In a follow-up study (Beckman and Frankel, 1985) it was suggested that patients who are interrupted are significantly more likely to raise further issues later in the consultation. These results led the investigators to conclude that 'overdirected interviewing at the beginning of the visit may obscure the very concerns that the initial segment of the visit is designed to capture (1984: 695)'. Moreover, more than 90 per cent of patients' formal complaints about their care stem from the way that medical staff communicate with them (West and Frankel, 1991).

'Good' communication between doctor/provider and patient has become so central to our understanding of the idealized doctor–patient relationship as to be something of a cliché. And yet for all that, there is considerably more agreement about what constitutes bad communication or 'miscommunication' (and they are not at all the same thing) than on what constitutes 'good' or ideal communication. Poor communication is frequently based on a failure of understanding, either of one party or of both. Paget (1983) considers questioning practices to be central to the success or otherwise of communication in the clinic, because, she says, these practices 'often construct the meaning of a patient's illness'. She remarks upon the typical developing discontinuities in the doctor–patient interview that she chooses to analyse, which involves a male doctor and a female patient. The doctor's (D) opening comments are worthy of note:

> D: I wan yuh tuh sit straight....
>   no
>   sit facing me
>
>   (3.4)
>
>   d yuh wear a hat by preference
>   or yer having anything wrong with yer *scalp*

The doctor's contribution here is not only directive and intrusive (both in terms of the patient's physical space and her choice of head-wear), but the remark on the patient's hat-wearing is expressed with a remarkable lack of sensitivity. Throughout the interview the doctor directs their talk, making commands and requests for action, introducing, developing and dissolving topics. Often he appears to ignore the patient's concerns entirely, which, Paget says, contributes to the discontinuity of their talk. Politeness forms are almost entirely absent from the doctor's contributions to the interaction. Typical of this impoliteness (which serves to enforce the dominance/ subordination roles) is his failure to answer the patient's questions, even ones framed as a direct request for help, here responded to with a command to 'look straight':

> [P=Patient D=Doctor]
> P: o:h I know it
>   but what m I gonna *do*
> D: w'll let's look straight

In a similar vein, the topic control exercised by the doctor ruthlessly terminates contributions by the patient that carry any affective significance. In the sequence below, where, according to Paget's commentary, the patient's turn is voiced with considerable feeling, the doctor offers no acknowledgement before giving the instruction 'now big breath':

> P: I I (think) I want to feel better
>   I I was- a . . . . .
>   *very* active person . . . . .
>   had many interests
>   n many hobbies

```
          n . . . . .
          uh I I still do
          but I find that I just
          haven't got the . . . . . . . .
          stamina . . . . .
          tuh tuh do it . . . . . .
          which is crazy
              [ ]
D:          uhm
P:    because I think I have when I start
          t do it . . . .
          n then I just fall apart
          (0.6)
D:    now big breath
```

It transpires that this patient has recently undergone surgery for cancer, and yet throughout the three encounters (the above extracts are taken from the first), there is none but oblique reference made to this shared knowledge. Scar, tumor, surgery, the remaining kidney (the patient has had a nephrectomy) are mentioned, but not, according to Paget, in relation to the patient's repeated expressions of pain. The doctor assesses symptoms and complaints, such as the patient's fear of death, as indicative of neurotic depression. He tells her that her basic health is good but that she is suffering from 'nerves'.

Her status as a cancer patient is never directly addressed. Both doctor and patient know that the patient had cancer, and each knows that the other knows, and furthermore each also knows that the oblique references recur without achieving expression. Often the unspoken topic, 'hovers on the verge of expression' in the questions the patient asks. However, attempts by the patient to pursue any line of discourse that might throw light on her cancer, the possibility of its metastasizing, are stymied by the doctor, either by interruption, or by abrupt change of subject. On one occasion, while examining the patient's back, the doctor whistles through a part of her explanation.

As the doctor manipulates the conversations away from the issue of cancer and the patient's experience of pain it is not surprising that the patient's evident nervousness increases. This feeds the doctor's assertion that all that is wrong with the patient is her nerves. In a final extract the patient volunteers some suggestions e.g.: 'do y think maybe the uhm (0.6) do y think maybe this kidney is is uh (0.4) overloaded or something'; 'oh they removed an adrenal gland'; 'I'm thinking maybe it's a ho:rmone deficiency or someth- ing'. The doctor ignores or interrupts her questions and responds irrelevantly:

> Two of her questions are interrupted in their course and the third seems not to have been correctly heard. All her questions refer to the impact of her operation on her health. He looks at the scar and inquires about the other end of it and says, 'it's beautiful surgery'. (1983: 70)

Paget's terse, eloquent paper presents us with some excellent and extreme examples of the discursive forms that doctor–patient asymmetry takes. Throughout there is a disharmony between what the patient says and what the doctor hears. By refusing to broach the subject of cancer in any but the most oblique fashion the doctor neglects the patient's humanity and understandable fear, preferring to belittle her concerns and consigning them to the psychosomatic netherworld of 'nerves'. He suggests that she would benefit from psychiatric aid. It is the norm that her questions remain unanswered and that her replies to his questions do not receive acknowledgement. He persistently assures her that her basic health is good.

In the follow-up questionnaires that both the doctor and the patient filled in, the doctor remained convinced of the correctness of his diagnosis. The patient however claims on *hers* that since the last appointment she has been to another hospital where she has been diagnosed as suffering from cancer of the spine.

Such studies, which acquired the reputation of 'doctor-bashing', dominated the literature of patient–doctor consultation in the 1980s. Interestingly, many of these accounts display an awareness of the highly gendered nature of 'traditional' doctor–patient relations where the doctor is a male and the patient a female. We shall be returning shortly to this theme in a discussion of the work of Fisher (1995).

THE 'VOICE OF THE LIFEWORLD'

Many studies of doctor–patient interaction have focused on problems of communication (Paget, 1983; Treichler et al., 1984; Silverman, 1987; West and Frankel, 1991; Fisher, 1995; Ainsworth-Vaughn, 1998), often caused specifically by a conflict of interest brought about by an imbalance in the relations of power. Mishler (1984), like others, identified this conflict as being based in the asymmetrical nature of medical consultations, but elaborated this conflict by developing the analogy of a struggle between voices. On the one hand, he suggested, we have the 'voice of medicine', on the other the 'voice of the lifeworld'; representing, respectively, the 'technical-scientific assumptions of medicine and the natural attitude of everyday life' (1984: 14).

According to this model, the medical practitioner is seen as pursuing a line of discourse determined almost exclusively by the biomedical model, or, as McKeown (1976) prefers it, the 'engineering approach'. Translated into a discourse strategy, the biomedical model is often at odds with the socio-relational bias of the patient's perception, which represents what Mishler terms 'lifeworld contexts' (1984: 7). Since the medical consultation is dominated by the voice of medicine, argues Mishler, any contribution from the voice of the lifeworld is regarded by the medical professional as an interruption.

Conversely, any literal interruption by the voice of medicine when the patient is speaking from the perspective of 'everyday life' is not an interruption at all, but a return to reality, that is, the 'specific normative order' (1984: 63) of the dominant mode of discourse. Typically, in an interview where the patient introduces the voice of the lifeworld and attempts to seize control of the consultation by reiterating 'lifeworld statements', the doctor's response is to attempt to bring the interview back around to the voice of medicine. The medical bias is perhaps most clearly indicated within the consultation itself by the typical and pervasive sequence of utterances. This follows the pattern, summarized by Mishler (1984: 61) as: physician question; patient response; physician assessment/next question. The tendency of doctors to use closed- rather than open-ended questions serves further to maintain the doctor's control of the interview. This in turn strengthens the biomedical model as the framework of discourse and permits doctors to carry out the medical tasks that most concern them – diagnosis and prescription. The intrinsic imbalance of the question-asking sequence gives the physician control over the turn-taking sequence. One might wonder why this bias towards the voice of medicine is so persistent, considering the emphasis placed by researchers on the ultimate benefits of adopting a patient-centred approach (Byrne and Long, 1976; Treichler et al., 1984; Stewart et al., 1995). However, it may well be that the coercive strengths of a normative style of discourse are so entrenched in social attitudes that such a discourse style has become naturalized (Fairclough, 1989: 92). Naturalization has occurred when neither of the participants regards a particular discourse style as oppressive or disempowering (consider, for example, the way in which doctors frequently select topics and avoid normal politeness forms). When these conditions are in place, and tacitly accepted by participants (adapting to fixed roles, or scripts, in Treichler et al.'s analogy), then the conflict between Mishler's two voices might be regarded merely as the 'sort of language medical consultations ought to be conducted in' (Fairclough, 1989: 101).

Mishler argues that the lack of any convincing social theory hinders interpretation of findings from the analysis of doctor–patient interaction. Although there is a history of research into medical interaction that identifies time and again the difficulties of communication between doctors and patients, there is (or was, claims Mishler, at the time of his writing) no thoroughgoing examination of these problems from the perspective of a general social theory. It should be noted that more recent work on medical discourse has been keen to embed itself more thoroughly in such a theory (see especially Sarangi and Roberts, 1999a). Mishler, however, draws on phenomenological sociology and critical theory in his search for an appropriate theoretical framework. First he refers to Schutz' paradigm, which has as two of its 'provinces of meaning' (states in which the individual experiences the world) the natural attitude and the scientific attitude (Schutz, 1962, cited in Mishler, 1984: 122). These correspond, according to Mishler, with his own lifeworld and medical voices. This paradigm 'proposes that the natural attitude and the commonsense world are the basic social "realities", and that all other attitudes are "modifications"' (1984: 123). In other words, the voice of medicine is perceived as a secondary construction, a marked version of reality (or not reality at all), compared with the 'commonsense' or 'natural' attitude, which is the unmarked position. He further suggests that the different attitudes sustained by these distinct 'provinces of meaning' are essentially irreconcilable, and that they cannot cohabit in any way that does not cause serious distortion of one of them. An example of this would be the singling out by the physician, during a consultation, of some specific element of the patient's account (for instance the presentation of a particular symptom), removing it from the context within which it was presented (that is, the lifeworld context) and re-presenting it as an element pertaining to the voice of medicine.

Mishler finds in Habermas' (1972) technocratic consciousness a parallel to his own 'voice of medicine'. Following Habermas' terminology, the voice of medicine is represented by purposive-rational action and its associated (technocratic) consciousness, whereas the voice of the lifeworld is referred to as symbolic action. As an example we can see how the province of meaning inhabited by the patient is redefined by the doctor in an extract (1984: 84–5) that occupies a considerable amount of Mishler's attention. This extract, or parts of it, has been reproduced elsewhere (notably in Fairclough, 1992; Elwyn and Gwyn, 1998). It is, however, still worth reproducing, if only on account of the commentary that it has generated:

```
[D=  Doctor  P=Patient]
    D:  Hm hm . . . Now what do you mean by a sour stomach?
    P:  . . . . . . . . .What's a sour stomach? A heartburn
        like a heartburn or something.
 5  D:                          Does it burn over here?
    P:                                             Yea:h.
        It li- I think- I think it like- If you take a needle
        and stick ya right . . . there's a pain right here . .
    D:          Hm hm  Hm hm                    Hm hm
    P:  and and then it goes from here on this side to this side.
10  D:  Hm hm does it  go into the back?
    P:                      It's a:ll up here. No. It's all right
        up here in front.
    D:  Yeah          And when do you get that?
    P:                                         . . . . . . .
15      . . . . . . Wel:l when I eat something wrong.
    D:                                      How- How
        soon after you eat it?
    P:                  . . . . . . . . . . . . . Wel:l
        . . . probably an hour . . . maybe less
20  D:                              About an hour?
    P:  Maybe less . . . . . . . I've cheated and I've been
        drinking which I shouldn't have done.
    D:              . . . . .
        Does drinking make it worse?
25  P:  (. . .)                    Ho ho uh ooh Yes . . .
        . . . Especially the carbonation and the alcohol.
    D:  . . . Hm hm . . . . . . . How much do you drink?
    P:                                          . . . .
        . . . . . . I don't know . . . Enough to make me
30      go to sleep at night . . . . and that's quite a bit.
```

```
     D:   One or two drinks a day?
     P:                              O:h no no no humph it's
          (more like) ten . . . . at night.
     D:                    How many drinks - a night.
35   P:                                            At night.
     D:                                                      . . .
          . . . . Whaddya ta- What type of drinks? . . . . . I ( . . .)
     P:                                            Oh vodka
          . . yeah vodka and ginger ale.
40   D:                        . . . . . . . . . . . . . . . . . . . .
          . . . . . . . . How long have you been drinking that heavily?
     P:   . . . . . . . . . . . . Since I've been married.
     D:                                            . . . . .
          . . . . How long is that?
45   P:                              (giggle) Four years. (giggle)
```

The patient's reference to a 'sour stomach', in its non-technical formulation, clearly belongs to the 'lifeworld', and the doctor seeks to 'translate' the concept into biomedical terms ('like a heartburn or something'). The patient also refers to eating 'something wrong' and to cheating, which locates her explanation in a lifeworld context of 'morality'. Interestingly though (which Mishler does not remark upon in his commentary), is that in her account of her drinking the patient partially slips into the voice of medicine, or at least an approximation of it, with her comment 'Especially the carbonation and the alcohol', in an effort to produce a more 'technical' explanation of the effects of her drinking rather than a purely 'moral' one ('I've cheated').

Crucially, according to Mishler, when the patient responds to the physician's question, 'How long have you been drinking that heavily?' (l. 41) with 'Since I've been married' she is locating her problem within a co-ordinate of subjective time. But, says Mishler, the physician presses her towards objective time – 'How long is that?' (l. 44): here 'he is reconstructing her practical interests into technical ones' (1984: 127). This view of medical discourse as a dialectic between the voice of the lifeworld and the voice of medicine is thus linked by Mishler to a more general societal conflict of representation: 'the technocratic expressed through a language of purposive-rational action, and the symbolic expressed through ordinary language' (ibid.). Unfortunately, Mishler does not elaborate on the exact nature of 'ordinary language', any more than he does 'the natural attitude of everyday life'. He merely presents them together as a *fait accompli*, a body of shared knowledge that the reader holds in common with himself and with patients at large, as distinct from physicians as a professional unit, who apparently operate as instruments of the 'technocratic consciousness'.

Despite the elusive character of this 'natural attitude to everyday life', Mishler regards it as the discursive style appropriate for patients in the medical consultation. For example, in his chapter entitled 'Attending to the voice of the lifeworld', Mishler provides the reader with a model consultation of kinds, with a doctor who pays attention to and seeks to communicate within the voice of the lifeworld. The strategies employed by this doctor include:

not interrupting; listening more; introducing questions by reference to the patient's own words and using an abundance of transitional phrases, thereby avoiding the rather disjointed tone of typical 'voice of medicine style' interviews (or rather the kind of typical interviews that Mishler employs to illustrate his presentation of the voice of medicine). The doctor here is consistently reassuring and supportive of the patient, provides precise uncomplicated explanations of what he is going to do or ask and at the end of the interview makes sure that there is not some area of complaint or concern that has been left uncovered during the course of the meeting. He also interjects with personal comments designed to make the patient feel at ease: for example, the patient says that she is 76 years old and the doctor retorts: 'You don't look 76 at all you're still pretty', which Mishler interprets as representative of speaking from within the lifeworld context (1984: 158). If this example is to be isolated as illustrative of a 'humane clinical practice' – and Mishler does employ it as such, referring to its 'expressive and slightly teasing quality' (ibid.) – then it invites attention on account of the doctor's insidious compliment-paying behaviour. Is there a terminal age for 'prettiness'? why shouldn't a person who is 76 look as though they are 76? While Mishler presents these procedures as models of 'humaneness' they disclose, on closer inspection, a wholly distorted and patronizing attitude on the part of the physician that only emphasizes the imbalance in power relations between himself and his patient, an imbalance exacerbated by their respective ages and genders.

Mishler's account provides umbrella solutions to specific problems by proposing the adoption of 'humane' principles of consultation throughout medical practice on the assumption that there is otherwise a contest between conflicting voices. This assumption fails to consider that each voice must itself be the aggregate of other, competing voices, and the whole conceptual framework seems to depend upon a somewhat naïve belief in a single social reality that produces the 'voice of the lifeworld'. However, as Potter and Wetherell (1987: 45) have observed: 'if a certain attitude is expressed on one occasion it should not necessarily lead us to expect that the same attitude will be expressed on another'. So we need not be surprised if people say conflicting things in different circumstances. Rogers (1991: 67), whose work was discussed in Chapter 2, writes on the same theme:

> Although people continually construct alternative versions of an idea, argument or account, they are often quite unaware of them. This is because one creates, in effect, a different version of 'reality', and hence people slip into and out of alternative 'realities' all the time, usually without any awareness that they are doing so.

The notion of a lifeworld that has a specific voice, deriving in part from the writings of Schutz and Habermas, is expanded upon in the medical contexts of Mishler's work to suggest that a commonsense view (Mishler, 1984: 123) is available to the mass of patients, and that this view is intruded upon and distorted by the voice of medicine, but – and as has been objected elsewhere (Silverman, 1987; Atkinson, 1995) – with regard to the voice of the lifeworld, why should researchers employ Mishler's concept of ordinary conversation as a model when the context of a medical interview is and has to be more precise and technically informed than an ordinary conversation? Questioning the patient is an eminently suitable way of establishing clinical facts. In support of this criticism, we might recall that in the extract cited above, where the patient claims she has been drinking heavily since she got married, Mishler suggests that the doctor's insistence on placing this information within an objective time scale somehow diminishes the lifeworld or existential value of the woman's statement. But, we might ask, does the physician not have a professional obligation to find out the length of this period in order to help him assess, for example, the possibility of liver damage to his patient? We cannot assume that a style of discourse is inappropriate or inhumane simply because it deviates from ordinary everyday conversation. Furthermore, it would be simplistic in the extreme to believe, as Mishler is evidently aware (1984: 103), that doctors and patients use only the voices of medicine and the lifeworld respectively. The issue, more precisely, is one of 'the relation between voices rather than the establishment of a single authentic voice' (Silverman, 1987: 196).

Silverman's 'Discourse of the Social'

If we regard Mishler's study as being representative of a line of enquiry into discourse studies that can be traced to its theoretical roots in the sociological writings of Schutz and Habermas, then Silverman (1987), although similarly concerned with the role of the patient within the interactive process, is at a remove from Mishler's liberal humanism, and acknowledges instead the dominant influence of Foucault. Silverman suggests that despite their pleas for humanism and equality, the proponents of the 'patient-centred approach', such as Mishler, are unwittingly reinforcing a central strategy of power in the doctor–patient relationship.

According to Foucault, the effects of power (such as 'naturalization') are least visible (and therefore most efficacious) when subjects themselves define and organize their behaviour according to normative parameters. These parameters are invariably the ones held by professionally defined bodies of knowledge. To argue against asymmetry in the doctor–patient relationship therefore misses the point since any attempted adoption of equality would only be a simulation and would leave intact the essential nature of the power imbalance, which is based upon specialized knowledge. Silverman, pursuing this line of argument, claims that the movement for 'patient power' which asserted itself in the 1970s to a large extent reflects a burgeoning consumerist mentality. Patient power arose in opposition to the system of medical treatment which, according to Foucault (1973) became established at the end of the eighteenth century, and with its emphasis on technology and specialization, created a clinical discourse that became ever more unintelligible to the patient. However understandable such opposition to clinical procedure might be, by focusing on notions of asymmetry, Silverman contends, the 'patient power' lobby misses the point for two reasons, to which I would add further suggestions.

First, professional expertise predetermines an imbalance in the doctor–patient relationship. The principle that a doctor should disclose all relevant information to a patient in order to help that patient come to an intelligent understanding of his or her course of treatment is itself asymmetrical. The situation is further complicated by the fact that the pace of developments means that generalists are often operating at the fringes of their knowledge when they refer patients for specialist treatment. I might add to this the axiom, driven home by the 'evidence based medicine' movement (Sackett et al., 1997), that there are relatively few clinical treatments which have the benefit of 'evidence', yet no shortage of 'expert' views. The consultation is therefore forever threatened with becoming the domain of 'other experts' in which, if any progress is to be made in terms of interactional symmetry, they will have to begin again from scratch.

Secondly, Silverman maintains, many patients want to keep the asymmetry of the relationship and would feel uncomfortable without it. They want the doctor to 'know best' and are likely to resent any shifts in decision making onto themselves. Again, I might add to Silverman's argument by suggesting that perhaps, too, patients accept the discourse strategies that dominate doctor–patient interviews because they are regarded, however subliminally, as an implicit part of their treatment, and by questioning the authoritative voice of medicine (by speaking out of turn, interrupting, initiating topics, etc.) they might be seen to be symbolically challenging the status quo of medical discourse, thereby causing covert damage to their chances of recovery.

If there is real consensus between patient and doctor during the later, decision-making part of the consultation, then professional dominance is surely not contentious. Merely employing criteria of patient-centredness is not sufficient in analysis of a medical interview in which the dominance of the professional is maintained by consensus. The great insight of Silverman's argument is that it makes use of a consensual notion of power in relation to the doctor–patient encounter, and thereby undermines the simplistic dichotomy of 'powerful doctor versus powerless patient'.

Why then should we see the problem facing medical practice as lying in the choice between patient-centred practice and doctor-centred practice? And why should we suppose that a programme of reform, institutionally sanctioned, will achieve a better medical interview? One recent development in patient-centred medicine, spurred on, in the UK at least, by government incentives to save money and involve a 'partnership with patients' (see special issue of the *British Medical Journal*, vol. 39, 1999), has been a move to include patients more substantially in the decisions relevant to their care. But – and this is a crucial consideration – either patients are at ease with the consensual acceptance of power asymmetry, or else they resist it; they view doctors' attempts to involve them more comprehensively in the decision-making process either with suspicion or else as bona fide attempts by the doctor to achieve fuller patient collaboration. Between these extremities lies the mass of consultations, in which roles are not clearly demarcated, but constantly shifting; and in which discourse plays a central part in the unfolding not only of the interaction, but of clinical outcomes also.

NURSE PRACTITIONERS AND GENDERED KNOWLEDGE

One area of interactive asymmetry in which the demarcations are relatively clear-cut is that of male physcians and female patients. Fisher (1995) presents an examination of the role of women in the provision of health care, observing that women are perceived primarily as nurses, and as such are 'carers', while men (predominantly the 'doctors') are perceived as 'curers'. We are educated into the belief that while male doctors are good at the real stuff of dealing with disease, women are perhaps better predisposed to bonding with patients, and providing the female/feminine virtues of nurturing and compassion. In reality, Fisher believes, it is only an institutionalized and gendered resistance to change that sustains such a view.

Fisher's data comes in the form of four consultations, two between physicians and patients, and two with nurse practitioners. Both of the doctors are male, both the nurses are female. This is an important factor, and one which Fisher utilizes in her deconstruction of the medical hierarchy as an essentially male and conservative domain. By contrast, she sees the nurse practitioners' concept of caring as profoundly and empathetically gendered, as they struggle to assert an autonomous identity. The emergence of this new force in American medicine is set by Fisher against the backdrop of an historical struggle, more social and political than scientific, and based on criteria of race, class and gender.

In the analysis of her two examples of nurse practitioner data, juxtaposed with material collected from two doctor–patient consultations, Fisher seeks to shed light on the divergences and correspondences between the two kinds of consultation, and as an additional strategy, to draw attention to the importance of viewing caring as a 'discourse of the social'. Focusing on the ways that nurse practitioners care for patients might, she suggests, change the way they are perceived and help rectify their second-class status within the medical hierarchy. The two male doctors that Fisher provides are suitably horrifying in their adherence to reactionary patriarchal practices, which no doubt was her intention in selecting them. The bulk of the first consultation is conducted with the patient and doctor speaking at cross purposes, and when at last the patient confides her fear that she might be pregnant, the doctor wrongly dismisses it as a 'remote possibility' since she is still breast-feeding. The second doctor provides a catalogue of social ineptitude and communicative churlishness, all the more striking in contrast with the nurses, who achieve (or set out to achieve) a firm rapport with their female patients based on a diminution of differences. They adopt a less domineering posture; they don't interject so many professional-centred questions;

they are, most importantly, of the same sex. Not that they get things all their own way. In a revealing section, Pat, an African-American patient, resists the emancipatory discourse of Claudia, the younger, white, 'firmly middle-class' nurse practitioner, over private sexual matters and responds in ways which covertly support the very normative structures which the nurse practitioner would have hoped to dismantle. Here then, the medical professional is being undermined by a resistance to resistance, and finds herself having to back down.

The two male doctors are seen to be guiding their patients towards behaviour that perpetuates hegemonic understandings of the role of the doctor and the patient, as well as the roles of men and women, and by doing this they sanction the dominant cultural distinctions based on class and gender. It is meant to be equally clear that the nurse practitioners do not. Yet (and here, as Fisher observes, is the inescapable irony of their position) they necessarily utilize the power imbalance in their relationship with patients to promote their own adversarial, oppositional discourse on questions of women's rights, gendered structures of oppression, class-based prejudice, and ways in which women might find modes of resistance. In other words, while acting as a revolutionary catalyst for social change the nurse practitioner is still recirculating the institutional authority associated with her professional status.

THE NEGOTIATION OF 'PARTNERSHIP' IN PRIVATE HEALTH CARE PROVISION

Ainsworth-Vaughn (1998), whose study reports on interactions which took place in private clinics in the USA, presents a resolutely upbeat picture of patients' ability and willingness to claim power in the medical encounter. Practising an ethnographic discourse analysis, she provides commentary on medical encounters in which the distinction between interview and conversation is brought into question, where patients are seen to be co-constructing not only the subjective 'meaning' of their illnesses but also their own diagnoses; where patients happily carry out face-threatening acts with their doctors and get away with it; are at liberty to frame the medical encounter in ways conducive to their own storytelling – aided and encouraged in all these activities, it would appear, by compliant, smiling and humane physicians. Moreover, her study contains quantitative data to support her qualitative analysis. The most extraordinary statistic that she provides is that, apparently, 40 per cent of topic transition in the consultations she studies is initiated by patients. Similarly 40 per cent of the 'true, unambiguous' questions (838 of them) asked in her 40 encounters were 'controlled by' patients. Interestingly, when the doctor was a woman, around 50 per cent of questions were asked by patients, compared to 26 per cent when the doctor was a man (1998: 184). This goes against the grain of our expectations of the doctor–patient encounter, one of whose trademarks is the strict control that doctors maintain over topic.

In a study where, in the ethnographic tradition, relevant details are provided about doctor, patient, and the contextual setting of the interaction, Ainsworth-Vaughn suggests that patients were seen to claim power, often with the co-operation of their physician (1998: 180–2). Patients achieved this through (1) the selection of topic; (2) the offering of candidate diagnoses; (3) the co-construction of diagnoses with doctors; (4) the challenging of doctors' diagnoses; (5) proposing treatment; (6) carrying out potentially face-threatening acts; (7) framing the medical encounter as friendly and invoking favourable cultural schemas in defining the self.

While it must be emphasized that these consultations take place in a private clinic, and that the patients and doctors have, for the most part, known each other over a number of visits, if not years, this list provides an extraordinary reversal of expectations when compared to much of the existing doctor–patient data, and the conclusions that are drawn from it stand in stark contrast to the examples selected by Treichler et al., Paget, Fisher, and other studies using first-visit encounters. However (and this holds true for conflicts arising from gender-related issues), it is a norm of private practice that if a patient dislikes or does not have rapport with his or her physician, they find another physician. This situation does not obtain quite so unproblematically in state-sponsored medical practice. It could therefore be argued that the above-listed strategies, if successful, are largely dependent on their taking place within private clinics. With this in mind, I would suggest that Ainsworth-Vaughn's claims on behalf of 'patient-power' are severely compromised.

The first item on the list, that of selection of topic being significantly under the control of patients, is a case in point. Ainsworth-Vaughn reports that speakers usually exercised their choice of topic transition after a sequence of reciprocal/power-sharing activities, as well as by using questions to control topic. While this is a refreshing inversion of most data on doctor–patient activities, in settings such as those described here, in which power-sharing activities have, to a degree, become normative, these findings fail to impress. They are not representative of any wider shift in doctors' attitudes towards non-private patients and would need to be replicated elsewhere before any significance could be attached to them. Nor, indeed, does the second item, patients offering candidate diagnoses, seem to be so odd. Patients frequently pose 'lay' explanations of illness to their doctors, but doctors are far less likely to derogate the opinions of paying clients. The same objection stands in relation to the fifth item on her list: that patients propose courses of treatment to doctors.

The issues that Ainsworth-Vaughn covers in items 3 and 4 on her list occur so infrequently as to be negligible, since she indicates only one example of a patient co-constructing diagnoses with a doctor and only two examples of patients challenging professional diagnoses. While of interest as case studies, the underlying tenet of Ainsworth-Vaughn's book is to combine quantitative and qualitative analyses in order to establish powerful statements about patients' ability to claim power in their talk with doctors. The rarity of these occurrences means that they cannot indicate anything of the kind.

The sixth item, that patients carry out potentially face-threatening acts (FTAs), is again an interesting position from which to argue the assertion of increased patient power. Individuals frequently and almost randomly carry out FTAs in professional encounters for a wide variety of reasons. It does not necessarily follow that the person doing so does so in order to rectify an inherently asymmetrical relationship. Ainsworth-Vaughn presents only two examples from her data, one in which a woman covertly questions her physician's competence, the other in which a male patient makes blatant sexual references to both his (female) physician and (off-screen, as it were) to female nursing staff. This latter case is complicated by the man being a patient with testicular cancer, whose own face is effectively threatened by his condition. While in the first example the woman is clearly claiming power in order to further her own medical needs, the same cannot be said of the second, where the intention of the speaker was, it would seem, to limit his own loss of face by resorting to clichéd sexist banter with all the women in the clinic.

Finally, in the seventh item in her list, Ainsworth-Vaughn asserts that patients 'frame the medical encounter as friendly and invoke favorable cultural schemas in defining the self'. The principal resource used by patients to achieve this is storytelling. It is worth examining this claim in a little more detail. After all, in medical encounters something rather more complex than the 'framing of the ... encounter as friendly' is going on, and it would be naïve to assume otherwise. In particular, it is difficult to see how the use of stories *per se* helps to achieve such beneficial ends. Treichler's, Paget's and Fisher's patients all told, or attempted to tell stories, most of which were ignored or interrupted by the doctors. Throughout her two chapters on this subject, Ainsworth-Vaughn defines 'story' as distinct from 'narrative'. According to her, a story is 'any narrative that is evaluated' (1998: 151). She cites Riessman approvingly, as struggling 'with a definition of story which rests on overt structural features' (1998: 200). I share that discomfort, but fail to see how it can be resolved by arbitrarily discriminating between 'narrative' and 'story' depending on the presence or absence of evaluation, since, as I and others have shown (Riessman, 1993; Edwards, 1997; Gwyn, 2000) evaluation takes place constantly and surreptitiously in the descriptive detail of a narrative rather than as a discrete structural feature.

For all that, a good deal of the talk in Ainsworth-Vaughn's study is convincingly analysed, and she makes valid points about the potential for systematic changes in our conceptualization of the doctor–patient phenomenon. However, its claim to be anything other than a one-off – reflecting the cosy relations between paying private clients in long-term arrangements with their largely sympathetic doctors – needs to be taken with considerable caution. The majority of patients, after all, do not enjoy a long-term relationship with a single physician, and in many respects this study reflects the particular details of a privileged minority rather than being a blueprint for the future management of all doctor–patient relations.

'SHARED DECISION MAKING'

Traditionally, medical practice has been divided as to the amount of influence patients are permitted in the making of decisions that affect their health, or the health of their children. At the one extreme there is *paternalism*, which assumes that the doctor should make decisions on behalf of the patient, based on his or her superior knowledge and experience. Little or no consultation with the patient takes place: the patients put themselves, literally, in the hands of the doctor. At the other extreme lies *informed choice*, in which the doctor lays out the pros and cons of each and every possible course of action without prejudice, and allows the patient to make a choice based on this information. In recent years a trend towards 'shared decision making' in the medical encounter has emerged, driven largely by government initiatives to 'democratize' institutional and professional relations, and evidenced in the UK by such policies as the various citizens' charters of the 1990s, the updating of the Freedom of Information Act, and more general governmental moves to 'involve the public' in policy making.

But shared decisions are not made in a vacuum, and it might be suggested that a situation of *equipoise*, that is, one in which options really *are* options, must exist in order for a shared decision to successfully take place and thereby justify the term. Shared decision making is a philosophy, or an approach towards doctor–patient consultation, and commitment to a philosophy of ideal practice should not be allowed to prejudice a practitioner in conditions where shared decision making is not well suited. For example, 'equipoise' might be a precondition in a setting where the patient is considering hormone replacement therapy (HRT) or treatment for prostatism, but would not be suitable for a child with a viral infection such as a sore throat. In such a case 'shared decision making' might be a misnomer, and although a 'shared decision' is reached, it would be more accurately described as an informed decision engineered according to doctor preference.

In order to be successful, shared decision making (SDM) involves four essential criteria. First, the decision must involve at least two (often many more) participants, the bare minimum being the doctor and the patient. Family members, friends, and the influence of other individuals such as counsellors should also be taken into consideration. Secondly, both parties (doctors and patients) take steps to participate in the process of treatment decision making; thirdly, information sharing is a prerequisite to shared decision making; and fourthly, a treatment decision is made and both parties agree to the decision (Charles et al., 1997).

There are, of course problems with the implication of shared decision making. It is time-consuming, usually needing more than the six or seven minutes typically allotted a family practice consultation in the UK. It is also threatening to the traditional power relationship between doctor and patient. Moreover, there is a lack of training and modelling for general practitioners in applying the method, a lack of skill in 'sharing' and 'involving' patients in decision making, a lack of information about risks and benefits, as well as a lack of skills in conveying that information to patients. Finally, and perhaps most significantly, patients are perceived not to like the 'doctor uncertainty' it may convey.

Patients may have views at odds with those of clinicians attempting to employ a shared decision strategy, and will call on their own 'evidence' – the recall of prior experiences, anecdotes received from relatives and friends, information from newspapers and television. A plurality of value systems is, it would seem, an inescapable characteristic of late modernity. The individual 'subject' is constructed as an accumulation of responses to a continual bombardment of 'facts', whether 'lay' or 'scientific', 'valid' or 'unreliable'. Under this assault, the emphatically consumable solution of a prescribed medicine often appears to have almost talismanic powers. As we saw in Chapter 1, medicines, including antibiotics, retain an intrinsic quality of 'charm', the key to their charm being in their concreteness: in them healing is objectified. In this respect, the medicine itself might be perceived as a metaphor for 'getting well', and what is being requested when a patient insists on a specific concrete therapy is this substance, or commodity, which is 'good to think with'.

AN EXAMPLE FROM CLINICAL PRACTICE

In the extract which follows, a general practitioner who is a professed supporter of shared decision-making strategies, and who regularly employs a 'SDM consulting style', is visited by a couple and their small son, Ali (not his real name). It is the first meeting between the doctor and this family. The child is suffering from a high temperature and vomiting. The father, a non-native speaker of English, does the talking. Ali's mother makes occasional background comments, and participates in the interaction only during the episode where the doctor attempts to 'share' the decision. But within that brief interaction she seems to have a decisive influence on the final decision. She is also vocal in the ritual/phatic language of departure, the 'sealing off' of the interview, and, in the context of this particular consultation, this is significant.

The example given here does not pretend to *resolve* the issue of SDM in a context where equipoise does not obtain, nor can it be ignored that the different cultural backgrounds of doctor and patient contribute to the issue of doctor–patient asymmetry. However it does present facets of how, within the context of a patient-centred approach, a doctor's decision-sharing strategies can be disrupted both by the inherent power imbalance of the consultation, and by the doctor's own preferences for treatment.

[D=Doctor; F=Ali's father; M=Ali's mother.]
001 D: okay how can I help?
002 F: yeah (.) he has a high fever (.)
003   since eight o'clock yesterday night

004		and he vomited yesterday night
005		and in the morning ag*ain* (.)
006		he:: doesn't eat anything (.)
007		refuses everything (.)
008		and (.) he's *weak* (.)
009		since (.) two days
010	D:	weak yes
011	F:	yeah
012	D:	(.) has he um had a *tem*perature?
013	F:	[M assenting] yes uh thirty *eight*
014	D:	thirty eight
015	F:	yeah
016	D:	for how long?
017		(2.0)
018	F:	yesterday night since yesterday night
019	M:	[*almost inaudible*: all day]
020	F:	[*quietly*] okay
021	D:	has he carried on eating or not eating
022	F:	*not* eating anything
		[
023	M:	[*quietly*] not eating
024	D:	*vomiting?*
025	F:	vomiting that's right yeah=
026	D:	=yeah? (.) any diarrhoea?
027	F:	no diarrhoea at all
		[
028	M:	no
029	D:	any *coughing?* [*simulates sound of coughing*]
030	F:	no at all
031	D:	not at all
032	F:	*not* at all
033	M:	[*quietly*] not at all
034	D:	okay
035		(.)
036	F:	not at all not at all

After a very open invitation from the clinician (l. 1), the father (F) begins
with an outline of his son's condition, (ll. 2–9). This information is immediately re-processed by the doctor (D), item by item (ll. 12–26). Although
this kind of repetition is a commonsense technique for confirming information, it has all been given already (temperature, rather than the unspecific
and dramatic 'high fever', vomiting, not eating). However, it is also a feature of talk between native speakers and non-native speakers that the native
speaker will seek to confirm utterances more frequently than with a fellow
native speaker, and in the context of the GP consultation this might be even
more marked. This mistrust of the father's capacity to understand is again
signalled in line 29, where the doctor simulates a coughing sound in order
to facilitate patient understanding, an event which in other circumstances
(and quite possibly here) might be interpreted by F as eccentric or patronizing. This event precipitates a bizarre sequence of chorusing wherein a phrase

is picked up and repeated by all three participants. The repetition comes about as the result of a second language learner's mistake (F saying 'no at all' instead of 'not at all') which D appears to 'correct' to 'not at all', prompting F in turn to correct himself, and his wife (as if in echo) to repeat the utterance, in a manner reminiscent of rote learning in the language class-room. After D closes the episode, indeed, indicates a shift with the discourse marker 'okay' (l. 34) and a pause, F takes it up again, repeating 'not at all' twice more, as though attempting to memorize the idiom.

```
037   D:   okay ( . )  I'd like to just have a look at him
038   F:   okay
039   D:   right you keep him on your lap there and I'll  ( . )
040        [to Ali] hullo  ( . )  what's your name?  ( . )  Ali yeah?
041        ( . )  maybe if we take the jersey off first of all
                                                [
042   F:                                        yeah
043   D:   (3.0) how old is Ali now?
044   F:   ( . ) two years and ( . ) eight months
045   D:   two years and eight months okay
046        I'll listen to the chest first if I may (2.0)
047   F:   okay [three syllables to A]
```

The doctor again initiates the shift into the next phase of the consultation with 'okay' (line 37) used as a discourse marker to indicate change of topic. The doctor engages in smalltalk with the child, suggesting tentatively that the parents help undress him (*'maybe* if we take the jersey off') followed by the permission-seeking 'I'll listen to the chest first *if I may*'). This use of modality ('maybe'; 'if I may') reflects the tentative nature of the cross-cultural encounter, as well as indicating sensitivity to the delicacy of con-sulting with a small child. The examination itself is preceded by the doctor asking Ali's age, a question whose tone of delivery is 'conversational' rather than 'professional'. This change of tone corresponds to the doctor moving *literally* into a different space (close to Ali) as well as securing a different interactional positioning, seeking to gain the child's confidence.

```
048        (18.0) [D examines Ali's chest]
049   D:   yes he's quite hot
050   F:   yeah uh do you know I've realized that uh
051        he has uh very big tonsils?
052        (5.0)
053   D:   the other side ( . )
054        let's have a look in this ear as well
055        (7.0) [D unwraps tongue depressor]
```

The examination prompts a single D assessment ('yes he's quite hot') which confirms the father's account of Ali's high temperature. F's 'yeah' therefore is almost dismissive (he's given that information already) and he immedi-ately changes the subject to remark on the size of Ali's tonsils. This change of topic is in turn ignored by D, who, being engaged in the *professional* act of examination, may not have heard it (Baron, 1985). The fact that D continues with instructions to the patient/carer, without responding to F's comment, would indicate that he is still 'listening', literally, with a stethoscope, or at least engaged in a physical examination, and that he is not yet ready to return to the consultation mode.

```
056  F:   open your mouth ah:: ah:: ah::
057  D:   very good
058  F:   good
059  D:   thank you
060       (2.0)
061       right (3.0) it's very clear what he's got
062       he's got some white spots on his tonsils=
063  F:   =I see
064  D:   yeah? so he's got um a sore throat=
065  F:   =I see
066  D:   in medical terms we call it tonsillitis
067  F:   yeah tonsillitis
068  D:   =okay ( . ) his *ea*rs are fine
069  F:   yeah
070  D:   *chest* is fine
071  F:   okay thanks very much=
072  D:   =so that's why he's got a high temperature okay?=
073  F:   =okay thank you
074       ( . )
```

Returning to the consultation, the doctor states his diagnosis (l. 64 'he's got ... a sore throat') and then the lay description is reformulated (l. 66): 'in medical terms we call it tonsillitis'. F repeats the word in a tone that suggests he is already familiar with it, after which D continues evaluating the patient's condition, to which F responds (l. 71) with a formulaic expression of thanks. Heath (1992: 242) provides an example in which a similar recycling of the clinical term takes place before the doctor, encouraged by this minimal act of confirmation, begins to discuss the diagnosis:

```
Dr   That's shingles.
     (1.2)
Dr   <that's what it is:
     (.2)
P    Shingles.
Dr   Yes
```

This section of the consultation is clearly marked off by F's 'thank you', and we move straight into the key sequence: elicitation of the shared decision.

'Sharing' a Decision?

```
075  D:   now (2.0)
076       did you have any ideas as to how we should
077       deal with this ( . ) problem?
078  F:   actually I have a ( . ) other *son* [D: mmm] ( . )
```

```
079        six and a half years old [D: mmm] ( . ) he had
080        lots of problem ( . ) about his tonsils  ( . )
081        the same problem ( . ) actually he [all come?] now
082        he finished this problem (1.0) he's coming to age seven
083        ( . ) so ( . ) I think it is better to keep the child from cold
084        ( . ) no cold drinks? something like that ( . )
085        I don't know any more
```

D begins this section again with a clear discourse marker, 'now', followed by a long (two-second) pause. He is preparing to offer F a turn to express any ideas he may have had about Ali's condition *before* he came to the surgery. This might be considered an unusual move in the normal script or formula of the doctor–patient consultation, but if he is surprised, F does not suggest as much. He responds to this invitation by delivering a brief account of a similar event that took place some time previously with another son. By doing this he claims prior experience of the situation and is therefore locating himself as one with a certain limited knowledge. This is a particular kind of strategy known as a 'category entitlement', by which individuals' experience entitles them to special knowledge about a topic (Potter, 1996). However, the only course of actual treatment that F suggests is that the child should be kept from 'cold drinks? something like that', the partial disclaimer indicating that he is not expert in any *real* knowledge on this account, a position reinforced by his next utterance: 'I don't know any more' (l. 85).

The plea is implicit rather than explicit: F is treating D's invitation to contribute as rhetorical, as though whatever he (F) says, he knows that D is the *real* purveyor of knowledge in an interaction of asymmetrical power, and therefore he chooses to say little, and qualifies that with a disclaimer – *even though* he has previous knowledge of the condition, or one very similar to it with another child. This reluctance would seem to undermine D's attempt to negotiate a shared decision from the very start, and provides a form of resistance to what Maynard (1992) has termed the 'perspective-display series', whereby doctors give parents an opportunity to express their view before providing a professional assessment.

```
086   D:   okay ( . ) the the ways we deal with tonsillitis ( . ) um ( . )
087        it's quite normal for children to have this kind of problem
088        ( . ) yeah? d'ya?
                          [
089   F:                   yes=
090   D:   =it comes and goes it's usually a viral infection
091        a virus okay? ( . )
092        which means that (1.0) I would like you to u::se ( . )
093        either Disprol or Calpol to keep the temperature down
094   F:   I see=
095   D:   =and I would like you to use that every four to six hours ( . )
096        regularly ( . ) plenty to drink ( . )
097        an' it doesn't matter what really
098        so long as it's ( . ) cold not too much sugar
099   F:   I see
```

D's reaction is to 'normalize' the condition by emphasizing its *regularity* (Potter, 1996). He does this by reassuring the parents that 'this kind of problem' (l. 87) is something that 'comes and goes'. He also takes the opportunity to establish that it is a viral infection or a *virus*, a term which he immediately defines in terms of its treatment ('which means that ...'). This explanatory sequence is followed by prescription and advice (ll. 92–8), but advice which *directly contradicts* F's only active contribution to the decision making process thus far, namely that it is better not to give the child *cold* drinks (l. 84).

```
100   D:   right? ( . ) now ( . ) some people then ( . ) like to use ( . )
101        antibiotics as well ( . )
102        but ( . ) I'm not so keen because
103        antibiotics don't deal with viruses ( . )
104        they just ( . ) are no use (1.0)
105        and they also cause some problems ( . )
106        they sometimes cause diarrhoea and vomiting ( . ) um ( . )
107        and it means that you have ( . ) problems for the future (1.0)
108        so ( . ) those are the kind of possibilities (1.0)
109        which ( . ) which way would you like to deal with the problem?
110        (1.0)
111   F:   actually if I use antibiotics for my children ( . )
112        the problem ( . ) is ending in a short time ( . )
113        which I ha ob observe ( . ) but the the another way ( . )
114        some paracetamol or things yeah (1.0)
115        it will end but a little bit more than the uh ( . )
116   D:   yes take a bit longer=
117   F:   =yeah take longer
118   D:   sure I understand ((yeah))
119        (1.0)
120   F:   so it's it's uh ( . ) family I mean the uh parents we don't (1.0)
121        want to see our children ( . ) going down I mean getting weak
122   D:   [quietly] sure=
123   F:   =so we want to take some ( . ) antibiotics
```

Having provided F with the information on drinks as though oblivious to his observation on the avoidance of the cold and of cold drinks, the doctor then explains why he doesn't want to prescribe antibiotics on this occasion ('they just (.) are no use'), a position he enforces by mentioning harmful side-effects ('diarrhoea and vomiting') as well as 'problems for the future'. After this bleak presentation of the possible harmful effects of antibiotics, the question 'which (.) way would you like to deal with the problem?' (l. 109) would seem to be a loaded one – but F too has a clear stand on the issue of antibiotics, one gained from his own experience ('the *same* problem', l. 81) of watching his children 'going *down*' (the metaphor of downward movement is here accompanied by a softening of tone in the speech of F) – and he is not so easy to coerce into the decision that D evidently wants him to make. Indeed, this passage seems most emphatically to question the underlying motivation of the 'shared decision' procedure, which on this occasion can be seen as the attempted imposition of a clearly preferred doctor's option. D goes along with F's explanation, appearing to (as he must) collapse his argument ('sure I understand', l. 118 – then 'sure' l. 122) in deference to F's forthcoming statement of preference (l. 123).

Making a Choice

This provides Ali's father with his choice, and it would have been possible to terminate the consultation here. But the doctor is not ready to finish yet.

```
124         (1.0)
125   D:    you would like to do that would you?
                                        [
126   F:                                  yeah
127   D:    yeah?
128   F:    yeah ( . ) it is too difficult to to explain but (2.0)
129         if we can uh (2.0) can be encouraged by doctors yeah
130         we can do some uh paracetamol
131   D:    sure=
132   F:    =[we cannot lie]
133         ( . )
134   D:    my own feeling is that
135         you're probably better to use paracetamol and fluids
136         rather than use antibiotics
137         because you can cause sickness
138         and also resistance for the future
                        [
139   F:                             I see
140         yeah I understand
141   D:    um ( . ) but if you feel strongly
142         that you would like to definitely have an antibiotic
143         we can do that as well ( . )
144         um the other possibility's for me to give you
145         a prescription for an antibiotic
146         and for you to wait
147   F:    I see ( . ) yeah
                  [
148   D:                                and and only use it
149         if things get worse
150         you can give me a telephone call or something
151   F:    yeah ( . )
152   D:    so which one of these possibilities would you like to do?
153         (1.0)
154   F:    okay [slight laughter in voice] let me ask my wife
155         [to M] which one paracetamol or ( . ) antibiotics?
156         ( . ) antibiotics?
```

There is a noteworthy pause after F's utterance (l. 124), after which D pushes for a restatement of this choice. F repeats this forcefully, again (l. 126), D questions it (l. 127), and F repeats (a third time) his preference for antibiotics (l. 128). He then launches into an unintelligible defence of his decision (ll. 128–30), which D appears to concur with ('sure' – l. 131), before F closes this turn with the ambiguous remark 'we cannot lie' (l. 132). However, D is not satisfied with this outcome, and attempts to change F's mind. This he does with an appeal to preventing future sickness that might result from the lowering of resistance (a technical term, or more precisely a metaphor, for which, this time, he offers no explanation). This is the 'firmest' position that D has taken so far, and it would have been interesting to see what might have happened had F become more strident in his request for antibiotics at this stage. He appears to back down, however, conceding 'I see yeah I understand' (ll. 139–40). D accommodates to this concession in F's stance by offering a compromise, stating that he is prepared to do a 'delayed prescription'. In this way he has actually presented three choices. They are: (1) paracetamol only; (2) paracetamol and antibiotics; (3) paracetamol and the possibility of antibiotics in a few days. However F seems to consider only a straight choice between paracetamol and antibiotics, a reduction of three choices to two, which is consistent with other research findings that patients will seek to redefine more complex options as a dualistic choice whenever possible (Parsons and Atkinson, 1992; Charles et al., 1998). Thus, D's question (l. 152): 'which one of these possibilities would you like to do?' becomes translated in F's version to his wife as 'which one paracetamol or (.) antibiotics?' He then repeats (with stress) his preferred choice 'antibiotics?' before M responds in their own language (unfortunately inaudible on tape).

Parents' Decision and Closure

The exchange between the parents is brief, beginning with M's short laugh, but the outcome is (in the context of F's previous stand) startling. In one short utterance (l. 157) F states his new preference and (while his wife continues to speak to him in a quiet voice) offers no further contribution whatsoever to the shared decision, only giving his son's age, the family's address, some minimal feedback and a farewell. It is as though the entire preceding discussion about the use of antibiotics has been discounted. His wife meantime is busy thanking the doctor and bidding him goodbye.

> [*After a subdued and brief laugh, M responds to F at some length in their own language, quietly and insistently*]

157	F:	yeah paracetamol this time please [*M still talking quietly to F*]
158	D:	okay (2.0) Disprol or Calpol?
159	F:	yeah
160	D:	which one? doesn't matter
161	F:	I see uh Calpol is uh eh better than paracetamol or euh which one? [*M whispers to F throughout*]
162	D:	children like it a bit better than most stuff [laughing]
163	M:	yeah=

```
164   F:   =okay
165   D:   Ali? [writing]
166   F:   [gives family name and spells it]
167   D:   and how old is he?
168   F:   uh two years and eight months
169   D:   okay and the address?
170   F:   [gives address]
171   D:   okay ( . ) plenty to drink
172   F:   okay
173   D:   Calpol every four hours please
174   F:   okay thanks
175   M:   thank you very much
176   D:   no problem and he's you know he'll be healthy fine
177   F:   okay
178   D:   okay no problem
179   M:   thanks very much
180   D:   bye bye now
181   F:   bye bye
             [
182   M:        bye
```

The preference for antibiotics expressed by F in lines 111–23 can be seen in the light of Van der Geest and Whyte's argument for medicines as a metaphor for 'getting well'. The choice is borne out by F's previous experience with another child in a similar situation, which we have described as a 'category entitlement'. This medicine is *known* to work, and therefore arguments against its prescription can only be secondary arguments, that is, they are working against the grain of personal experience and shared knowledge. What the doctor achieves is to present the parents with a choice in the issue of prescription, a choice which he then effectively undermines by arguing against the father's preferred alternative. The father offers to confer with his wife, and finds his own choice overturned, a potentially face-threatening outcome. However, the hasty concession is, to a certain degree, face-*saving*, because the father qualifies the decision as being appropriate to this particular occasion.

We might recall that at the end of the examination, the doctor tells F that his son has 'some white spots on his tonsils' (l. 62), and then goes on to explain the effect of this for Ali: 'so he's got um a sore throat' (l. 64). However, D's next utterance: 'in medical terms we call it tonsillitis' (l. 66), while ostensibly (and harmlessly) presented as a piece of 'incidental information' which 'includes' F and his family in the 'technical version' of the diagnosis, is, in terms of SDM, quite unnecessary, and could be seen, were we to accept Mishler's terms for a moment, as an intrusion of the 'voice of medicine'. The effect of doctors' use of the 'voice of medicine' in order to appropriate or else discount patients' 'lifeworld' versions of events is documented at length by Mishler (1984), and Fairclough (1992), who suggests that doctors might use the voice of medicine to maintain power asymmetry in the consultation. If we were to go along with this model, we might imagine that D here is alienating the patient by employing the specialized discourse of the clinic, or in Mishler's vocabulary, taking the description out of the lifeworld and into the world of medicine. From now on, following Mishler's logic, F is disadvantaged. However, against this view, we would argue that doctors frequently provide patients (or parents) with just such an opportunity to respond to the medical assessment (Heath, 1992: 242), and such an offer is not intrinsically rooted in any 'voice of medicine' but can be, and more obviously *will* be, offered as a way of sharing terms from clinical discourse in an unobtrusive way, thereby involving the patient in the language of diagnosis.

Immediately after giving the explanation for Ali's sore throat and temperature, D asks 'now (2.0) did you have any ideas as to how we should deal with this (.) problem?' (ll. 75–7). This, in terms of the present consultation, is the initial stage of eliciting a shared decision – a variant of which might be the question 'before you came along to the surgery did you have any idea how we might treat this?' And here F is able to state his previous experience of the condition, or a similar one, and his account of treating his other son. We ascertain that D and F are both speaking from positions of shared knowledge about what constitutes 'tonsillitis', however differently that knowledge has been formulated. But D has already reframed Ali's illness as 'tonsillitis', and is therefore speaking from a position of professional authority, whereas F (who doesn't use the term tonsillitis, except to repeat it after D), speaks of his other son having had not only 'lots of problems (.) about his tonsils', but 'the *same* problem'.

Furthermore, his hesitant response to the question 'how we should deal with this (.) problem' (ll. 76–7) suggests that, rather than not having anything to say on the topic (he has, after all, had the 'same' problem with his other son's tonsils), he simply does not want to say something foolish. In other words he is treating D's question as a *rhetorical* question, one that he knows that D knows the answer to. His closing words in this turn: 'I don't know any more' would appear to confirm this. Such a confession of ignorance presumes a superior knowledge on the doctor's part, and would be consistent with Heath's observation that: 'Even in cases where the doctor displays uncertainty in diagnosis, and thereby encourages discussion of the medical assessment of the condition, it may be observed how the patient's contribution preserves the contrasting status of the two versions of the illness and in particular embodies the subjective and lay standpoint of their own opinion' (Heath, 1992: 262).

By introducing new terminology, initiating the turn-taking sequences and controlling the topic choice, the doctor is effectively sabotaging the chances of a genuinely negotiated shared decision from the outset. That the father treats the doctor's 'decision-sharing' question as rhetorical only emphasizes that an embedded consensus on power asymmetry in this consultation will work against any shared decision even in a situation (like this one) where the father already has views, gained from previous experience, on how his son's complaint might best be treated.

The analysis of this consultation exposes a fundamental problem of any decision-making process carried out between professional and patient, namely, how to account for the way in which the embedded power asymmetry operates so as to facilitate a decision that the doctor feels is in the best interests of the patient. Whether or not this process can legitimately be termed a 'shared decision' is therefore open to question – it might be better qualified as a shared decision made with the proviso that the patient's preferences are at least commensurable with their own best interests: interests which, ultimately, are determined by the doctor, and which Silverman (1987, 1997) refers to as 'persuasion'.

CONCLUSION

The doctor–patient relationship has long been regarded as the pivotal interactive encounter in the treatment of illness. Other carers are not perceived as being so central, even though many patients spend considerably more time talking with nurses and other health care workers than they do with doctors. The reason the doctor's role is seen as crucial in Western culture is that the figure of the doctor is invested with considerable importance, and consequently there has arisen a literature which takes as its starting point the asymmetry in relations between doctor and patient. The conflict of voices in the consulting rooms has been seen as crystallizing into two dichotomous and opposing 'voices', which Mishler (1984) stylized as 'the voice of medicine' and the 'voice of the lifeworld'. The voice of medicine is based upon a biomedical model of reality. The 'voice of the lifeworld' speaks from the everyday experiences of individuals and is rooted in a 'commonsense' reality. Within this paradigm, in their dealings with patients, doctors are seen to control topic, ask most of the questions, and generally minimize or obstruct patient contributions from the 'lifeworld' perspective. 'Patient-centred' medicine emerged in the 1970s as a way of contesting this medical hegemony, and, accompanied by a burgeoning consumerism, led towards a greater involvement of patients in all phases of the medical encounter, and particularly in the decision-making process.

However, some researchers felt that an oversimplification was taking place: there was not a clear-cut divide between two conflicting voices. On the contrary, power was asserted and manifested in minute and 'capillary' modes. If talk were studied in close detail, it could be seen that speakers' positions were constantly shifting and realigning, and that both doctors and patients spoke in more voices than one. Moreover, any appeal to commonsense reality had to be treated with extreme suspicion, since common sense is a discursively constructed phenomenon, as liable to manipulation, fusion and fluctuation as any other normative device.

While recent studies, notably by Fisher (1995) and Ainsworth-Vaughn (1998), have been presented by their authors as possible blueprints for a changed order within the carer/patient relationship, they remain unconvincing. The first displays an extreme antagonism to the traditional, especially the *gendered*, roles of doctor and patient – in order to profile dramatically the more humane and patient-centred strategies of nurse practitioners. The second presumes that the improved quality of doctor–patient relations and the relative lessening of patient asymmetry in private clinics can somehow have a wider resonance when doctor–patient relations are not influenced by specific financial considerations.

Finally, when we considered a case in which a doctor attempts to carry out a piece of 'shared decision making' we saw that the efforts of the doctor are turned back on him, as it were, with the realization that the patient appears to have taken the doctor's invitation to participate more fully in the decision as simply hypothetical or rhetorical.

As Silverman insists, professional expertise predetermines an imbalance in the patient–doctor relationship: many patients want to keep the asymmetry of the relationship and would feel uncomfortable without it. They *want* the doctor to 'know best' and are likely to resent any shifts in decision making onto themselves. Crudely speaking, if one feels that one has taken responsibility for a decision oneself, one is robbed of the option of blaming another should things go wrong. But for patients who want more say in the decision-making process, and in those relationships where both parties actively seek to achieve collaborative decisions, simply employing criteria of 'democratic' or 'shared' decision making is not sufficient in medical interviews where the dominance of the professional is sustained by consensus.

The Media, Expert Opinion and Health Scares

4

In the last chapter we looked at the issue of power asymmetry in the medical consultation and saw how the doctor's professional position and assumed scientific knowledge maintains legitimacy through consensus. Traditionally, patients are given the 'facts' by professionals who *know*. Likewise, the conventional construction of professional 'voice' in media stories on health and illness functions as a vital element in the presentation of medical facts as authoritative and legitimized. From British and American television dramas of the 1960s, such as *Dr Finlay's Casebook* and *Dr Kildare*, up to and including more recent shows like *Casualty* and *ER* this identification of the (predominantly male) doctor as an heroic figure invested with almost godlike qualities reflected a cultural projection of 'the doctor' which popular culture still finds hard to resist. In the past ten or fifteen years there has been an unending supply of television hospital dramas, supplemented by 'family practice' dramas, as well as the now-standard regimen of 'fly on the wall' documentaries of life in a doctor's surgery. Public eagerness to consume dramas and documentaries on medical topics has been paralleled by an increase in news stories documenting the atrocities committed by individual medical practitioners, horror stories of malpractice (such as 'Struck off at last: Richard Neale, "botcher gynaecologist"': *Independent*, 26 July 2000) and even of murder committed by doctors, the most infamous of whom, Harold Shipman, a general practitioner in Manchester, was found to be responsible for the deaths of more than 250 of his patients (*Independent*, 5 January 2001).

For whatever reason, stories about doctors and their patients have a special resonance in our society (perhaps reflecting how the medical profession has replaced the clergy as custodian of sacred or arcane knowledge) ensuring that people will watch their televisions when anything from a hospital drama to a documentary about a newly discovered disorder is screened. And while media discourses on health, illness and the medical professions are often focused on specifically topical issues such as public spending on health care, any health-related topic creates a spin-off which draws in other health topics, and, just as in those fly on the wall documentaries that more refined viewers might claim to detest, a sense of voyeurism and *schadenfreude* usually wins out, allowing television producers to make more and more programmes dedicated to health, illness and the world of medicine.

In this chapter I will examine distinct representations of health, disease, medicine and practitioners across different media and consider how such representations are objectified in the public domain. Having considered a range of stories (from hyperactive children to world plague) in cinema, television, the radio and printed news media, I will then consider the accounts given, and dialectics of, two particular examples: HIV/AIDS and the bacterial infection widely known as 'killer bug' disease.

MEDICAL ISSUES IN MEDIA CULTURE

At least since the last decade of the old millennium, there has been an increasing preoccupation with world plague and apocalypse, a discourse which parallels the concurrent ones on the loss of tropical rainforests, ozone depletion, the melting of the polar icecaps and ecological disaster generally. Perhaps the most alarming of the illnesses to have emerged from our threatened rainforests in the last quarter of a century is Ebola. The (normally restrained) *Independent* newspaper ran a leading story on the disease (17 October 2000), under the headline:

> **There is no cure for Ebola. It kills everyone**
> **in its path. And it is back with a vengeance**

It seems that one of the conventional ways of writing health scare stories in British newspapers is to liken the disease, or some of its characteristics to 'science fiction'. This is, as we shall see, typical of early representations of HIV/AIDS as described by Sontag (1991). The *Independent* opens its Ebola story with the following paragraph:

> In surreal scenes worthy of science fiction coming to the Third World, masked men and women dressed in sterile overalls will today start quarantining the crowded Gulu district of northern Uganda where 63 cases of the highly contagious Ebola virus have been confirmed.

The 'surreal' qualities of the epidemic are reiterated later in the article, when an American epidemiologist, David Heymann, is cited as saying: 'There was blood everywhere. Blood on the mattresses, the floors, the walls … There were people dying everywhere and the women were wailing. It was surreal.' This tendency in reporting health scares to invoke concepts of the 'alien' and the 'surreal' is an instance of *intertextuality*, in which representations from the cinema and television have been expropriated and applied to 'real life', rendering real life as being 'like' the simulated or cinematic version of itself. In this way, 'reality' begins to 'imitate' the images provided by the 'society of the spectacle' (Debord, 1994, first published 1967), a notion taken up by both Baudrillard (1983) and Eco (1990).

The 'science fiction' register of the majority of such news reporting is accompanied by the insistence on shocking detail, preferably attributed to an expert or authority on the given topic. In the *Independent*, a second article on the same page quotes a passage from *The Hot Zone*, a best-selling book on the history of Ebola outbreaks by Richard Preston: 'Your mouth bleeds, and you bleed around your teeth, and you may have haemorrhages from the salivary glands – literally every opening in the body bleeds, no matter how small ... The surface of the tongue turns brilliant red and then sloughs off, and is swallowed or spat out. It is said to be extraordinarily painful to lose the surface of one's tongue.' The ghoulish attention to detail in this extract, and the attribution of this fascinating insight to an unacknowledged source ('it is *said* to be extraordinarily painful'), contribute a vicarious quality to the horrifying catalogue of symptoms. It is a measure, too, of how potent are the images of sudden, violent and messy physical degeneration in an era and society in which death and disease have been sequestered from the majority of people's everyday experience. Thus we are able to peruse from a safe distance the horrifying ravages of a disease such as Ebola, even to buy a bestselling 'biography' of the disease, which treats its subject almost as a form of pornography.

It is when such an illness ceases to be confined to its distant and exotic place of origin, however, that the news media begin to mobilize against individual 'carriers', and the possibility of an 'African' plague being imported into a European setting. A report in the London *Evening Standard* described the arrival in the British capital of a Zairean family suspected of being 'infected with' Ebola, and the following day (19 May 1995) the *Times*'s front page reported that 'a woman and her two daughters from Zaire are being held in a secure hospital in north London suspected of having the deadly Ebola virus'. Later in the same article, however, a health department spokesperson was quoted as saying: 'we do understand that it is thought unlikely that they have the Ebola infection.'

Not surprisingly, the movie industry has chosen to focus on the most horrible and terrifying possibilities of plague, apocalypse and incurable disease in its depiction of illness. There is a recurring theme even in the most sensationalist account of invading bugs and killer viruses – the role of the professional doctor/scientist within the overall representation of illness and mortality. A defining feature is the insistence on a life and death struggle against disease in which doctors fight a bloody but ultimately victorious battle against the serial killer that is disease.

Outbreak

The 1995 film *Outbreak* provides a fascinating dialogue between a self-conscious 'authenticity' and pure fantasy. Interestingly, the film is cited in Crawford's (2000) history of viruses, an inclusion noted by Meek in his review of that book (2001: 17), claiming that virologists are drawn to the movie because of its depiction of long-standing and dramatic human struggle against viruses. Before the film begins, a quotation appears on screen, attributed to 'Nobel Laureate Joshua Lederberg PhD'. It reads: *The single biggest threat to man's continued dominance of the planet is the virus.* The film then begins with a compact narrative set in the jungle of Zaire in 1967. A war is taking place, and among the soldiers are American mercenaries. The soldiers are dying of a mysterious disease which the camp surgeon can do nothing to avert or stall. An unmarked helicopter lands in the settlement and two Americans dressed in anti-contamination suits and masks tour the improvised hospital and inspect the dying and the dead. One of the Americans assures the camp surgeon that he will organize a supply drop immediately. The next sequence shows a plane with blacked-out insignia dropping the 'supplies' by parachute. The camera focuses on the surgeon's horrified expression as it dawns on him that this is no ordinary cargo of medicines but some kind of bomb. After the explosion, only a few monkeys are seen scampering from the scene of burning wreckage in what remains of the makeshift village.

The next scene introduces the audience to the 'United States Army Medical Research Institute of Infectious Diseases (USAMRIID) at Fort Detrick, Maryland. The time is the present day. Inside the building we see 'scientists' in protective costume, working with test tubes and glass containers of presumably virulent substances. As the credits appear on screen we are shown around the different sections, or 'biosafety levels' of the Institute, beginning with the innocuous 'Biosafety Level (BL) 1' ('minimal biohazard. Study of low risk infectious agents: pneumococcus, salmonella'), up through BL2 ('hepatitis, Lyme disease, influenza'); BL3 ('anthrax, typhus, HIV'), the music becoming steadily more menacing alongside the nastiness of the viruses under investigation. Eventually we arrive at Biosafety Level 4 ('extreme biohazard. Maximum security. Infectious agents: Ebola, Lassa, Hanta viruses. Highly virulent. No known cures or vaccines'). It is clear that this is the level with which we are concerned, where scientific knowledge is at the frontiers.

In this skilfully orchestrated introduction the audience is made aware not only of background to the plot, whose relevance only becomes apparent later in the film (the officer who ordered the bombing of the village is now a power-crazed general; the one who opposed it is caught between two moral camps), but also, and most importantly for our purposes, we are let in on easily digestible (but important-sounding) 'facts' about the relative dangers of different viruses. This provides a degree of 'authenticity' which movies and hospital dramas need to sustain in order to appear credible. In Hollywood movies such as *Outbreak*, this is seen as necessary to a realistic grasp of the 'facts' within a fictional setting. By being introduced to the 'meaning' of different 'biosafety levels' within the secure wing of a research institute, we are immediately prepared for the following scene, in which Sam (the army virologist played by Dustin Hoffman) picks up the phone and Billy (played by Morgan Freeman) says: 'Looks like we have a level four, Sam'. We have been given members' knowledge of a particular kind, at the same time as being invited into a pseudo-scientific community.

In Sam's house:
Sam: Hi Billy, what's up?

Billy: Looks like we have a level four, Sam
Sam: How many dead?
Billy: Don't know. There aren't any numbers yet.
Sam: What do you think it is?
Billy: Too early to say. The World Health Organization is preparing a team, but I want you there first.

Billy, it transpires, was one of the two masked American officers responsible for the firebombing of the African settlement 30 years before. The virus is identified as the same deadly variant (with one significant difference) that the two officers encountered in the jungle, and the film develops into a morality tale along predictable lines.

One of the most interesting things about this film is the way in which the masked figures (soldiers, scientists) who feature so prominently can be regarded as *metonymic* of the virus itself. There is an elusiveness, a 'face-lessness' about the virus, which makes it very difficult to 'read' (for example, the scientists cannot determine whether or not it is airborne, or communicable only through bodily contact). This facelesness is perfectly analogous with the robotic visages of the investigators and soldiers who mill around the small American town where the caucus of virus-carriers is eventually tracked down. That this metaphor is extended to the military is fitting in the light of the predominant metaphor of illness being a fight, or war, against disease. Moreover, there is an extreme nihilism, an anti-humanitarian rapaciousness, evident in the villain of the piece (Donald Sutherland), who is eager to destroy the threatened American town (just as he gave the order to firebomb the African village all those years ago) in order to protect the virus and allow its development as a biological weapon at the service of the US military machine. The character played by Sutherland suggests nothing less than the kind of aimless destruction associated with the virus itself, which finds an echo in the words of Williamson (1989, cited in Tulloch and Lupton, 1997: 9): 'Nothing could be more meaningless than a virus. It has no point, no purpose, no plan; it is part of no scheme, carries no inherent significance'. The virus only spreads chaos and destruction (as against the professional dedication and selflessness displayed by Dustin Hoffman and his medical colleagues). In the final outcome, the film suggests, the moral supremacy of the doctor-hero is absolute.

Lorenzo's Oil

Another movie, one in which the interplay of professional and lay responses to illness is explored in a more subtle and persuasive manner, is *Lorenzo's Oil* (1992). Based on the actual experience of an American-Italian family, this film tells the story of Lorenzo, a five-year-old boy who is discovered to be suffering from a rare and hereditary disease, adrenoleukodystrophy (ALD). An extremely bright and apparently healthy child, Lorenzo begins to display signs of dementia, and rapidly loses both his sight and hearing.

Lorenzo's parents are told by their doctors that he will die within two years. However, the parents, Augusto and Michaela Odone (played by Nick Nolte and Susan Sarandon), refuse to accept the diagnosis, and the movie charts their search for a cure. Despite their lack of medical training, they begin a tireless search for information and research data that might help them to find solutions to their child's condition. They investigate every known aspect of the illness and attend international conferences, often to the chagrin both of medical professionals and of parent support organizations, both groups opposing their autonomous search on the grounds that they provide false hopes for the parents of sick children, who are already resigned to watching their own sick children die. But while this opposition is troubling to the Odones, who regard several of the parents as being far too subservient to the pessimistic prognoses of the medical profession, it is the opposition of the medical orthodoxy that provides the greatest source of conflict for Lorenzo's parents. They are regarded as outsiders, non-medics, who cannot possibly understand the biomedical complexities of ALD. Even after the treatment that they develop is found to be eliciting positive responses in Lorenzo, some medical professionals and parents are still set against them, since they have upset the ritual code of behaviour between parents and doctors. Their offence lies in a symbolic contravention of roles, of not play-ing the doctor–patient (or doctor–parent) game according to the rules. As Lupton has observed, the film is particularly adept at depicting the problems and sense of helplessness often encountered by lay people when attempting to penetrate the 'arcane mystique of medical science and the arrogance of specialist doctors' (1994a: 54). Not surprisingly the film was criticized by some members of the medical profession for presenting medical researchers as insensitive and research programmes as being driven by motives of profit (the small numbers of ALD sufferers meaning that sales of drugs would never cover the research costs incurred). And yet, as Lupton points out, scientific medicine, if not individual doctors, is vindicated in this film, and it is the couple's dedication to the task of finding a cure for their son's illness, and their faith in the ability of medical science to help them do so (by obsessively exploring and scrutinizing the medical literature), that ulti-mately provides them with a possible cure and hope for future generations of ALD patients.

Both *Outbreak* and *Lorenzo's Oil*, in their different ways, provide inter-esting perspectives on the ways in which doctors are perceived in contem-porary culture. In *Outbreak*, the doctor-as-hero is pitted against the twin foes of a mindlessly destructive virus and a mindlessly destructive general, the two becoming analogous in our reading of the film. Our faith in the ulti-mate ability of medical science and human ingenuity to defeat rampant nature is never called into question, but the possibility of an individual doctor abusing the power vested in him by taking decisions for reasons of personal interest or self-seeking is central to the film's narrative strategy. Meanwhile, in *Lorenzo's Oil*, the Odones are only encouraged in their investigations as long as they do so unobtrusively and without making claims which might threaten the self-sufficiency or perceived competence of the medical profession. In both cases the power vested in doctors simply on the grounds that they *are* doctors reflects a wider cultural acceptance of the role of doctor-as-expert and one which is widely promoted in other popular media, whatever the attempts of more progressive or enlightened medical professionals to change their image in society.

TELEVISION HEALTH DOCUMENTARIES

Health documentaries on television provide another set of perspectives on the ways in which professionals and lay people are represented. We can divide these documentaries into two categories: those which take a fly-on-the-wall approach, and follow the daily activities of a health professional or group of health professionals, most frequently doctors in general practice; and those which seek to be informative about a particular condition or disease, and are essentially aimed at being *educational*. I shall consider both of these in turn, using examples from recent British television.

In an article on television health documentaries, Hodgetts and Chamberlain (1999: 317) assert that '[D]epictions of lay people serve to personalize and normalize medical care and to legitimize medical surveillance and intervention.' Drawing on the social theory of Zola (1972) they put forward the argument that television coverage of health issues generally endorses a *medicalized* view of society, one in which the dominance of medicine as a social force is unquestioned, and that 'medical ways of thinking' are not restricted to the clinic but are evident in many other aspects of daily life, serving as a type of social control. As a consequence of this, lay people come to rely on a medicalized version of health and of ways of treating illness rather than being encouraged to question the wider social and economic factors surrounding health issues. Although there is evidence (as discussed in Chapter 1) that the patient as 'active consumer' is in the ascendant (Lupton, 1997), along with demands for greater doctor accountability, the medicalization thesis is still evident in widespread cultural expressions such as advertising for health products, and the 'passive patient' is still (in a manner of speaking) alive and well. As Hodgetts and Chamberlain observe (1999: 326): 'The use of lay depictions to support a medicalized perspective is highly salient in health documentaries. The use of lay depictions as sources of challenge to medicine are much less prevalent.'

Doctors' Orders

There is little in the 1998 BBC series *Doctors' Orders* to suggest a radical questioning of medical practice by either patients or practitioners. Set in a small coastal town in the west of England, the series affirms stereotypes of

English rural life, with the local GPs playing in a charity cricket match, a large and personable doctor bonding with one of his female patients by simultaneously going on a diet with her, and the same doctor having to hurriedly absent himself from his duties in order to oversee the birth of a litter of piglets at his own home. The programme charts the daily running of the practice over six episodes using the friendly but paternalistic personae of the doctors to illustrate not only the homogeneity of an idealized and disappearing community lifestyle but also, implicitly, to endorse it. It is, runs the subtext, largely through the vocational and dedicated aspects of doctoring that this community is held together. The characteristic fabric of the community is on display in the surgery, as in the cricket match jollity, displaying features of a kind of society many of its viewers will be unfamiliar with, one in which the traditional verities of community spirit (not to mention social class) play no small part.

As distinct from straightforward fly-on-the-wall documentaries, in this series the camera is addressed intermittently by the doctors (but never by the patients), and extracts in which the camera is used in this way serve as linking devices, providing narrative thread to the illness story being enacted, or contextualizing events within a broader case history. One of the more compelling episodes showed Dr Paul Slade (the dieting, pig-farming doctor) attempting to comfort and console an elderly man whose wife is dying from cancer. He is presented as accomplishing this demanding and anguished task with considerable compassion and sensitivity. It is illuminating to contrast Paul Slade's deeply understanding position in relation to this elderly patient with his consulting style in respect of another patient, a recidivist drug addict who has been caught augmenting his regular methadone prescription with illicit drugs. In the sequence that follows, a mixture of voiceover, flashback and the doctor addressing the camera directly is used in order to present the narrative detail as economically as possible:

Voiceover: Paul [Dr Slade] has a delicate relationship with his next patient, Paul Bradley, a heroin addict who is bound by a strict contract. Three weeks ago their relationship was put to the test when Paul discovered he'd been hiding the truth. [*Threatening, rhythmic percussion sounds, which continue throughout early part of sequence*]

Doctor: [*to patient, in flashback*] You've got to be honest. You've *got* to be honest, haven't you. I know it breaks a lifetime's habit but let's try and start it now yeah?

Voiceover: His contract bans him from using illegal drugs while being prescribed methadone, a heroin substitute...

Doctor: I'm *really* disappointed in this.

Voiceover: The urine tests revealed that he's been using heroin and amphetamines.

Patient: [*dramatically, whining*] This is the first time I've ever done this. You should give me a chance, for God's sake, Doctor Slade, I'm *sorry*.

Doctor: You had your chance last time. I'm *not* prescribing for you any more.

Voiceover: Paul Bradley was refused any more methadone. But the surgery decided the episode would serve as a warning. Now the guidelines are even stricter.

Doctor: What I intend to stick to with you is to make your contract with me to be very tight indeed, on checking urine tests, and your daily dose.

Patient: Yeah, I agree with that, that's Ok.

Doctor: And on that basis I'll continue to prescribe for you, and then we know *exactly* where we stand and er any going off that contract from your side then we end our relationship. You're fully understanding that, are you?

Patient: That's right yeah.

Doctor: And I'll want a urine test from you on Mondays and Thursdays. What day is it today? It's Monday. *What* a good day. You go and do this for me now. [*handing patient sample container*] [*to camera*] He was beginning to mess us about, I pulled him right back, and now, you know, he's back on the level again, and er, between us, with Bridget [one of the other GPs] and I seeing him regularly I hope we'll stay all right with him.

While it is a commonplace that medical interactions with addicts do not conform to patterns observable in less controversial instances of illness, it is worth noting that the extremely paternalistic and controlling approach adopted by Dr Slade here is reminiscent of a more authoritarian perspective altogether, which might once have been more familiar in, for instance, the army medical corps, and which may nowadays be more readily observable in addiction treatment centres. Textual examples of this controlling language, even in this short and edited extract, are (a) the use of grammatical modality ('You've got to be honest'); (b) the patronizing use of the first person plural ('let's try and start it now'); (c) the use of directives ('You go and do this for me now'); and (d) threatening or at least affective declaratives: 'I'm *really* disappointed in this'; 'You had your chance last time'; 'I'm *not* prescribing for you any more'.

Furthermore, Dr Slade seeks confirmation that Paul Bradley has understood the terms of his contract by an emphatic utterance suffixed with a question tag ('are you?'), adopting, unusually, the present continuous form for the main question: 'You're fully understanding that, are you?' rather than the more predictable 'You understand that, don't you?' The use of the present continuous lodges the requirement for understanding in an *ongoing* present, one which needs to be continually reasserted and of which the patient needs to continually remind himself. It represents a shift in Dr Slade's repertoire, and serves also to enforce the medical orthodoxy in which he, as prescribing doctor, is both gatekeeper and provider. In this sense, the episode makes it abundantly clear that television documentaries perpetuate accepted notions of a medicalized society, even (or especially) in a supposedly reprobate case like that of a heroin addict. Finally, the episode graphically affirms the sort of 'surveillance' in contemporary health care described by Foucault (see Chapter 1), in which the medical gaze penetrates the social domain, with the doctor monitoring, as here, the urine samples of the addict in order to check that he has fulfilled his side of the 'strict contract' imposed on him.

Attention Deficit Hyperactive Disorder (ADHD)

In 1998 BBC2 ran a series of short introductory documentaries on different aspects of children's health such as dyslexia, diet and hyperactivity. Hyperactivity in children is an excellent example of a condition which has become increasingly medicalized. As the voiceover in the introduction to the programme asks: 'When is a naughty, energetic child simply a bright spark, or displaying a pattern of behaviour that indicates something much more serious? Attention deficit hyperactive disorder (ADHD) can wreck the lives of children and parents.'

The programme was designed to present parents' views, children's views and the professional perspective of a Professor Eric Taylor. There are also sequences in which a child actor acts out some of the typical symptoms of ADHD. The most salient of these flash up on screen in red as a voiceover lists them: *lack of attention leading to mistakes; difficulty interacting with others; forgetfulness; being unable to sit still or to calm down; impulsiveness; constantly interrupting others; engaging in physically dangerous activities without considering the consequences.*

We are introduced to two families with ADHD children, Rosie and Richard, aged nine and eleven respectively at the time of filming, who have displayed disruptive behaviour from a very early age. Richard's parents appear together on the sofa in their living room, and are clearly distressed by the effect that Richard's condition has had on their lives. The father says: 'We used to joke "where did he get his energy from?" but we knew because he *sucked* it out of us, like a vampire.' Rosie's mother sounds similarly ill-disposed towards her daughter: 'She'll try anything on anybody. She can be a compulsive liar and can be quite deceptive in regards to what she wants and what she wants to get away *with*.' A remarkable feature of the programme is the extent to which the parents go to present their own children in such a negative light. Richard's father again: 'These children are masters at manipulation. Richard just knew every button to press. He knew every way to continually wind you up.' Both children speak with received pronunciation and seem remarkably articulate and self-aware concerning the nature of their condition and the trouble it has caused their parents. They talk of themselves as being 'naughty' and 'out of control'. Rosie's words resonate with therapist-talk or echo the dietary concerns of her mother : '... hitting people, getting angry. When I'd get angry with myself I didn't take it out on myself I'd take it out on other people ... Some things make me grumpy and misbehave and one of those is Smarties and fizzy drinks.'

The issue of medicalization is most clearly raised by Richard's mother, who takes comfort in the knowledge that the condition (and hence her son's behaviour) is being framed medically and can be treated by a drug ('just as insulin is used to treat a diabetic child', is the analogy chosen by the father). She says that her reaction to her son's condition was one of overwhelming guilt and that 'although I loved him as my child, I disliked him intensely as a person. *All* his behaviour *all* his life was horrendous as far as we were concerned. But he couldn't help it. I personally found the label of ADHD very very helpful.' By having the problem of hyperactivity medicalized, the parents of Richard and Rosie are spared the social onus and personal stress of having to deal with what otherwise would be termed 'naughty' children. Rosie's mother describes how at an early age Rosie stopped being invited to parties because 'a child would get hurt', 'things would get broken', and so on. With treatment, Rosie is seen to be on the path to recovery, reciting a list of things she wants to be, which includes geologist, artist and Olympic athlete. And Richard's father sees the current regime of treatment as a constructive step towards managing the more negative aspects of his son's behaviour: 'I don't know if Richard ever *will* grow out of ADHD. I think what he *will* do is learn to manage some of the more negative aspects of his behaviour. My *hope* is that he'll find some way of using that energy in a very *positive* fashion and of being able to ensure that the negative side doesn't take precedence too much.'

Although there is some ambiguity about the disease status of ADHD given by Professor Taylor – 'ADHD isn't exactly a disease in the sense of something that you have or don't have, with a single cause. It's a bit like having a blood pressure problem' – the labelling of this distressing condition lends it an institutional authority which is clearly welcomed by the parents of these children. As Professor Taylor says:

The *brain* of children with ADHD is *not* hyperactive. Parts of the brain are *under*active, and the parts of the brain that are underactive are those that are particularly involved in in*hibiting* things that we do when we shouldn't do them, the sort of things that are involved in *waiting*, in *refraining* from an action, in *resisting* temptation. It's those uh controlling and inhibiting centres of the brain that are *under*active in children with ADHD.

This accounting for ADHD, and its framing as a medical rather than a solely behavioural problem, ensures that the lay depictions of ADHD conform to the perspective presented by Professor Taylor. This too conforms to the position argued by Williams and Calnan (1996: 257, cited also in Hodgetts and Chamberlain, 1999: 331), that:

lay views on the merits of modern medicine are likely to differ according to whether it is being considered in general or personal terms. Indeed, when viewed at a distance there appears to be considerably more room for skepticism. In contrast, when considered in the context of personal or family illness, the picture is likely to be very different.

In other words, if you are personally affected by a condition which others might consider 'marginal', or by one of those illnesses, ranging from drug addiction to cancer, which are still considered by many people to be somehow 'brought upon themselves' by individuals, you are far more likely to subscribe to a view of that illness or condition in which it becomes medicalized. Indeed, as we saw in Chapter 2, 'discourses of truth' become what they are through a process of objectification which involves the 'naturalizing', or the 'mainstreaming' of once-marginal discourses. In respect of media representations of medicine in general, including television health documentaries, whatever questions are raised in the more sensational denunciations of medical practice from time to time, we are far more likely to encounter lay representations which support a consistently medicalized perspective, rather than ones which act as sources of challenge to medical orthodoxy.

COMMONSENSE REALITY AND 'TEST-TUBE BABIES'

Also in Chapter 2, we examined the notion that the members of any human community, however defined, will share certain 'commonsense' beliefs. Central to an understanding of common sense is that one must be in possession of at least some of it in order to recognize what it is and is not, or, as the anthropologist Geertz wrote epigrammatically in his essay 'Common Sense as a Cultural System': 'generally, the notion of common sense has been rather commonsensical: what anyone with common sense knows' (Geertz, 1983: 77).

Naturalization, argues Fairclough, is the 'royal road to common sense' (1989: 92) and is particularly insidious when a dominant discourse mode becomes accepted as commonsensical, achieving, in Bourdieu's words, 'recognition of legitimacy through misrecognition of arbitrariness' (Bourdieu, 1977, cited in Fairclough, 1989: 91).

Whereas Fairclough regards the process as one of naturalization, Moscovici defines common sense as a social representation that has been *objectified*:

> Common sense is continually being created in our societies, especially where scientific and technical knowledge is popularised ... In the process the store of social representations, without which a society cannot communicate or relate to and define reality, is replenished. (1984: 59)

Frequently we are dealt a lesson in common sense by politicians or the media on the implicit understanding that the truth value of that common sense is not open to question. In 1999 the British Conservative party leader, William Hague, attempted to challenge that assumption by inverting the paradigm with the slogan 'the common-sense revolution'. By this Hague was suggesting that the policies of Tony Blair's Labour government were anti-commonsensical, and a revolution was needed in order to re-establish common sense as normative.

Fairclough's conception of common sense as an ideological tool used in the maintenance of a consensual reality can be illustrated with an example from the *Daily Mail*. This 1994 newspaper article describes the establishment of a government body for the regulation of fertility clinics, the 'Human Fertilisation and Embryology Authority' (HFEA). Above the banner headline:

NEW LIFE IN THEIR HANDS

we were informed that

'Commonsense people will have final say on birth controversy'.

The article proceeds:

> Eighteen people are to have the final say in the fierce debate over test-tube babies ... Besides medical experts, they include actress Penelope Keith, BBC radio managing director Liz Forgan and Rabbi Julia Neuberger. It will be up to them to frame rules covering 'retirement pregnancies' of older women, the question of 'designer babies' and the use of ovaries from aborted foetuses. Though most of the names on the list have obvious qualifications – Rabbi Neuberger, for example, is a noted moral commentator – others are slightly more surprising. The explanation is that the membership is intended to reflect a wide range of society's views, and bring expertise in fields like the media as well as individual common sense. (*Daily Mail*, 4 January 1994)

The adjectival use of 'commonsense' in the introductory phrase, 'common-sense people will have final say' alerts us to the symbolic force of the representation before we read the article. The assertion that there exist people who by definition exhibit the faculty of common sense promotes an assurance of their normative authority. It is then established that common sense is an 'individual' commodity, but also one that can be supported and reinforced by both scientific and moral expertise. In this sense the 'experts' are capable of common sense just like *us*, and the possibility that *our* common sense (voiced by 'commonsense people') is simply a reformulation and popularization of received 'expert' knowledge (*their* knowledge) is neatly eclipsed. In referring to France, where a law is said to be planned to prevent 'post-menopausal women' from becoming pregnant, the French Health Minister is cited as politician, doctor *and* moralist, thereby, one would conclude, exerting maximum force as a purveyor of expert (but also, as we shall see, of 'commonsense') judgements: 'Health Minister Philippe Douste-Blazy, a doctor himself, said artificial late pregnancies were "immoral" and dangerous for the health both of mothers and children'.

This is an exemplary case of expert scientific opinion informing the consensual view, which Moscovici (1984) refers to as the process of *anchoring*. When we classify, or name something ('test-tube babies', 'retirement pregnancies', 'designer babies') we always compare it to a conceptual prototype (e.g. 'normal babies', 'the correct age to have babies', etc.), and always ask ourselves whether the object compared is normal or abnormal in relation to that prototype. In this way, science and its experts generate new social representations: or, put another way, they fabricate common sense. New theories and information are reproduced at a more immediate and accessible level and in the process acquire an authority of their own. In the *Daily Mail* article, the non-expert ('commonsense') members of the governing body of HFEA express the same normative values as the experts, thereby endorsing the commonsensical nature of both.

Health promotion projects are notable sources for this kind of anchoring, as of course is advertising in general. A series of British government publications on 'sensible eating' under the generic heading 'Food Sense' was available from doctors' surgeries in the UK in the late 1990s. These pamphlets, prepared by experts from the Food Safety Directorate of the Ministry of Agriculture, Fisheries and Food, provide 'guidelines for a healthy diet': 'Food is one of the most important parts of our lives', readers were informed. 'It is there to be enjoyed, and shared with family and friends. If you follow these guidelines there is every reason why you should enjoy your food as much – or even more than before.' The advice given constitutes 'sense' because it has been compiled by 'experts' who agree with one another. In the pamphlet, *Healthy Eating* (HMSO, 1991) uniformity of belief among experts is stressed: 'In spite of confusing publicity, there is wide agreement among experts on what is a healthy style of eating'. Until it disappeared from supermarket shelves in the late 1990s, the British public also had the option to consume expert opinion more literally: Kellogg's produced a breakfast cereal called Common Sense, now, apparently, discontinued.

To revisit the arguments I presented in Chapter 3 for a moment: if we are to accept this reading of the way that common sense is fabricated, then the kind of talk that Mishler sees as incorporating the 'voice of the life-world' is itself a reconstituted version of science. That is to say, patients in their talk with doctors will present a version of the world which accords with their common sense. If that common sense is established by the anchoring of scientific ideas in everyday discourse (through the media and our frequent exposure to 'expert' views on television and the radio), the patient is doing little more than giving a *consensual* version of a scientific 'truth'.

'Common sense', therefore, is largely constructed through the reification of a mode of discourse transferred from the world of science and expert opinion; and is sustained by the normative reiterations of a compelling and invasive mass media and its accompanying popular wisdom.

RADIO: FAIRCLOUGH ON 'MEDICINE NOW'

We might explore one aspect of the foregoing discussion a little further. The development of an authoritative position is familiar from the way that television and radio shows introduce the 'expert voice' into a discussion. Within the news media this kind of attribution is particularly relevant. As Fairclough observes:

> the attribution of news statements to authoritative sources is a key part of the rhetoric of factuality, profoundly affecting the structuring of news texts with respect to the construction of complex embedding relationships between voices (interviews, reports, film sequences, and, of course, discourse representation). (1995: 93)

Fairclough uses critical discourse analysis (CDA) to examine a BBC Radio 4 broadcast in the series *Medicine Now* (Fairclough, 1995). The programme outlines ways in which epileptics might devise strategies for controlling their own 'mental states', in order to avoid fits. There are three phases to the item: first the presenter introduces the topic, essentially that 'conscious attempts to avoid certain states of mind help to prevent epileptic seizures'. In the second phase the presenter interviews a doctor from the Institute of Psychiatry, an interview in which there is apparent equality between presenter and expert, each of them having an ascendant role – the interaction being overtly 'managed' by the presenter, but the doctor being the provider of expert opinion. In the third phase the presenter interviews a patient, Kathleen Barker: here the presenter restricts himself to using information-eliciting questions:

```
[P:    Presenter
KB:    Kathleen Barker]
P:     what Kathleen . ar – is the situation on the circumstance or the thoughts
       which tend to bring on a seizure in your case
KB:    in my case guilt
P:     . when did it start
KB:    e: when I was quite young . . . . . attacks started occurring
       epil
       [
P:     epileptic attacks
KB:    yes . . . .
P:     and did this pattern continue . for for years
                              [              [
KB:                           yes            yes
P:     after
KB:    there are certain attacks that I know were induced by guilt
P:     what about e more recent times
KB:    on two very important occasions ...
```

Here, as Fairclough comments, 'the patient's narrative has been divided up into topical chunks for presentational purposes, with the presenter's questions controlling the topical development, moving from what causes her attacks, to when they started, to how long they went on, to what's happening now' (1995: 134). In other words, in these exchanges the mediating and managerial work of the presenter as interviewer is quite overt. It could, comments Fairclough, be suggested that the degree of control the presenter exerts over the patient's story is motivated by the need to make it more easily digestible for the audience. But no such effort is made when the presenter interviews the doctor. More likely, it indicates that the presenter sees the patient as needing more guidance. Also relevant is the fact that while the doctor is not addressed directly, the patient is called by her first name.

In several important ways, this programme assumes the voice of medical and pedagogic authority, expressed in different ways by both presenter and medical expert; a voice which is not challenged by the patient and which despite its radical approach to the subject matter is presented as authoritative.

The contentiousness of this approach to the treatment of epilepsy (above all, the implication that epileptics are 'responsible' for their attacks by somehow failing to identify and check the preconditions for their occurrence) is nowhere engaged with. The accommodation made by the doctor to the audience style is 'made from within the profession on the professional's terms' (1995: 135). The packaging and presentation of the programme leave us in no doubt as to the factuality of the topic and the professional authority of its interlocutors. It is a legitimizing and authoritative discourse which asserts itself through a combination of factual data and rhetorical strategies.

HIV/AIDS AND THE NEWS MEDIA

A similar concern with issues of authority, legitimacy and the rhetorical strategies used to implement government prevention policies has been evident in discourses of HIV/AIDS in recent years. This has accompanied a wider interest in the discursive construction of AIDS in clinical interaction, in ethnographic interviewing as well as in the media (e.g. Peräkylä, 1995; Lupton, 1994b; Silverman, 1997; Jones, 1997; Tulloch and Lupton, 1997). According to Lupton (1994b), in the early days of AIDS awareness common lay notions were that AIDS was largely a matter of bad luck (serendipitous logic), and that the virus was easily transmitted (miasmic beliefs). Beliefs also emphasized the *endogenous* nature of HIV infection, explaining the common distinctions between 'innocent' and 'guilty' people living with AIDS. Many people believed that even if they did contract the virus, there would be a cure in time. Additionally, AIDS was seen as being caused by certain individuals who engaged in particular kinds of sexual practice, particularly gay men, and by intravenous drug users, rather than by a virus, and therefore there was a new emphasis on selecting the 'right kind' of sexual partner. Many such beliefs originated in and were generated by press reporting. As Lupton writes,

> In the case of AIDS, the popular media, especially the news media, have played an extremely important role in drawing upon pre-established knowledge and belief systems to create this new disease as a meaningful phenomenon, particularly in regions dominated by the mass media such as westernized countries. From the time that the symptoms of AIDS were first recorded, in the absence of other sources of easily accessible information, the news media have defined AIDS for the developed world, set the agenda for public discussion of AIDS issues, and influenced key decisions of policy makers. (1994b: 4)

From early days, news reporting of AIDS had an enormous impact. In 1983 a TV AIDS documentary sparked a study in the *British Medical Journal* about the number of patients with anxiety about AIDS. Individuals who watched the documentary complained of acute depression, malaise, night sweats, impairment of concentration. One individual had watched the programme over 30 times and had contemplated suicide. The authors of the

BMJ article believed that their patients' conditions were precipitated by media coverage of the AIDS epidemic (Lupton, 1994b: 9). These patients represent extreme cases, of course, yet they encapsulate much of the speculation about the impact of news media on everyday beliefs about AIDS. News media coverage of AIDS peaked in 1985 with the death of Rock Hudson, the movie star, from an AIDS-related illness, and his name was only the first in a list of 'celebrity status' AIDS casualties.

In Britain, the first major AIDS-prevention advertising campaign was launched in 1986. Advertisements carried the slogan: 'Don't die of ignorance.' The billboards and television advertisements used 'apocalyptic, forbidding images of coffins, tombstones, pneumatic drills, icebergs and volcanoes' (Tulloch and Lupton, 1997: 36). However, the campaign was criticized both by gay organizations and medical authorities for its 'unrelentingly negative stance, its ambiguity and its attempts to arouse fear, anxiety and guilt in the audience' (ibid.: 36 citing Rhodes and Shaughnessy, 1990: 56).

In 1987 the Australian government launched a campaign aimed at raising public awareness of AIDS. It became known as the 'Grim Reaper' campaign because of the central icon employed in mass media adverts. Television, cinema and print advertisements drew on medieval and horror movie imagery, portraying the Grim Reaper, a skeleton swathed in black cloak and hood, carrying a scythe and a bowling ball. Instead of ten-pins, a collection of 'ordinary Australians' were knocked down by the Reaper's huge bowling ball: a housewife, a baby, a little girl, a footballer. The intention was to render the abstract notions of death, danger and risk more familiar, and to demonstrate that people are like ten-pins before AIDS, vulnerable and unable to protect themselves. The print advertisement warned that:

> Anyone can get AIDS. It doesn't matter who you are, it's what you do that counts. At first it seemed that only gay men and IV drug users were being killed by AIDS. But now we know all sorts of people are being devastated by it. The fact is, experts say that in Australia over 50,000 men, women and children now carry the AIDS virus.

Accompanying press releases emphasized the message:

> TWO MILLION AUSTRALIANS ARE NOW AT RISK FOR AIDS, SURVEY SHOWS – National AIDS education campaign (NACAIDS) launched to warn Australians that 'prevention is the only cure we've got' – safe sex, single partners, abstinence, education, caution and condoms will prevent the further spread of AIDS.

Referring to Strong's (1990) concept of 'epidemic psychology', Lupton (1994b) points to an apocalyptic element in health reporting which dominated during this period. Just as in times of war or revolution, disease epidemics create an atmosphere of lack of control within societies, an 'emotional maelstrom' which brings about intense feelings of fear, suspicion, moralization, irrationality, panic and the need to take decisive and immediate action. The mass media, insists Lupton, played an important role in transmitting such fear. The 'Grim Reaper' campaign was the response of a government and a society in the grip of a psychosocial epidemic just as Strong describes.

Campaigns in the Australian media (replicated elsewhere in the world in similar formats) included television advertisements which emphasized the need to wear a condom, since one could never be certain of one's partner's sexual history (or even of one's own, with regard to possible HIV infection). For example, in 1988, an advertisement targeted at young, sexually active heterosexuals depicted a naked young couple passionately embracing on a double bed, panning out to show numerous other beds containing couples engaged in the same activity in the widening space around them. The voiceover then said:

> Next time you go to bed with someone, ask yourself, 'Do you know how many people they've been to bed with?' Because it's quite possible that they've had several partners and it's just as likely that these partners had several partners too. And they've had partners and so on and any one of them could have been infected with the AIDS virus and passed it on. But you don't know. That's why you should always use a condom. Because you can never be sure just how many people you're really going to bed with. Cover yourself against AIDS. (in Tulloch and Lupton, 1997: 43)

A similar advertisement was shown at this time in Britain. A variation on this theme appeared in 1990, in which a young couple are seen kissing and embracing in an atmospherically darkened room. We are then shown a flashback of the young man embracing a 'previous' female partner in the same way. The voiceover warns us that the person you're about to go to bed with might have slept with 'someone who's been doing drugs, and shared a needle with someone who shared a needle with someone who had the AIDS virus. And that means any of these people could have passed on the AIDS virus to your partner. Because when you sleep with someone, you're sleeping with their past'. The next image is of a large mattress covered with hands holding syringes, tips upward. The couple are seen to tumble in slow motion onto the mattress, suggesting that they 'will be impaled upon the needles as they continue their clinch and fall onto the bed' (Tulloch and Lupton, 1997: 45).

Moral ambivalence regarding different kinds of illness, particularly those considered to be epidemic, has become a marked feature of health discourses since the arrival of the HIV virus, and HIV/AIDS can be used as a yardstick for the moral valency attached to other disease outbreaks. Jones (1997: 394) suggests that people with HIV/AIDS are subject to the contradictory discourses of both an amoral 'medical model' and a morally suspect 'stigma model' according to which people affected by these media-driven definitions take on the opposing roles of 'innocent victim' and 'guilty agent'. Meanwhile, Strong (1990: 251) has argued that the first psychosocial dimension of any epidemic is fear. He goes on to suggest that it is possible, within an epidemic psychology, 'for great waves of panic and fear to spread among a population even when almost no-one has actually been infected'

(1990: 253). Recourse to the folk memory of plague (the 'Black Death'), along with the scaremongering and apocalyptic imagery in the popular media that accompany actual disease outbreaks (for example, the Ebola scare of May 1995), combine to create a siege mentality, in which potential fifth columnists are identified and scapegoats are pursued.

The representation of AIDS as invader, of the 'war with AIDS', is one that Helman (1984: 101), writing at the onset of AIDS hysteria, saw as being attributable to identifiable groups of foreigners (Africans, Haitians, etc.) as well as invoking the science fiction interest of an alien body lodging itself in the normally healthy body of the host. As Helman pointed out, it was not difficult to associate the one with the other and to create xenophobia from a virus. AIDS as *war* was a metaphor according to which normal society could be seen as defending itself against the degenerate lifestyles of a sexually promiscuous, deviant, drug-abusing nucleus of 'carriers'.

The resonance of the war against an invasive disease is central to an understanding of illness as something *external* to the individual, an *exogenous* entity to be battled with, and in this respect corresponds to Herzlich's (1973) perception of the intrinsically healthy individual pitted against a health-threatening society (see Chapter 2). However, there are times, as Strong suggests, when society is itself under threat, and these are the occasions which prompt a spirit of resistance (*the war against cancer*, *the battle with AIDS*, etc.). An example, from May 1994, is the breathless and irresponsible coverage in the news media of the apparent proliferation in cases of necrotizing fasciitis, better known as the 'killer bug', which I shall consider below. One of the objectives of this chapter will be to ascertain the difference in representation between the moralizing hysteria that accompanies militarized representations of HIV/AIDS and the media-generated panic accompanying the 'killer bug invasion' (Gwyn, 1999b).

First, however, I would like to pre-empt the next chapter by examining briefly the twin metaphors of invasion and war. Sontag (1991) states that the military metaphor first came into general use in the 1880s, when bacteria were identified as the agents of disease. Montgomery (1991) traces the metaphor back to the Middle Ages, and records images of disease portrayed as an '"attacker" armed with spear or quiver' (cited in Lupton, 1994a: 61). However, it is the germ theory of disease that has caught on as the predominant feature of twentieth-century Western medical beliefs. 'Illness is ... a microscopic invader, intent on entering the body and causing trouble. "Germs" are commonly believed to have motivation and evil intentions' (Lupton, 1994a: 61–2). It is no mere accident, claims Montgomery (1991: 368) that the development of 'germ theory' by French scientists in the 1860s and 1870s coincided with a period of insecurity and mobilization among the great powers of the time, specifically with Prussian militarization and the subsequent invasion of France.

The power of the military metaphor lies in its ability to arouse people into a state of fear and preventive activity, to mobilize against an emergency. In the reification of the 'germ', and more so the 'bug', the 'enemy' is one that can be pictorially imaged: Helman (1984: 113) claims that some bugs are thought of as tiny insects – it is known that certain bugs visible to the naked eye (the louse, the flea, the nit) can cause illness, and so it is a short step to imagine a 'stomach bug' in similar terms. Texts abound from the Edwardian period onwards (Lupton, 1994a: 62) in which the war against germs is promoted as though it were like any other war, with children especially being targeted as at risk from 'bacteria ... anthropomorphized into wily aggressors, deliberately changing themselves to elude detection and attack from their human foes' (Lupton, 1994a: 63).

The particular way in which the HIV virus lodges itself in its human host secures for science writers a free pass into the domain of science-fiction. Sontag refers to a *Time* magazine article from late 1986, which captures the flavour of an invasion from outer space as well as any of its contemporaneous movies or space invader games: 'On the surface of that cell, it finds a receptor into which one of its envelope proteins fits perfectly, like a key into a lock' (1991: 104). Here, echoing Lupton's Victorian bacteria, the invading disease is seen as a diabolically clever agent of destruction: *it* knows the secret way to the body's frail secret, namely that it can be turned *against itself*. It takes over the body's own cells in familiar science-fiction fashion, so that the victim's cells *themselves* become the invader.

Sontag's by now well-known (and frequently contested) argument states that the military metaphor is dangerous because it implicitly provides the rationale for widespread oppression in the guise of protecting civilian lives. Already we are familiar with the representation of heterosexuals as innocent bystanders felled by the crossfire in the triangular war waged between the medical establishment, AIDS, and the cohorts of homosexuals, blacks and junkies who, we are informed, constitute the greater part of people with HIV/AIDS (never mind the continent of Africa, where HIV is transmitted overwhelmingly through 'innocent' heterosexual contact, a vision of AIDS that has only relatively recently seeped into Western, or at least European, consciousness). The representation of the HIV virus as an invasive, alien and murderous entity can only impose upon its sufferers, or 'carriers' (and note the implicit moral rebuke in the term) the stigma of alien and destructive intent. To defend oneself against such a monstrous enemy is not only just, it is obligatory. The military metaphor thus provokes the cry for institutionalized marginalization and repression, such is the moral consensus surrounding the perceived 'carriers' of the virus.

And yet the same is not true of *other* disease outbreaks represented as invasive forces, and, as we shall see, these other diseases, where the 'innocence' of the sick people is unquestionable, might even be juxtaposed *against* AIDS as a competing discourse – most notably as a means of challenging public spending on AIDS research. In the reporting of the killer bug disease, for example, patients were not subject to any of the accusations of complicity reserved for people with HIV/AIDS, and blame for its supposed proliferation was deflected onto the Secretary for Health at the time (Virginia Bottomley) and on spending cuts at the Public Health Laboratory Service.

THE MANUFACTURE OF A HEALTH SCARE

On Tuesday, 24 May 1994, preliminary reports appeared in the British newspapers The *Independent*, *The Times* and the *Daily Mail*, indicating that a microbial infection was responsible for the deaths of three people in Gloucestershire, England. These deaths were discovered to be the result of *necrotizing fasciitis*, itself caused by *Streptococcus pyogenes*, commonly associated with a throat infection, acute pharyngitis. Necrotizing fasciitis is carried in the bloodstream and can destroy fatty tissue, muscle and muscle sheath beneath the skin. If treated early with antibiotics, the spread of the bacterium can be halted, but untreated patients need to have infected areas removed by amputation, or else they deteriorate rapidly and dramatically, with severe accompanying pains and high fever. Often the spread of infection into vital organs is the cause of death.

The 'outbreak' had first been reported by The *Independent* two weeks earlier, but it was not until 23 May that the Communicable Disease Surveillance Centre at Colindale, north London, gave out a formal warning to public health departments. On 25th May, these headlines appeared in the national newspapers:

Independent:	Killer Bug may become even more virulent
Sun:	CURSE OF THE KILLER VIRUS
	New Mum is victim Number 9 of deadly flesh bug
	It devours in 1 hour flat
Today:	Horror Bug kills a new mum in hospital
Guardian:	Sixth killer bug death reported
	Return of the killer bug
Daily Telegraph:	Flesh-eating bug claims sixth victim after 'complete cure'
Daily Mirror:	Doc who discovered flesh-eating bug warns Britain:
	'DITHER AND YOU DIE'
Daily Express:	Squad to Beat Killer Bug

Several newspapers displayed maps charting the geographical distribution of casualties of the 'killer bug'. These maps gave the impression of a military campaign, reminiscent of wartime depictions of 'the front'. In the *Daily Mail*'s illustration and map a masked 'scientist' is depicted grimly examining the contents of a test-tube. Behind him spreads the map of Britain, with the names of towns marked to signify their 'frontline' status. The caption informs us 'how the virus has spread' (see Figure 4.1).

The 'killer bug' was from the outset a reified enemy, and its progress across the country and the deaths that it incurred were charted (or so we were led to believe) in scrupulous detail by the nation's press. *Today*'s report openly acknowledges what Sontag (1991: 103) refers to as the 'science-fiction flavor, already present in cancer talk ... even more pungent in accounts of AIDS':

> It sounds like something from a horror movie – a creeping, flesh-eating super-bug which literally devours its victims, killing them within hours. (*Today* 26 May 1994)

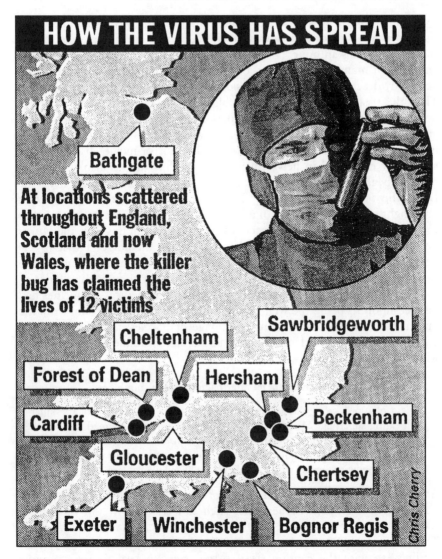

FIGURE 4.1   Map from *Daily Mail* (25 May 1994) illustrating the spread of the 'killer bug', erroneously termed a 'virus'

The metaphor of a spreading disease, an insurgency and a fanning-out, complements the primary metaphor of military invasion. The 'bug' is seen to 'arrive' in Britain after having wreaked its havoc elsewhere. The *Sun* (26 May) under a subheading 'The scourge of Europe' tells us that 'The bug is killing across the continent. Twenty-one people have died in Holland over the past 18 months and another 132 infected. Many were saved by having limbs amputated.' Horror-film terminology and Gothic imagery were a staple of the tabloids during these days: 'A young mum told yesterday how the flesh-eating superbug turned her leg into an horrific bloated mess in just four hours' (*Sun*); 'It was horrible, the thing just ate away at her abdomen. As fast as the doctors cut away the flesh, it was spreading – as fast as three centimetres an hour' (*Today*). This degree of reification pervaded the language of many cited 'victims' of the bug: a nurse from Boneybridge in Scotland 'described watching the skin on her stomach turn transparent. Then the tissue underneath it went black as the bug marched across her body' (*Today*). This language of mutilation and violation owes much to the genre of the horror film: the 'thing' eating away at the flesh: the bug 'marching' across its victim's body. Although this horror-movie discourse was repeatedly employed in news coverage of the bug, it was also referred to reflexively, in opposition to the 'reality' of the bug's deadly effects. Thus the *Daily Mirror*'s 'Comment' concludes: 'An epidemic of a flesh-eating killer bug might sound like the plot of a horror movie. But its effects are only too real. Virginia Bottomley had better realize that now.' In this way, the *Mirror* presents itself as standing outside the discourse of the horror movie (by its 'responsible' call on the Health Secretary to act), while maintaining, within its storylines, the same Gothic discourse and imagery to which it alludes.

The notion that the bug was a mystery (although medical authorities had insisted upon its being the well-known streptococcus A bacterium from the outset) took hold, compounding the image of 'facelessness'. So the *Daily Express* (25 May) could print under its banner headline ('Squad to Beat Killer Bug'):

Medical chiefs to act after bacteria claims ninth life

A team of top doctors was set up last night to solve the mystery of the killer flesh-eating superbug. Medical chiefs moved as the disease claimed its seventh victim this year, a young unmarried mother who was thought to have been cured ... MPs accused the Government of not doing enough to find the source of the 'galloping gangrene' which is believed to have killed at least nine people ...

Amid pleas 'not to panic' (*The Times*, *Sun*) there was a general incitement to do just that, prompted by headlines such as KILLER BUG ATE MY FACE; I WAS LUCKY ... IT WAS ONLY MY LEGS; ORDEAL OF VICAR ATTACKED BY BUG (*Daily Star*). The *Sun* provided its readers with a full-colour half-page photograph of a victim's leg with the caption FLESH EATING BUG DID THIS TO MY LEG and I THOUGHT I WAS GOING TO DIE, SAYS MUM. The imagery of war (amputated limbs, sudden death) was reinforced by 'facts' given by the newspaper as to how the medical profession was fighting (and apparently losing) the war on 'our' behalf:

10 facts from docs fighting the disease

DOCTORS believe they can combat the disease if caught in time. Here are ten facts on the bug:

The 'ten facts' are actually a list of increasingly horrific details about the long-term inefficacy of antibiotics (but the apparent need to take them as soon as possible); the virulence and speed with which the bug 'strikes'; and the 'fact' that it is a 'mutation', and therefore resistant to treatment:

6. The bug is a mutant strain of streptococcus, a bacteria which usually causes sore throats.
7. Overnight mutations have made other bugs resistant to antibiotics.
8. One – cryptosporidium – has no known cure and can get into water supplies, causing diarrhoea.

By this stage the account has shifted from the subject under investigation:

9. New forms of cholera, bubonic plague and TB are beating known vaccines.
10. Using too many antibiotics or failing to finish a course of the drugs can make mutant bugs develop.

The 'mysterious' and 'alien' aspect of the bug is now completed in science-fiction terms by its description as 'mutant'. This completes the demonic trinity: in the catalogue of potential invading hordes (and newspaper sales) a faceless mutant alien is a considerable prospect. Despite its calls on the Minister of Health to confront reality, the *Daily Mirror* caught on to this facet of the story from the start, and on each day the story ran, accompanied its texts with the bug's very own logo: a fly-like representation of the supposed structure of the bug itself. This enabled readers to reify the bug along the lines of the *Mirror*'s model, as reproduced in Figure 4.2.

Although, throughout the 'killer bug' scare, the presentation of the story and the imaging of the 'bug' was absurd and a certain misinformation and

FIGURE 4.2   The Daily Mirror's model of 'the bug' featured every day the story ran

'incitement to panic' was evident in press coverage, the casualties were not stigmatised or perceived to form any sort of cohort that might attract moral reprobation (in spite of the *Daily Express* irrelevantly, but typically, referring to one victim as an 'unmarried mother'). Inaccurate reporting, however, helped to spread one particular misrepresentation: that the bug was in fact a virus. A virus is an organism which is capable of reproduction only in the cell of a host, but the term is often erroneously used to cover bacilli, cocci, vibrios and many other organisms. Journalists who referred to necrotizing fasciitis as a virus condition were therefore highly irresponsible, utilizing, as they did, a 'hot' word like virus, with all its popular connotations and misapplications (Helman, 1978) to describe a specific bacterial infection. The *Daily Mail* in particular, in its article 'On the trail of the killer bug', and its accompanying map, 'How the virus has spread' was guilty of misinformation in this respect. By contrast the *Today* report speculated that 'the extreme virulence of the disease might be the result of the bacteria itself being invaded and supercharged by a parasitic virus'. This was feasible (as the *Sun* also reminded us), but in the event an incorrect supposition.

Today's correspondent, Nicki Pope, made imaginative use of the metaphor of the flesh-eating bug in her critique of government spending on public health. Praising the Public Health Laboratory Service, Pope claimed that this organization was itself 'being eaten away by a disease that should worry us at least as much as the flesh-eating bug. A disease called Government cutbacks'. She warned that 'frontline workers' were set to lose their jobs and that the system which acts as a defence against conditions such as necrotizing fasciitis was under threat by a serious paring of government support. In this way, as in other reports, the blame for the bug's progress was laid with government policy on health spending, even if (as in the case cited in the *Today* newspaper) these particular cuts had not actually taken place at the time of writing.

Some newspapers conceded that necrotizing fasciitis was by no means a new phenomenon. The *Times* and *Daily Telegraph* produced reports which played down the outbreak, and *The Times* cited Kenneth Calman, the Chief Medical Officer, as being 'doubtful that some of the cases reported in the media were necrotizing fasciitis and [he] repeated that nationwide figures had not exceeded the normal incidence'.

So, why then did the 'killer bug invasion' attract so much attention in the popular media, given that it affected so few people? Employing Bell's (1991) criteria of news values (see also Galtung and Ruge, 1965), it is possible to identify 11 of the 12 aspects of newsworthiness listed (1991: 156–9) as being applicable to the killer bug story: *negativity* ('damage, injury or death' being vital concepts in making of news); *recency* ('the best news is something which has only just happened'); *proximity* ('geographical closeness can enhance news value'). We have noted the presentation of maps and diagrams: proximity was made more explicit in regional news media, such as the story run by national newspaper of Wales, the *Western Mail*, whose headline for 26 May ran: 'Flesh-eating bug claims Welsh victim'). Further criteria fulfilled by the story were those of *consonance* ('people have a mental script for how certain kinds of events proceed', thus headlines like 'killer bug ate my face' fulfil (and exceed) a popular conception of plague; *unambiguity* (the clear-cut fatalities caused by the bug); *unexpectedness* (closely linked to the suddenness and supposedly unknown provenance of the outbreak); *superlativeness, relevance, personalization, attribution* ('doctors' and 'experts' are quoted liberally) and *facticity* ('locations, names, numbers'). Bell's criterion of 'continuity' is also satisfied if we invoke the recurring dread of killer outbreaks cited by Strong as a feature of folk memory since the Black Death. After all, in news value terms, Plague is a story that will run and run.

But within a week, killer bug stories vanished from the news media. Statements from government sources assured us that there was no cause for alarm, although it was conceded that possibly a slightly higher incidence of necrotizing fasciitis than might normally be expected had occurred in one or two geographical clusters. The killer bug ceased to be newsworthy as rapidly as it had achieved its initial moment of fame. Yet it is precisely via the paradox of the killer bug's newsworthiness that we are able to return to our initial consideration of HIV/AIDS reporting in the news media.

By far the most disturbing article that emerged in the course of the week was the *Daily Star*'s leading article of 26 May 1994. Headed 'Silly Buggers', it is worth reproducing in full (emphasis as in original):

> The killer bug which eats victims' flesh has been around for a long time. Government medical chiefs knew about it at least a decade ago, but they spent a paltry £150,000 on research, then dropped it.
>
> **Yet £15 million a year is being thrown at AIDS, although the number of cases is a fraction of predictions.**
>
> You don't have to look far to find the reason.
>
> The Government has let itself be brow-beaten by the militant gay lobby, with its powerful, politically correct pals.
>
> **While scientists working on equally or more deadly diseases have gone begging.**
>
> A team has been put on necrotising fasciitis, but years have been wasted, when a cure might have been found.
>
> **While people are dying in agony. That's a tragedy – and a scandal.**

Sontag's grim forecast that people with HIV/AIDS would become scapegoats, that the disease itself would become reified in its sufferers so that *they*, the sufferers, and not AIDS, would represent the real threat, could not be more clearly exemplified. The homophobic title of the editorial, with its pun on the word 'buggers' gives a hint of what is to follow. The government, we are told, 'throws' vast amounts of research money at AIDS, despite the number of cases being 'a fraction of predictions'. An appeal to commonsense knowledge reminds us that 'You don't have to look far to find the reason.' The synthesized personalization (Fairclough, 1989: 62) of the pronoun 'You' involves the reader directly in the editorial discourse. A group of 'politically correct' subversives has 'brow-beaten' government into this course of action, the spending of money that should rightfully have been used on finding a 'cure' for people who are now 'dying in agony' (is the implication that people with HIV/AIDS do *not*?).

Fairclough (1989: 85), writing on implicit assumptions, argues that 'Texts do not typically spout ideology. They so position the interpreter through their cues that she brings ideologies to the interpretation of texts – and reproduces them in the process.' The implicit assumption being made in the *Star*'s editorial is that people with HIV/AIDS are not worthy of the 'vast amounts at money' being spent on research, money which might instead be directed towards research into streptococcal infection. Texts such as this are aimed at provoking readers' unease, casting a projection of 'otherness' onto people with HIV/AIDS (cf. Tulloch and Lupton, 1997) in contrast to the killer bug casualties, whose diversity (and yet whose unifying innocence) is emphasized by 'cosy' categories such as 'new mum' and 'vicar'. And it is this quality of innocence that distinguishes the discourses surrounding the 'victims' of the killer bug disease so radically from those concerning people with HIV/AIDS, for whom a dominant metaphor has been one of 'AIDS is deviance' (Lupton, 1994a: 124). Metaphors have a tendency to merge with other metaphors, and the one about war and invasion can easily become one in which the 'body politic' must be purged of its 'unhealthy' parts (Sontag, 1991: 180). The *Star*'s editorial comment helps to demonstrate some of the means by which this particular representation of disease is encouraged by biomedical discourses and propagated in the news media, to be readily consumed and reformulated as commonsense knowledge.

The bug's Gothic horror credentials coincided perfectly with the image of an invasive destructive force already circulated several years earlier in popular representations of AIDS. But the difference was that this invasion was represented as being all the more terrifying in that it presumed no implicit culpability in the 'host' body, no discourse of deviance. Its terror lay in the horrific manner of its progress through the body, its entirely exogenous provenance, and in the uselessness of any known medical or therapeutic response unless it was detected in the preliminary stages. By 1994 AIDS had lost its shock value and AIDS stories had become 'stale subject matter for the news media' (Lupton, 1994b: 140). The 'killer bug invasion' provided a sudden jolt for a news-consuming public that was becoming complacent, if not indifferent, towards apocalyptic visions of AIDS, at the same time reactivating the plague mythology that has been a feature of European cultural consciousness for at least the last 600 years.

CONCLUSION

In this chapter we have taken a look at some of the ways in which health issues and the practice of medicine are represented in the media. As a rule, illness stories do not make megabucks (after all, most lack any easily identifiable 'feelgood factor'). So while cinema is more likely to treat only exceptional instances of illness as a major theme, especially ones which can be presented in a terrifying or apocalyptic light, there are occasions when a story which incorporates the ideological ingredients of an individual struggle in the face of overwhelming odds will be successful. What is discernible in both the films we considered is a sense of the health professional as somehow 'set apart' from ordinary humanity, either in the utterly dedicated but obsessive character of the Dustin Hoffman character in *Outbreak* or else as the senior doctor played by Peter Ustinov in *Lorenzo's Oil*, who ultimately distances himself from and belittles the attempts of Lorenzo's parents in their quest for the precious cure.

Television documentaries are commonly either of the fly-on-the-wall variety, pursuing the daily events in a doctor's surgery ('docusoaps'), or else set out to be more straightforwardly instructive, such as the short films produced by BBC2 on topics of interest to parents, such as the one on ADHD children. In both types of documentary the discourses of medicine are seen as authoritative and inviolable. The theme of *medicalization* is reiterated in the way in which patients are seen to reproduce the kinds of discourses that accept medical hegemony in areas which might reasonably be considered behavioural or even lifestyle concerns. Thus the disputes between a GP and a heroin addict are framed ambiguously within the context of a surgery otherwise given over to the more conventionally described practice of family medicine; a learned professor is seen to go to lengths to define the difference between 'naughty' behaviour and a neurological condition (which can however, still be framed in terms such as 'resisting temptation', a designation that would be more familiar to Victorian children) in order to cast the cloak of medicalization over yet another area of everyday life.

In investigating the ways that news reporting has covered, respectively, HIV/AIDS and the 'killer bug' disease of 1994, we are able to discern the prevalence of what Strong has called 'epidemic psychology', and a kind of vicarious delight in making the most of any health scare story which can in some way be seen as presaging the end of the world/'life as we know it'. In discourses on HIV/AIDS, patients are caught ambiguously between a 'medical model' and a media-driven and morally suspect 'stigma model'. Recourse to folk memory of 'plague' and images of apocalypse have devolved a particular kind of 'otherness' on people with HIV/AIDS, which can be exploited indiscriminately by certain sectors of the news media.

In all these instances, the discursive formulation of these issues – whether of doctor–patient interaction, radio presenters communicating with lay people, public understanding of 'complex' medical issues, or campaigns aimed at reducing HIV/AIDS – is central to our understanding of them, and the ways in which we elect to respond to these representations help define us both as patients and as human beings.

Metaphors of Sickness and Recovery 5

Since the time of Aristotle the study of metaphor has been divisive, opposing those who supported its use, on the one hand, with those detractors who deemed metaphor a mere ornamentation, a rhetorical device useful for poets but not worthy of serious analysis (Steen, 1994: 3). Until quite recently it was seen as relevant to the 'art' of literary criticism rather than the 'science' of linguistics. Indeed, the distinction between science, with its 'hard facts', and the 'arts' might be exemplified by the rejection or acceptance of figurative language. Even at the turn of the millennium, as Gibbs observes, science denies metaphor any 'autonomous cognitive content':

> Modern positivists do not radically alter the standard view of metaphor in science. The distinction between the cognitive and emotive aspects of language, along with the belief that scientific knowledge can be reduced to a system of literal sentences, implies that metaphor has no cognitive import. For the positivist, the language of science *refers*. (Gibbs, 1994: 170, my italics)

The positivist tradition teaches that so-called 'literalism' is the hallmark of a truly scientific method. Metaphor is the subversive, the heckler at the back, the reprobate, the fly in the ointment of literalism. This view is also held by religious fundamentalism, as evidenced by the Puritans' attempts to banish 'sinful extravagance in language' (Mair, 1976: 247). At the end of the seventeenth century there was even an attempt to pass an Act of Parliament to forbid the use of '"fulsome and luscious" metaphors' (ibid.). In scientific writing there is a decidedly ambiguous attitude towards the employment of metaphor (Gentner and Jeziorski, 1993; Kuhn, 1993; Knudsen, 1999). Knudsen, for example, illustrates how molecular biology utilizes a metaphoric structure based on 'writing', 'translating' and 'interpreting' in its explanation of DNA production. Meanwhile Sontag (1991) and Lupton (1994a) find the talk of medical professionals to be thick with tropes. However, there remains a belief in professional scientific circles that description is routinely achieved using literal language; that one might engage in metaphor as an explanatory or pedagogic device, and only then as a 'last resort' (Gibbs, 1994: 172). And therein lies a key. Positivists speak of 'resorting' to metaphor in much the same way that an otherwise worthy bank robber might have cause to 'resort' to violence. 'Resorting' to metaphor implies the normative and superior nature of literalism. However,

Gibbs finds the definition of 'literal meaning' or 'literal language' to be too elusive by far: there simply exists no comprehensive account of 'literal meaning':

> Literal meaning cannot be *uniquely* determined, since our understanding of situations will always influence our understanding of sentences. To speak of a sentence's literal meaning is already to have read it in light of some purpose, to have engaged in an interpretation. What often appears to be the literal meaning of a sentence is just an occasion-specific meaning where the context is so widely shared that there doesn't seem to be a context at all. (1994: 71)

Understanding one thing in terms of another is the simplest formulation of metaphor, and this understanding is guided by principles of analogy. A central tenet of the contemporary theory of metaphor (Lakoff, 1993) is that metaphor represents *a mapping across conceptual domains,* which takes the earlier work on metaphor by scholars such as Richards (1936) and Black (1962) a step further, suggesting that there is in fact a cognitive *preference* for 'thinking in metaphors'. Lakoff and Johnson (1980) talk of a broader definition of metaphor, in which practically all of what we think, say or even do is steered by what they term 'conceptual structures', which function like groups of association engraved in the mind and which are linked to one another by key linguistic representations.

However, when it comes to the study of the metaphors themselves, it seems it is only a change in terminology, an added layer of complexity that is being argued by Lakoff and Johnson, since the essential understanding of 'transfer' between one concept, idea, or state to another lies behind all metaphor. (This sense of 'transfer' or 'translation' can be perceived nicely in the most mundane, or 'literal', of settings: the city of Athens public transport system, whose buses go conveniently under the name of METAPHORI.)

So, crudely speaking, the fundamental principle at work in metaphor and figurative language is for an idea, image or thought, to be expressed by another analogous idea, image or thought. For example, in the metaphorical construct: *Love is a journey,* the 'source domain', or 'vehicle' (Richards, 1936) of *journey* is mapped onto the target domain, or 'topic' (ibid.) of *love* (Lakoff, 1993: 208). Meanwhile Lakoff's *source domain* and *target domain* correspond closely to Black's (1962) *focus* and *frame* respectively. It is noteworthy too (if unavoidable, according to these same theorists' position) that the terms with which they choose to label elements of the metaphor should themselves be metaphoric (target, source, frame, vehicle, etc).

For the purposes of the present chapter, we might ask ourselves the hypothetical question 'How is metaphor understood?' – which itself can be elaborated by less abstract ones, such as: How are individuals' biographies presented in relation to metaphor? What metaphors are employed in the descriptions of illness and, more importantly, what metaphoric positions are adopted by patients or their kin in resistance to or accommodation of illness?

An examination of metaphor seems appropriate to analysis of texts in terms of speakers' own perceptions and explanations of illness, but also from the perspective that an illness *conceived* of in metaphoric terms might be *come to terms with and responded to* in metaphoric terms also. This does not confine our understanding of metaphor to linguistic representation. We shall therefore examine conventional linguistic metaphorization, from the perspective both of medical professionals and of patients, briefly considering the study of metaphor across cultures before focusing on the more controversial and less well-defined field of symbolic action as metaphor.

MEDICAL METAPHORS

Metaphors of illness have been discussed overwhelmingly from a lay perspective. Conceptual frameworks of illness have been compared by medical anthropologists, often focusing on specific cultural formulations such as *shinkeishitsu* in Japan (an obsessional anxiety), *koro* in China (a belief that the penis will retract fatally into the abdomen), or *crise de foie* in France. Other formulations such as *susto* (loss of soul) and *nervios* in Costa Rica and elsewhere in the Spanish-speaking world have broad correlatives in other cultures, but hold specific local meanings (Helman, 1984). Many such formulations are essentially problematic for a western medicine based in observable, quantifiable science. However, in their metaphoricity they are little different from the formulations of medical professionals, which afford a perspective on biomedical reality that frequently appears at odds with scientific positivism.

Just as medical professionals adopt the 'soft' approach of narratives in order to frame their accounts of case histories and individual illness careers (Hunter, 1991) so too is metaphor an important feature of in-group talk among doctors and nurses (Ibba, 1991; Vidal, 2000). But, as the writings of Lakoff and others suggest, language is not the only focus of conceptual metaphor. The transfer from one domain (a medical training) to another (the marking of one's dress and formal appearance) constitutes precisely the kind of action that might be deemed metaphoric in the broader sense permitted by the conceptual structure theory. The donning of the white coat, is, for a medical student, a significant symbolic manifestation of status which 'declares the wearer ... as a "medical" person to others in the hospital' (Atkinson, 1981: 45). The stethoscope, that unmistakable symbol of professional authority, might be worn ostentatiously by first year clinical students, while world-weary fourth years in an equally self-conscious act of identity stuff them deep in their pockets (ibid.). The ritual of the 'Round' is learned, with students obediently trailing behind a domineering and often belligerent senior consultant. The students learn, for example, that they must always approach a patient from the patient's right-hand side. When the senior doctor asks students to report on what they have observed on a round, the older doctor is permitted to scorn their answers and ritually insult them, calling individual students by names such as 'moron' or 'buffoon', and generally making them 'vulnerable to the weapons of sarcasm, humiliation and degradation' (1981: 25). Right down to its finer manifestations in the self-presentation of its practitioners the medical world is profoundly influenced by what Strong (1979) has called the 'ceremonial order of the clinic'. Ceremony is, by definition, ritualistic: and ritual is symbolic activity, in turn a kind of metaphor, as we shall see.

In a world so dense with symbolic performance it is only to be expected that linguistic tropes should form an important part of doctors' in-group talk. We have already noted how scientific discourses use metaphor to convey fundamental concepts. Doctors of medicine, too, make use of a quantity of in-group metaphoric terms to describe illness, not only as a means of fulfilling a positive social identity based on displays of sardonic humour; but also, and more significantly, because some of these terms might be used in a teaching hospital in the presence of patients, where the patient has not yet been informed of the nature of their illness. So, *neoplasm* or *space occupying lesion* might be used to describe a cancer; *acid fast infection* for tuberculosis; *specific* or *luetic* disease for syphilis. Among themselves, doctors might speak of a *blue bloater* or a *pink puffer* to refer to the appearance of a patient with lung disease. There is a marked tendency among both clinicians and pathologists to use food and kitchen similes, metaphors and allegories for disease processes. This would suggest something along the lines of a Hallidayan 'antilanguage' (Halliday, 1978), facilitating comprehension for peers while obfuscating meaning to patients. For example, in acute pericarditis the pericardium is referred to as a *bread and butter* pericardium. This is because a fibrinous deposit on the visceral and parietal pericardium gives the appearance of a folded piece of bread and butter which has been pulled apart. After the acute phase of pericarditis has passed, white patches appear on the surface of the pericardium where the fibrinous exudate has been invaded by fibroblasts. These patches are known as *milk spots*. Another culinary example is found in the description of the stools of a cholera patient, which are likened to *rice water*. Certain tumours are harder than others and are said to be 'scirrhous' (as in scirrhous carcinoma of the breast). The cut surface of such a tumour is likened to the cut surface of *an unripe pear*.

Gynaecology has more than its fair share of culinary and domestic equivalents, reflecting the male-dominated clinical tradition. For example, there are a number of different types of ovarian cyst, one of which, the endometrial cyst, tends to fill with old blood and to assume a dark reddish-brown colour. These are known as *chocolate cysts*.

In the lungs, tuberculosis causes cavitation of the lung tissue. This was very common before the introduction of streptomycin in the 1950s, although recent years have seen a return of tuberculosis in many places. The first lung lesion is one of several infected nodes known as *miliary* tubercles (i.e. the size of a millet seed). These enlarge or coalesce to cause an area of coagulation necrosis known as *caseation* – cheese formation.

Animal metaphors also occur: in cardiac patients (those likely to suffer a *heart attack*), there is a condition of fatty degeneration which produces a flabby ventricular heart muscle with a speckled appearance due to fat infiltration. This is known to pathologists as *thrush breast heart* or *tabby cat heart*.

A cursory inspection of the index of a household medical encyclopaedia (Smith, 1990) reveals many metaphoric lay and medical terms to designate illness, abnormality, deformity, or parts of the body. Thus we find *balloon angioplasty*; *the bends*; *bile duct*; *brainstem*; *buck teeth*; *canine teeth*; *cauliflower ear*; *chicken pox*; *the clap*; *claw-toe*; *cleft-palate*; *clergyman's knee*; *club foot*; *cluster headache*; *compartment syndrome*; *conjugated oestrogens*; *cowpox*; *crab lice*; *deciduous teeth*; *dental cusp*; *drop attack*; *dumping syndrome*; *elephantiasis*; *eye teeth*; *fish skin disease*; *floppy valve syndrome*; *frostbite*; *funny bone*; *glue ear*; *ground itch*; *hare-lip*; *heart attack*; *horseshoe kidney*; *housemaid's knee*; *irritable bladder*; *jogger's nipple*; *lockjaw*; *lunacy*; *mallet toe*; *marble bone disease*; *mosaicism*; *occult blood*; *parrot fever*; *pernicious anaemia*; *pigeon toes*; *port-wine stain*; *prickly heat*; *river blindness*; *rocky mountain spotted fever*; *rodent ulcer*; *rooting reflex*; *Saint Vitus' dance*; *salmon patch*; *sickle cells*; *spider naevus*; *swamp fever*; *tennis elbow*; *trench mouth*; *tricuspid incompetence*; *trigger finger*; *whipworm* and *witches milk*. Most of these terms are 'overtly' metaphoric; and this is not to begin on the quantity of figurative terms employed in psychiatry such as *split personality, derealization* and *free-floating anxiety*. A list of expressions such as this could never be exhaustive, however, since the more closely we examine the etymology of medical terms, the more likely we are to find a metaphor behind every dictionary definition. Thus 'cancer' is itself a metaphor of the creeping motion of the crab. Malaria, from the Italian *mala aria* (bad air); measles, from the middle English *mesel* (a leper); mumps, from sixteenth century English *mump* (to grimace) are further examples. The list is endless if only because the metaphoric faculty is the primary source of conceptualizing, and nowhere, apparently, do we experience the need to interpret a thing in terms of another thing more than in the domain of sickness.

Within intensive care units, colloquialisms such as 'heart sinkers' (patients with a poor prognosis); 'crash call' (emergency call to a patient who has suffered cardiac arrest): 'tubed' (the insertion of a tube into the patient's trachea to facilitate breathing); and a variety of euphemisms for dying might be common among health care workers (Vidal, 2000: 49). Vidal also suggests that one of the reasons that forms of wordplay, euphemism and metaphor are prevalent among healthcare professionals is to foment a particular kind of in-group solidarity. As she observes, 'the often highly obscure nature of these neologisms and acronyms makes it unlikely that members of the outgroup, i.e. patients or their relatives, would be able to retrieve the meaning from these displays of wit, should they be overheard.' (2000: 125)

Diekema (1989, cited in Ibba 1991) applies the conceptual structure approach to consider issues wherein relative truths present differing moral stances: one is in the expression 'removing foetal tissue' which is the terminology of choice for pro-abortionists, a term which anti-abortionists would paraphrase as 'the murder of unborn children'. Another metaphorical concept examined by this author is 'the body as machine', which we examine below. Within such a conceptual frame, the human body is seen as nothing more than the sum of its parts.

The subject of pain – often described by patients after being elicited by doctors – perhaps because of its inchoateness, most evidently lends itself to metaphorical expression. As Lupton writes, 'metaphors enable people to render indefinite physical sensations such as pain more concrete' (1994a: 55). Atkinson cites ways of describing pain through the use of colours such as 'an angry red pain' or a 'dull grey ache' (1981: 100). The most common referents for pain volunteered by patients to one GP (Humphreys, personal communication, 1994) include *stabbing*; *gripping*; *burning*; *as if stung by nettles*; and *as if stung by a swarm of bees*. Other common terms are: *stiff as a poker*; *tight as a drum* (referring to a swelling); *like a bunch of grapes* (referring to prolapsed haemorrhoids). Swellings may be *as big as an egg*, or, if inflamed, *like a piece of raw beef* or *brawny*. Pallor is, routinely, *as pale as a sheet*.

METAPHOR ACROSS CULTURES: TRADITIONAL CHINESE MEDICINE (TCM)

Despite suggestions by Lakoff (1993) to the contrary, research into the metaphoric representation of illness does not appear to support claims for cross-cultural congruity. According to Ibba '[M]etaphorical concepts vary according to the culture within which the speakers verbally interact' (1991: 610). However, within two broadly similar medical systems in contemporary Europe, Ibba undermines his own argument by illustrating that many pathological conditions are referred to by metaphorical constructions that translate easily between Italian and English, such as:

thrush breast heart	*cuore a petto do tordo*
cake kidney	*regne a focaccia*
green stick fracture	*frattura a legno verde*

Ibba concludes that while there is likely to be discrepancy in metaphorization across disparate cultural systems, there is a reasonable chance that descriptions of a condition/metaphors of pain might overlap to a certain extent in European languages.

In China, doctors trained in conventional Western medicine (CWM) are prone to the same metaphorical framework as Western doctors (Stibbe, 1996). However, traditional Chinese medicine (TCM) operates a different metaphoric system: balance, not warfare, is the key metaphor here. Equilibrium is good health, and imbalance bad health. The 'source domain' of balance consists of two weights, and systems are in balance when the weights are equal. This notion of balance is expressed in the concepts of *yin* and *yang*, the pervasive opposites of Taoist philosophy. Yin and yang are themselves defined by intrinsic properties, so yin is perceived to contain all that is dark, soft, cool, wet, receptive and feminine while the properties of yang are bright, hard, hot, dry, active and masculine. In effect, health is constructed by sets of interconnected balance metaphors: hot–cold, soft–hard, dark–bright, etc. within the superordinate categories of yin and yang. Imbalance (and consequently illness) is caused by an excess or deficit of

CWM	TCM
Illness is an invader	Illness is an imbalance
Curing illness is a fight	Curing illness is redressing balance
The body is a machine	The body is an energetic system
Illness is a mechanical breakdown	Illness is a blockage of energy

FIGURE 5.1   Comparison between conceptual models of illness and the body in conventional Western medicine (CWM) and traditional Chinese medicine (TCM) (Stibbe, 1996: 186)

either yin or yang (Stibbe, 1996). The following passage from a TCM book on treating cancer illustrates this:

> The main reason for the formation of tumors includes the loss of balance of yin and yang in human bodies, too much yin and too weak yang, which cannot promote the normal circulation of vital energy and blood. When the blood is cold it becomes frozen. The stagnation of vital energy and blood at a certain part of the body forms the tumor, therefore the treatment should begin with the root of the problem, adopting the 'internal warming treatment' which warms and nourishes the kidneys and yang, enriching the yang qi [energy]. (Zheng Wei-da, 1994: 10)

Clearly there is an incompatibility between the two systems operational in Chinese medicine. As Stibbe reminds us, this incompatibility extends to the CWM metaphor of the body as machine and the TCM metaphor of the body as an energetic system. This, and related discrepancies, can be structured as shown in Figure 5.1.

Stibbe remarks that if part of a machine breaks, then attention is normally directed to that part to fix it. Likewise, in CWM, if there is a particular problem with, say, a kidney, then the kidney is treated or operated on, or replaced if it is beyond repair. By contrast, in TCM, the body is seen as being made up of 'interrelated channels of energy'. So a problem with the kidneys could be treated by acupuncture at any point along the kidney meridian or related meridians, or else treated by affecting the elements associated with the meridians using herbal medicine. In this way, claims Stibbe, 'the metaphor of energy flow has the effect of unifying all aspects of the body, while the metaphor of body as machine divides them into discrete parts' (1996: 186).

In answer to the hypothetical question I posed earlier: how is metaphor *understood?*, Gibbs writes, 'no single theory provides a comprehensive account of how people understand all kinds of metaphorical language' (1994: 262). Moreover there is, as Hawkes (1972) has observed, an elusiveness to the very nature of the object of study that precludes a 'clear' exposition of it. 'In the long run', argues Hawkes, 'the "truth" does not matter because the only access to it is by means of metaphor. The metaphors matter: they are the truth.' But again (and as Stibbe reminds us), by analysing the metaphors used to help construct cultural precepts such as 'being ill', we can gain a better understanding of how people conceptualize reality and formulate their truths across cultures.

METAPHORS OF INVASION AND WAR

We encountered the ideas of Sontag, the writer most commonly associated with metaphor and illness, in Chapter 4. Her two essays, republished in one volume (1991) examined the metaphors associated with, first, tuberculosis and cancer, and several years later, with AIDS. It is an inevitable irony of Sontag's task that in arguing for a metaphor-free view of illness, she finds herself constantly seduced by, and reverting to, a rich and potent supply of metaphoric devices to put forward her argument. Thus, at the very start of *Illness as Metaphor* we are told: 'Illness is the night-side of life, a more oner-ous citizenship. Everyone who is born holds dual citizenship, in the king-dom of the well and in the kingdom of the sick' (1991: 3). And throughout Sontag's elegant work we are reminded of the difference between the things she wants to say and the means by which she must say them. She wishes to 'de-mythicize' disease and over and over again reiterates that 'my point is that illness is *not* a metaphor, and that the most truthful way of regarding illness ... is one most purified of, most resistant to, metaphoric thinking' (ibid.).

En route, Sontag collates an abundant supply of metaphoric representa-tions from various sources: cancer is a 'demonic pregnancy' (1991: 14), and a 'degeneration'. 'In cancer the patient is "invaded" by alien cells, which multiply, causing an atrophy or blockage of bodily functions'. Further descriptions of cancer inform us that 'it crawls and creeps like a crab'; that it is an 'unholy granite substance'; that it represents 'repression of passion', 'frustration', 'emotional resignation', 'giving up'; she uses the words 'to resign' and 'to shrink' and says that the personality of the cancer sufferer is 'unemotional, inhibited, repressed' and that the disease is 'an outlet for ... foiled creative fire'. We hear of a 'fight' or 'crusade against cancer'; of the 'killer disease'; of a 'scourge' that is 'invasive'; one that will 'colonize' 'set-ting up outposts', a veritable 'tumor invasion', whose *treatment* is to be 'bombarded with toxic rays, chemical warfare' in order to 'kill the cancer'. Cancer is the 'disease of the Other'; it is 'an invasion of "alien" or "mutant" cells, stronger than normal cells' (*Invasion of the Body Snatchers, The Incredible Shrinking Man, The Blob, The Thing*). It is a 'triumphant muta-tion' (ibid.).

If we can accept that metaphor is a central tool of our cognitive appara-tus as suggested by the Lakoff/Gibbs school of argument, it seems difficult if not impossible to conceive of illnesses – especially those, like cancer, that have become established metaphors in our cultural mythology (e.g. a 'cancer in society') – existing without further reproduction in everyday dis-course. We might recall Vico's (1968) aphorism that 'metaphors are myths in miniature'. Sontag herself admits to once writing 'in the heat of despair over America's war on Vietnam, that "the white race is the cancer of human history"' (1991: 85).

One of the strongest criticisms of Sontag's argument is that illness is never simply illness, but is the focus of a culturally experienced phenomenon. To reiterate, the passage from Fox (1993: 6) cited on page 47:

illness cannot be *just* illness, for the simple reason that human culture is constituted in language, *that there is nothing knowable outside language*, and that health and illness, being things which fundamentally concern humans, and hence need to be 'explained', enter into language and are constituted in language, regardless of whether or not they have some independent reality in nature.

Scheper-Hughes and Lock (1986), meanwhile, claim that Sontag's conclusions only support the notion of the reification of disease, and do not empower those patients who employ such metaphors. DiGiacomo (1992: 117) agrees, commenting:

> No one ever experiences cancer as the uncontrolled proliferation of abnormal cells. Indeed, we can experience anything at all only through and by means of culturally constructed and socially reproduced structures of metaphor and meaning.

Most convincingly, as we saw in the previous chapter, Montgomery has argued that we should no longer even consider the military metaphor to be a metaphor at all in the biomedical arena. So if the metaphors of invasion/ war are no longer truly metaphors in relation to illness, are there other strategies that may be termed metaphoric, which individuals *do* use in order to come to an understanding of, or to find an explanatory model for, their own chronic illnesses or the illnesses of those around them? Individuals might, like the novelist Marilyn French, react against the redundant metaphors of militancy – the frequent references to making war against cancer, attacking it, destroying it. She writes, in response to her own cancer, 'I could not bear to think in terms of fighting ... because the thing I was supposed to fight was part of myself. So I visualized my white cells surrounding the cancer in an embrace and shrinking it, not in hate but as part of a natural process, transforming the cancer into something benign.' Conversely, she describes a friend who has cancer as having felt 'great bitterness toward her body for inflicting this terrible disease on her. She hated her body for it' (1998: 85). The woman who hates her own body for giving her cancer dies – French, while enduring a horrific ordeal through chemotherapy and undergoing a two-week coma as a consequence of her treatment, comes through.

So how is a command of metaphor employed in people's accounts of illness? Is metaphor a purely conceptual and linguistic concern, or is it in some way translatable into action; that is, quite apart from thinking and speaking metaphorically do people 'act metaphorically'?

THE USE OF METAPHOR IN CHRONIC ILLNESS ACCOUNTS

In an attempt to answer these questions, I will be drawing upon ethnographic research I conducted with people who had experience of chronic illness themselves, or had looked after a family member who suffered chronic illness (Gwyn, 1997, 1999a). Although I asked a series of questions later on in each session, the larger part of our talk involved the interviewee's response to the question 'What is your experience of illness?' As with the Ryans in Chapter 2, talk that ensued fell into the category defined by Wolfson as 'conversational narrative', in which the role of the researcher is to encourage the interviewee to speak freely, to introduce his or her own topics, and to tell stories (1976: 196). By having myself introduced, or introducing myself, as somebody engaged in research who was making audio-tape recordings with people relating to their experience of illness and health care, I avoided the term 'interview'. Moreover, by verbally assuring my informants that I had sought out their 'help' in my project I was, to a degree, assigning to them the role of collaborator, which, according to Mishler (1986: 126) is a way of reducing the power differential in interviews.

Studying the interview transcripts my interest focused not so much upon the 'conventional' types of metaphor associated with illness (invasion, struggle, battle) but on those instances in the text where reality is viewed through a distinct domain of experience, and a transfer takes place as a means of explaining or coming to terms with the lived experience of illness. The idea that metaphor is not simply an 'as if' phenomenon, but suggests a transference of 'domains of experience', corresponded well with another thread of my investigation, namely the belief that storytelling is a longstanding human resource for understanding experiences. The resulting synthesis of narrative laced with metaphoric detail provides the basis for my analysis, and is close to that described by Radley (1993a: 110):

> adjustment to illness, if it is to be self-legitimating, needs to have a certain communicative structure. This structure is most readily seen as metaphor, or rather as one kind of metaphor among several that are used by patients to give expressive form to their condition.

Radley cites as an example the case of a male cardiac patient who 'always insisted on digging his garden even though he knew it upset his wife'. It is worth quoting the relevant passage from Radley in full:

> The act of digging can be seen as important because it signified to those around him the attitude that he took to his illness. It was not the only act of this kind, but it was readily specifiable as such. What might it be meant to convey? That he was active? Certainly. That he was healthy? Only in part. For the digging was only salient in the context of his heart disease, something known to his family and friends. Therefore, this action can be seen to stand for a relationship of the man to his illness and to the world of health. It said – perhaps more powerfully than words – that he refused the sick role in spite of the doctor having diagnosed him as having a serious illness. It becomes understandable in terms of his relationships to his wife and to his work ... in the way he could signify with bodily potentialities of sexuality and maleness. In this example, the digging can be read as standing for the man's relationship to other areas of life, including his role as husband in the home and as someone still capable of doing a day's work if need be (he was a retired manual worker). This is a metonymic relationship in that the physical actions involved are also constituent 'parts' of other areas of life, which (were they to be put into words) might be described as benefitting from 'putting one's back into it' or 'getting stuck in'. (Radley, 1993a: 117)

Metaphor, then, need not be restricted to the medium of language, to what can be said in words, since '[T]he idea of reflecting one domain of experience through another is a way of intending a meaning, engaging the world' (ibid: 116).

Another way of describing this might be to say that perceptions and actions are recorded in language that lends shape to the speakers' relationship to illness, quite apart from the 'conventional' metaphors that populate my recorded accounts of illness experience. I consider these perceptions and actions to be as 'metaphoric' as any of the linguistic tropes which we are accustomed to think of as being metaphors proper. Such a belief originates in the work of Richards (1936). Richards included as 'metaphoric, those processes in which we perceive or think or feel about one thing in terms of another'. For Richards a command of metaphor could 'go deeper still into the control of the world that we make for ourselves to live in' (1936: 135–6, cited in Mair, 1976: 249). He further suggested that what psychoanalysts term 'transference' is another name for metaphor: 'how constantly modes of regarding, of loving, of acting, that have developed with one set of things or people, are shifted to another' (ibid.). Again, Radley states (1993a: 113) that metaphor need not be restricted to the medium of language, to what can be said in words, but that it is a way of 'reflecting one reality through another'. A first example from my interviews (Gwyn, 1999a) will serve to illustrate this proposition. (In this chapter, as elsewhere in the book, the names of interviewees have been changed.)

Metaphor and Re-figuration

Nerys Williams is describing the nine years she spent nursing her youngest son, who had cancer. A brain tumour was diagnosed when Joey was 10: he died at the age of 19, seven weeks before the interview took place. Nerys, a 50-year-old social worker, frequently employs the metaphors of war in the course of her interview, along with references to the speed of growth of the malignant tumour:

> because if it had been a very fast growing tumor then it had come back then he would have died probably within the year whereas *what it bought us was lots of time* (.) um (.) so (.) at the time obviously your your child's life is so precious that even if you're being told well you know *he's got a fighting chance* and um it's a slow growing tumor and you think well that's great you know we're not looking at a crisis this month next month the *frontier's been pushed back*.

The conventional metaphorization of time as a buyable commodity (cf. Lakoff and Johnson, 1980; Gibbs, 1994: 441) might seem to ring hollow in the context where what is being 'purchased' is a temporary reprieve from early death. However, we are sharply reminded that this struggle is a fight to the end ('he's got a fighting chance'), that on the battlefront of cancer, some ground has been won ('the frontier's been pushed back'). Following

Montgomery, we might argue that these metaphors no longer *sound* like metaphors to our ears, but more like commonsense representations.

Elsewhere Nerys speaks of the 'more aggressive surgery' that had to be employed in the later operations to counteract the faster-growing tumour, of a 'great big thing swelling up inside your head'. At her first meeting with the consultant who informs her of Joey's condition she says: 'I've I've never experienced a shock quite like it I felt as if I'd been physically *hit* (.) I really felt (.) my stomach turn over'. These reactions and the descriptions of the fight against Joey's cancer correspond to the first category of metaphor described by Radley, that is 'the way that individuals use figures of speech in how they represent their illness to themselves and to others' (1993a: 110). Radley's second category, 'the way that certain adjustments involve a re-figuration of the subject in his or her dealings with other people' (ibid.) can perhaps be illustrated by a passage immediately following the breaking of the news to Nerys, when Joey, aged 10, is invited into the consultant's room to be told that

> your headaches are caused by (.) pressure inside your head and we're going to have to get you in to hospital to have an operation to remove the pressure (.) true (.) and he sat there and he said oh and she said we'll have you in on Monday and we'll shave your head and do the operation and then you won't have any more headaches.

For some cancer patients, hair loss through chemotherapy seems to act as a poignant metaphor for all that the illness entails. It symbolizes the dehuman-izing and desexualizing effects of cancer, and is a visible stigma, a marking and humiliation of the surface of the body that corresponds to the internal ravages of the tumour. This stigmatized identity is typified in Marilyn French's account, when the author confronts her loss of hair through chemotherapy, reporting that she 'felt like a leper, as if my limbs were shriveling and drop-ping off' (1998: 71). In Nerys' interview it is a theme that is taken up later, when throughout Joey's teenage years he suffers hair loss because of radio-therapy. However, that is to pre-empt the narrative because at this point in time Joey knows nothing of his cancer. He reacts to the news as follows:

> so we came out of the room and Joey then promptly had a tantrum as we walked down down the corridor saying *he* was not having his head shaved there was no way he wanted his head shaved and rather he'd have the headaches he'd rather have the headaches thankyou very much

Over the years that follow Joey undergoes brain surgery six times, experi-ences extended bouts of chemotherapy and radiotherapy, continues going to school, taking GCSEs and later, when very ill, his A levels. At 18 he is told that the tumour is back and growing faster and that a new course of radiotherapy may be his only hope. Nerys, Joey and a visiting nurse sit down together to formulate a plan of action:

> so we had to get a big piece of paper out and put for and against and it was things like (.) against having it was that you'd lose your hair you'd be ill um (.) and the for was (.) you're going to live longer

The prominence attached to this side-effect of his illness seems to add significance, retrospectively, to the episode of Joey, aged 10, throwing a tantrum because he doesn't want his head shaved. It is possible to read into Nerys' account precisely that 'backward action of selfunderstanding' that is central to the process of narrative reconstruction (Churchill and Churchill, 1982: 73). It might even be suggested that Joey's violent rejection of having his head shaved provides an anticipatory rejection of the tumor and of all that it entailed. What can be stated with certainty is that the associations of hair loss (depersonalizing, de-sexing and degrading) that the teenage Joey so disliked were anticipated by the obligatory shaving of his head for the preliminary operation, something that was repeated at intervals thereafter; and that the loss of hair, either through shaving or through radiation treatment, came to represent the same thing to Joey, namely his 're-figuration' through illness. Now *metonymy*, we might recall, is a widely used figure of thought or speech whereby we take one clearly demarcated aspect of something to represent the thing as a whole. This re-figuration, then, would appear to be constituted in a *metonymic* relationship, one in which a part of the body comes to represent the body subject to illness. The hair, or at least the head, is the most easily perceived aspect of any individual, and a shaved head would therefore stand in clear relation to the illness as something quite specific and meaningful.

Symbolic Action as Metaphor

On 2 December 1995 a story appeared in the Welsh newspaper The *Western Mail*, which helped confirm to me the significance of hair loss in relation to young cancer sufferers. Under the headline KINDEST CUT IS A REAL SNIP it told the story of a 13-year-old girl, Andrea Matthews, who had 'all her hair shaved off as a touching gesture of support to her sister, who has lost hers through chemotherapy' (see Figure 5.2). The article continued:

> On Thursday, we reported how 13-year-old Andrea planned to lose her shoulder-length locks in sympathy with sister Amanda, 16, whose treatment for leukaemia has meant the loss of her own long blonde hair ... Before an assembly of 100 classmates, Andrea took the stage at Tredegar Comprehensive and spoke about the meaning of her sister's illness, before family friend and hairdresser Lorraine Rees shaved off her crowning glory.

We are then told how Andrea decided on the public haircut in order to raise awareness of the problems raised by her sister's illness, particularly with regard to the hair loss: 'Amanda ... was rejected by some of her friends when she became ill and felt even worse when her hair fell out as a result of the treatment'.

Here is an example of what we might conveniently term symbolic action – and one involving a *conceptual transfer from one domain* to another: the healthy younger sister shows her support and solidarity by transferring the perceived sufferings of her sick sister, through symbolic sacrifice, onto

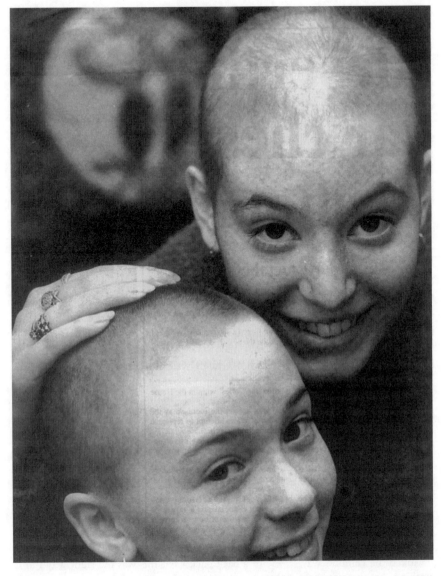

FIGURE 5.2   UNITED: Andrea Matthews, left, and her sister Amanda, for whom she had her blonde locks shorn (photo courtesy of The Western Mail)

herself. It is precisely this kind of action which merits the description 'metaphoric', and if we are to follow Lakoff and Gibbs into an acceptance of metaphor as constituting the principal mode through which people conceptualize their experience and their understanding of the external world, then we must be prepared to make this leap from the social semiotic of language into the domain of symbolic social action.

In the story of Andrea Matthews, therefore, we can again refer to the explicit relationship between the shaved hair and the suffering individual as *metonymic*, in that the part (the hair) stands for another feature of the body (its illness) or for the body itself.

Symbolic action is significant in the account given by another speaker. Bill Morgan, 55, describes his coronary condition in exquisite detail. As a successful young construction engineer in the Far East, Bill led a hedonistic lifestyle, ate and drank excessively, and weighed over 19 stone. At the age of 34 he suffered two heart attacks in quick succession, and a third one seven years later. Back in Wales, and at the age of 50, he suffered a fourth heart attack. On being discharged from hospital, Bill found he had great difficulty in walking and breathing. He began an exercise programme to combat this, despite a longstanding dislike of walking anywhere ('walking was something I hated doing in my life'). Within a month, however, he had begun mountain walking and within six months undertook his first long-distance walk:

> what happened in the twelve months twelve months I continued that programme was an awful lot of long-distance walking (.) walking about seventy miles a week plus doing four long distance back packs

Bill had to go in for a four-way bypass operation at the end of the year he refers to here, but by this time he was walking everywhere. I would argue that, as for Radley's digger, walking had become the metaphor of his opposition to heart disease. Bill's own account appears to support the positive aspects of such a stance: 'I felt that what I was doing was doing me good'. Just as digging can be seen as a process of discovery (digging *for* something), walking is the simplest means for an able-bodied person to get from one place to the next. The metaphor of the journey is a fundamental one. Western culture is steeped in the mythological tradition of the journey, from the *Odyssey* onwards (see Gibbs, 1994: 188–92 for a discussion of journey myths). Specifically, we walk 'the road to recovery', we get 'back on the right track' we 'get better one step at a time'. Bill lived out the ambulatory metaphor to its full:

> I had the operation I *walked* to the hospital nineteen miles to have the operation (.) I *felt* I could walk home but they insisted on me going by taxi (.) and (.) within a week I was back I was back out walking and (.) six weeks after I walked the Pennine Way (.) with a back pack I felt this was the right way I'm a bit of an obsessive personality

For some heart attack victims (Helman, 1987; Radley, 1993a) the adjustment to a new regime can be seen as a means of renouncing the lifestyle which led to the heart attack in the first place. If, as Helman argues, Western societies regard the heart attack victim as a figure of moral ambiguity, then such a renunciation might be seen as a metaphoric departure, hence the appropriateness of the kind of physical response involved in digging and long-distance backpacking. In fact Helman refers to recovering cardiac patients engaging in narrative reconstruction of their life-stories with the specific end of imaging the heart attack as a kind of nemesis – the only one appropriate to the accepted mythology of their predetermined careers as heart attack victims (see also Cassell, 1978; Cowie, 1976). Moreover, writing of coronary bypass surgery, Scheper-Hughes and Lock refer to the 'powerfully metaphoric effects of the [bypass] operation as a cosmic drama of death and rebirth' (1987: 30).

Metaphors of Struggle and the Dialectic of Faith

The third example I will draw upon is that of Yumiko Thomas, who at the time of interview was working for a Japanese electronics company in Wales. Yumiko grew up in Japan but came to Britain after marrying a British seaman. Yumiko begins her account, atypically, by categorizing herself as chronically ill. Her own comments locate her more eloquently than any third-person description would:

I was ill all my life (.) because as you know I was born in Hiroshima in 1948 three years after (.) that horrific incident had occurred and now we know uh we have knowledge about nuclear (4.0) effect but then [they] didn't know you see so people who ate vegetables from contaminated areas and ate fish from contaminated water so I was actually um (.) wasn't there I wasn't born then because [the] atomic bomb was dropped in 1945 still my body was to a certain degree contaminated

Yumiko's Buddhist faith sustains her in what she regards as a lifelong struggle with illness. The 'conventional' metaphors decorate her account, but throughout the interview there is another agenda, an underlying epic beneath the surface description of 'battle being done' with illness, and that is one which depends upon acceptance of the Buddhist notion of *karma*. To employ her own terms, the challenge to 'change her *karma*' lies at the very heart of Yumiko's story, and the location of her birth, as well as her illnesses and hardships are presented as illustrations of, or better still as metaphors for, her capacity for victory in that other, greater task:

usually when I become ill I almost if you like prepare (.) that is I psyche up myself and chant a lot and make conscious effort from corner to corner do everything that I have to do in order to overcome this illness and I become so if you like fighting machine mental physical that's how I approach that but this time it is very solid but very relaxed and I'm going to fight and I'm going to win I know that and keep saying that but not like uh standing on the cliff or edge of cliff not that sort of desperate just I know I can do it but I've got to do it in a short time

For a Buddhist, illness might be represented as a metaphor for an underlying spiritual struggle, that is, the external manifestation of an 'internalized' condition (and this connects with dominant themes in Oriental and holistic medicines). It is, too, a well-documented feature of folk beliefs about illness, one which might be indicated by a patient stating that 'I'm not feeling good in myself', which suggests a kind of internal disharmony or displacement that is integral to 'objective' illness (cf. Macleod, 1993). In fact the Cartesian body/mind dichotomy that preoccupies the Western scientific tradition and the biomedical description of illness seems to be far from happily installed in folk beliefs (Helman, 1978) and is overtly rejected in Yumiko's representation. The anthropological literature provides a wealth of examples of the making of metaphors in illness and body imagery that break down or ignore biomedical dualism, the distinction between mind and body (as well as the distinction between 'self' and the 'other'). One example will suffice here, reflecting on how an 'inner' dis-ease can produce a transference to the physical production of human milk: Scheper-Hughes reports that impoverished Brazilian mothers perceive their breastmilk as 'sour, curdled, bitter, and diseased, a metaphorical projection of their inability to pass anything untainted to their children' (Scheper-Hughes, 1984, cited in Scheper Hughes and Lock, 1987: 17).

If we consider the holistic notion that illness may occur because there is something amiss in another area of one's life (emotional, psychological) we are again faced with the question of transfer from one domain of experience to another. What holistic and Oriental medicine systems seem to hold in common is the belief that an imbalance in one's emotional or psychological state predisposes one towards a physical illness. Whereas these traditions regard the mental and the physical (*psyche* and *soma*) as two facets of a single integrated system and therefore treat interplay and transfer from one 'domain' to the other as the norm, Western medicine tends to isolate the two domains one from the other and consequently denigrates the effect of psyche on soma as 'psychosomatic illness'. Or, as one account summarizes: 'while modern medicine tends to view the ailing part of the body in isolation from the rest, treating it alone as if one were fixing a malfunctioning part of a machine, Buddhist medicine views disease as a reflection of the total body system, or life itself, and seeks to cure it not only through medical treatment but also through adjustments in the person's lifestyle and outlook' (Ikeda, 1988: 69).

The three speakers I have discussed here present distinct metaphoric perspectives on their experience of illness. Nerys Williams, through identifying an episode in her son's illness that carried continued significance for him (and her) until the end, provides an emotionally charged and visual representation of one aspect of what it meant for Joey to have cancer. To say that his hair loss 'symbolized' his cancer is to say that he was *marked* by cancer, that his illness was visible for all to see. I have suggested that in Joey's case, his hair held a *metonymic* relationship to his illness. The newspaper story about Andrea and Amanda Matthews seems to add credence to this perspective. A teenager is able to support her sister through symbolic action which succinctly marks her out as *more alike*, acting at the same time as a reprimand to those in her school who had stigmatized her sister on account of her illness.

Bill Morgan adopted a position towards his heart condition that seemed to involve a rejection of the lifestyle that led to his coronary. He left behind him his (on his own admission) gluttonous and bibulous lifestyle to become a vegan and a long-distance walker. A positivist might suggest that this is not metaphoric at all, but simply a survival strategy. However, seen in the light of Helman's writings on heart disease and the cultural construction of time, the heart attack can be conceptualized by the victim as a kind of nemesis, and the only suitable response would be the adoption of a new 'metaphor for living' (Mair, 1976). This is particularly interesting when compared with Radley's digger, whose digging seems to stand for a restatement of his 'old self' rather than the radical re-figuring of himself as a consequence of his cardiac condition. Both are metaphoric responses, perhaps diametrically opposed ones, but no less metaphoric for that.

Yumiko Thomas sees her lifelong physical illness (along with the time and place of her birth) as the metaphoric correlative of her karmic state. She believes that her life mission is to challenge that condition through her religious practice so that not only can she triumph over her illnesses but she might use those struggles to develop herself personally into a 'fighting machine' against whatever 'destiny' brings to her. She refuses to be like a 'puppet', or like somebody 'standing on the edge of the cliff'. She is the 'captain of [her] own ship'. The metaphor is apt, certainly, with respect to this particular speaker, a woman of apparently indefatigable certitude:

> I'm glad I'm quite strong enough to take it and I may get [laughs] graceful possibly [laughs] (.) and if there are pains the pain's absolutely minimal (3.0) and I feel that I always wanted I don't want to be manipulated by the environment I don't want to be like a puppet like my (.) upbringing in Hiroshima those horrendous experiences or karma or whatever des destiny manipulating your life (.) because of that in your life you don't know what's next what happens next year or even next month some people have that sort of life (.) I don't want to be like that my life is my own I want to be uh captain of my *own* ship that ship called Yumiko that's always what I wanted

In their critique of a biomedicine still in the clutches of a Cartesian dichotomy, Scheper-Hughes and Lock (1987: 30) alert us to the dangers of thinking reductionistically about the mind–body split. According to this model most sickness can be viewed mechanistically, as an isolated event. But 'to do otherwise', they suggest, 'using a radically different metaphysics, would imply the "unmaking" of our own assumptive world and its culture-bound definitions of reality'.

The study or pursuit of metaphor is a means of questioning the assumptions, descriptions and definitions of a literalistic and constricting outlook on reality. The ability of ethnography to present alien cultures as *not-so-strange* and our own as *strange* might therefore be a metaphor itself for the distinction between 'literal' and 'metaphoric' thought. Research that uses ethnographic and reflexive perspectives in order to establish conceptual structures of metaphor in talk is one way in which researchers can approach questions of representation and meaning in language. The body and its illnesses serve as a perfect locus for the investigation of our most involved and expressive emotions and language. 'Sickness', as Scheper-Hughes and Lock remind us, 'is a form of communication … through which nature, society and culture speak simultaneously'. It is in that simultaneity that metaphor thrives.

CONCLUSION

Historically, metaphor has been sidelined by the scientific, positivist tradition in western societies, and treated as though it were relevant only to artistic and literary enterprises. However, since the late 1970s there has been a shift towards a wider acceptance of metaphor as a topic worthy of study by cognitive scientists, especially by psychologists, anthropologists and linguists with an interest in studying fundamental aspects of categorization in language and cognition. Subsequently, it has been pointed out that much that has passed for literal or factual description in the 'hard' sciences has in fact been achieved through metaphor. Medical science is no exception to this, and the in-group talk of doctors is laden with metaphoric and other figurative descriptions of illness and the sick.

Although not yet adequately researched, there appears to be enormous scope in the field of metaphor studies across cultures. Medical metaphors have been shown to have a limited but concise translatability between European languages such as English and Italian, whereas the broader discrepancies of formulation between Chinese doctors trained in the Western medical tradition and those trained in traditional Chinese medicine poses an intriguing confrontation between medico-cultural systems. The fundamental notion of balance in TCM, resting on a belief in balancing the complementary categories of yin and yang, represents a metaphor framework distinct from that of the 'illness as invader' and 'body as machine' preferred by Western medicine.

Sontag has been criticized for demanding that illness be treated 'simply as illness', an attitude perceived by her critics as too idealistic to be credibly sustained. Furthermore, it is questionable whether the military metaphor should really be considered a metaphor at all, or whether, as has been argued, its metaphoric currency is now dead. However, the illness = invasion and body = machine metaphors are perhaps merely the most obvious linguistic expressions in the range of metaphors and metonyms associated with illness experience and recovery. People with chronic illnesses often draw upon their own resources to redefine or 're-figure' themselves within the new context of their illness. Examples from the research literature and from my own ethnographic interviews suggest that metaphor need not be restricted to the medium of language, and that if we are to engage fully with the broader meaning of metaphor and symbolic action we should include the ways in which individuals express one domain of experience through another. The types of action-trope illustrated here are as thoroughly metaphoric as linguistic metaphors, and help us to expand our understanding of discourse, and to regard it not as a result of discrete and peculiar mental processes, but as intimately interwoven with action.

Narrative and the 6
Voicing of Illness

Storytelling is one of the oldest and most quintessentially human of activities. Since the 1980s there has been a renewed interest in the theory and practice of narrative, in the study of what has become known as narratology (Bal, 1985), and in 'life stories' (Josselson and Lieblich, 1993). Developments in both postmodern cultural theory (Lyotard, 1984) and cognitive science (Bruner, 1990) acknowledge the central role of narrative in the way that people make meanings, and it has even been suggested that human grammars arose out of a proto-linguistic need to narrate (Bruner, 1990: 138). Whatever the claims of a reductionist position such as Bruner's, it is through the telling and retelling of stories that human beings have always come to frame, if not to understand, their experiences. As Kerby (1991: 53) writes:

> The stories we tell are part and parcel of our becoming. They are a mode of vision, plotting what is good and what is bad for us, what is possible and what is not – plotting who we may become. But in the telling we seem also to be immediately involved in generating the *value* of a certain state of affairs or course of action, of judging its worth, ethical or otherwise.

Since the 1990s the appeal of narratives has taken a substantive turn towards the pathologized body and the experience of terminal, or at least chronic, illness experience. Perhaps this fascination with self-related decrement and self-disclosure on themes relating to mortality and death is the logical progression of an increasing tendency towards self-reflexivity in western culture generally (as well as in the social sciences), or perhaps it bears some relation to the more arcane and apocalyptic manifestations of the millennium. Whatever the reason, recent years have seen a sudden deluge of biographical accounts of illness experience, written by media celebrities (innumerable), authors (Marilyn French, John Updike), journalists (John Diamond, Ruth Picardie), and academics (Allon White, Arthur Frank, Susan DiGiacomo, Irving Zola). Some of these accounts have received a great deal of exposure, such as journalist John Diamond's 'cancer column' in *The Times* (and the spin-off TV documentary), and Ruth Picardie's account of her own terminal illness in the *Observer*. Some of the motives behind these accounts have been described as questionable (see for example Aitkenhead (1998), who considers such narratives to be 'emotional pornography'), but the fact remains that they appear to have a market, and the guiding force behind the marketability of these accounts seems to be that people want to hear stories of illness, decrement and death.

In this chapter, we will consider the time-based nature of narrative, that is, its relationship to the cultural concept of linearity, at least within the Western concept of narrative (and of time!), before moving on to consider the ontological basis of what have been termed 'sustaining fictions' (Hillman, 1983), or the explanatory models by which individuals account for their experience, specifically their experience of illness. We then examine three models of narrative, from the fields of sociolinguistics, semiotics and sociology respectively. In the second half of the chapter we shall examine a short extract of narrative from a medical consultation in which a patient visiting her GP recounts a key episode in her own explanatory model of illness.

NARRATIVE IN TIME

A narrative account involves a sequence of two or more bits of information (concerning happenings, mental states, people, or whatever) which are presented in such a way that if the order of the sequence were changed, the meaning of the account would alter. It is this sequentiality which differentiates narrative from other forms of conveying and apprehending information. Narrative can therefore be regarded as depending upon a specific construction of temporality, in which events occur within and across time. Narrative is the form of human representation concerned with expressing coherence through time: it helps to provide human lives with a sense of order and meaning. By imposing an orderly sequence of events upon an inchoate mass of experience, expanses of time can be *retrospectively structured* and, in the process, made meaningful, an ambiguity which did not escape the philosopher Kierkegaard, who observed that we lead our lives facing forward, but account for them looking backward (Kierkegaard, 1987: 260). Ensuring sequentiality between events, imposing a beginning, a middle and an end, can serve to assure human lives of direction and growth: and at the very least, as Barthes put it, what is narrated is 'hemmed in' (Barthes, 1982).

However, there is considerably more to narrative than merely iterating a series of events in sequence, although the 'progressive' nature of much illness lends itself to 'storied' form, that is, a sequencing of events in chronological order (Labov and Waletsky, 1967; Labov, 1972; Mishler, 1986; Cortazzi, 1993; Riessman, 1993). Most people construct a narrative around their experiences of illness, and it is the *process* of reconstruction, this telling and retelling, that I wish to examine in this chapter. I will be investigating the *hermeneutical*, or explanatory, basis of narrative rather than analysing in depth different theoretical models.

It is through the hearing and telling of stories that human beings have always come to understand their experiences. Narration, as Churchill and Churchill have expressed it, echoing Kierkegaard, 'is the forward movement of description of actions and events which make possible the backward action of selfunderstanding' (1982: 73). Such a back-tracking in order to make narrative sense of what has happened to oneself is a typical feature of illness stories, as we shall see. Hunter (1991) discovered that storytelling was by no means the prerogative of the *victims* of illness. In her study of doctors' ways of communicating with each other, she discovered that the most hardened clinicians (despite evident attempts to retain an objective and literalistic presentation) would frequently interrupt a research seminar with an account that began with the words 'there was this one guy...' She continues:

> Whether the case was introduced informally in seminars or presented formally in grand rounds, the method of presenting the data of clinical science was familiar to me ... They were stories, narrative accounts of the action and motives of individual human beings, physicians and patients ... Stories had been the last things I had expected to find in a medical centre. Isn't medicine a science? Aren't such stories mere anecdotes? (Hunter, 1991: xii)

It seems that narrative, the purposeful reconstruction of past events across time, is an essential vehicle for talk about illness as much within the medical institution as in the 'lay' community.

'SUSTAINING FICTIONS'

A narrative account of illness helps to reproduce, and is itself a confection of, what the psychologist Hillman has called an individual's 'sustaining fiction' (1983: 17). Psychotherapy is a good place to start when studying autobiographical stories, whether of sickness or not. The kind of free-associative delivery suggested by Freud allows patients to develop narrative themes unhindered by the interpellations of therapist/physician, in contrast to the typical doctor's surgery, where, as we saw earlier, doctors are prone to interrupt the flow of a patient's account frequently.

Hillman writes of a basic human need to tell autobiographical stories; stories, he says, that will in turn constitute a version of 'how things are'. We are constantly adding new stories to the sustaining fictions of our own biographies. With time these fictions become the fabric of memory. For Hillman this is largely a creative or 'imaginal' enterprise, that is, the teller's imaginative resources have time to 'go to work on' their experience, resulting in a story which is meaningful to them personally: 'the manner in which we tell ourselves about what is going on is the genre through which events become experiences' (1983: 23).

Hillman suggests that people are guided by what he calls a 'sustaining fiction', by which they interpret events in their lives. He uses examples from the practice of psychotherapy to illustrate this argument:

> A colleague once told me about a new patient walking out on her when she challenged the thematic mode of the patient's story. The patient presented himself as a rather sick case, having been more or less steadily in therapy for fifteen of his thirty-six years ... My colleague said: 'For me, you are a new case, and I

don't accept that you are as sick as you believe you are. Let's begin today.' By refusing his web of constructions, she also cut him off from his supporting fiction. He did not return. His story still made sense to him: an incurable, but still a dues-paying member of the therapeutic traffic. He wanted analysis and the analyst to fit into his story. A second case, this one from my own practice: psychotic episodes, hospitalizations with medical abuses, seductions, and violations of rights, shock treatments and 'helpful drugs'. I took this story like a past another woman might tell of falling in love in high school and marrying the boy next door, having a loving husband, children and a spaniel, a story of making it. In other words both are consistent accounts exposing a thematic motif which organizes events into experience. Both of these women, this one from her percale sheets and the other from her canvas strait jacket – to put the fantasy figuratively – might come in to therapy, desperate, saying precisely the same thing: 'It doesn't make any sense; I've wasted the best years of my life, I don't know where I am, or who I am.' The senselessness derives from a breakdown in the thematic motif: it no longer holds events together and gives them sense, it no longer provides the mode of experiencing. The patient is in search of a new story, or of reconnecting with her old one. (1983: 16–17)

A sustaining, or supporting fiction thus contains the entire apparatus by which an individual provides a sense of self and identity, and is as flexible or as rigid, as multi-faceted or as unitary, as the identities or personae of that person. It needs to be stated that I am not using the term 'fiction' in a deprecatory fashion as indicating that what a person believes is fundamentally or in any other way 'untrue', nor does Hillman mean to suggest this (1983: 48). What I am suggesting is that the voicing of illness is achieved by way of narrative, which narrative is itself nurtured and developed in the manner that Hillman suggests. A sustaining fiction represents a model of the 'way things are' to the individual's subjective understanding and its 'truth value' (for what it is worth) is not under investigation. So, although the term 'fiction' presents initial problems for anyone whose cultural bias and education dichotomizes 'fiction' and 'fact', I find the term wholly appropriate to my argument.

In the context of illness a sustaining fiction might support, or act as, an 'explanatory model' (Kleinman, 1988). The narrative acts as the vehicle for the whole process of self-presentation in the manner described by Kleinman:

> The illness narrative is a story the patient tells, and significant others retell, to give coherence to the distinctive events and long term course of suffering. The plot lines, core metaphors, and rhetorical devices that structure the illness narrative are drawn from cultural and personal models for arranging experiences in meaningful ways and for effectively communicating those meanings. Over the long course of chronic disorder, these model texts shape and even create experience. The personal narrative does not merely reflect illness experience, but rather it contributes to the experience of symptoms and suffering. (1988: 49)

Like Kleinman's patients, the people with whom I have spoken in my own research experience often seem to be seeking to establish the *meaning* of an illness through their talk. For this reason, I see the purpose of narrative research in a medical context as identifying individual grains of meaning that together might constitute, for a given individual, the 'voicing' of illness. From the practitioner's perspective, this means honing an ability to listen constructively to what a patient has to say. Although this sounds easy enough, it is well established that the majority of complaints made against medical practitioners concern a perceived failure of communication in the clinical setting. Central to 'good' communication is an ability to listen, without continually interrupting. As we saw in Chapter 3, there is a high frequency of doctors interrupting patients during their first speech turn (Beckman and Frankel, 1984). Moreover, it has been suggested that by interrupting patients, thereby suppressing a source of information, doctors might be creating rods for their own backs (Stott, 1983). 'Unfinished business', in the form of complaints that are left untended during a visit, only resurface later in the patients' illness trajectory, and are often exacerbated by not having been attended to in the first instance. However, the pressures of doctors' heavy workloads, constraints of time, and a lack of training in communication (and especially listening) skills conspire to condemn the mass of doctor–patient interviews to a routine and scripted predictability with consequent frustration for the patient. By focusing entirely on the clinical evidence at the expense of the patient's story, doctors are in danger of missing out on invaluable evidence. An excellent allegory for this is presented in the paper by Baron (see page 82), in which the author/doctor, while listening to his patient's chest with his stethoscope, interrupts the patient with the words 'I can't hear you while I'm listening' (1985: 606). The irony lies in the fact that it is precisely because he is 'listening' to his patient's chest through the stethoscope, that emblem of medical authority, that the doctor is unable to 'hear' what his patient is 'really' saying.

Recent writings by medical scholars have seen a turn towards narrative as a means of developing a more holistic approach to patient care and as a potent reserve to be explored in the formulation of new therapies. Thus a strangely designated 'narrative based medicine' (Greenhalgh and Hurwitz, 1999) has arisen in counterpoint to the equally peculiar-sounding 'evidence-based medicine' (Sackett et al., 1997) (what, one wonders, had doctors based their treatments on *before* this strain of practice emerged?). Although it might be contended that narrative-based medicine is simply a case of re-inventing the wheel, considerable interest is being generated in medical circles, and in the pages of medical journals, by the phenomenon of narrative.

It is standard form for a scholarly fashion to do the circuit of disciplines, and the 'narrative turn' has been well documented in a number of studies in literary criticism (Scholes and Kellogg, 1966), linguistics (Labov and Waletzky, 1967; Labov; 1972; Toolan, 1988), anthropology (Geertz, 1988; Kleinman, 1988; Good, 1994) psychology (Bruner, 1990; Kerby, 1991), and the sociology of health and illness (Atkinson, 1995; Frank, 1995). By a process of cross-fertilization the narrative seed has germinated in certain areas of the medical establishment, which traditionally has had strong literary connections of its own (one thinks of the many doctors who became successful authors, such as Chekhov, Céline and Williams, quite apart from that consummate storyteller, Freud).

I would like to consider three models of narrative, which will appear quite distinct from each other and which originate in different scholarly traditions. A topic like narrative broaches all human affairs, and cannot be seen merely as attached to 'literary studies', 'linguistics', 'psychology' or 'anthropology'. The writers whose work I discuss are the linguist Labov, the semiotician Greimas, and the sociologist Frank.

NARRATIVE IN NATURALLY OCCURRING OR ELICITED DISCOURSE

In *Language in the Inner City* (1972) Labov analysed the structure and linguistic features of 'natural narratives'. Of course, it could be pointed out that the kinds of narratives elicited by sociolinguists like Labov are *not* naturally occurring, since they are 'collected' with the clear intention of providing 'data' for scholars. However, the structural features that occur seem to be common to narratives recorded in 'naturally occurring' conversations as well as in literary texts.

According to Labov, a narrative may contain (for example) four independent clauses which together refer to successive events in a temporal sequence:

a   Well, this person had a little too much to drink
b   and he attacked me
c   and the friend came in
d   and she stopped it

(Labov and Waletsky, 1967: 20)

Such a narrative, Labov tells us, is complete in itself: it contains a beginning, a middle and an end. However, there are more fully developed types of narrative that contain a combination of, or all of, certain standard features.[1] These are:

1. Abstract   an optional précis of the plot
2. Orientation   the time, the place, the players
3. Complicating action   what happened?
4. Evaluation   so what?
5. Result or resolution what happened in the end?
6. Coda   a means of 'bridging back' to present

(adapted from Labov, 1972: 370)

The *abstract* is an optional device that acts to summarize the whole story in one or two clauses. The abstract is seen as standing outside the narrative proper and is in no way essential to the telling of the story. Labov states that the abstract is not given *in place of* the story, nor does it act as an advertisement or a warning (1972: 364), this last view being at odds with Toolan, who writes: 'abstracts are often advertisements or trailers for stories, making exaggerated claims for what will follow, promising more than gets delivered' (1988: 154). The standard pattern is for the speaker to give the abstract and then proceed with the full story. An example of a 'well-formed abstract', according to Labov, would be:

a An' then, three weeks ago I had a fight with this other dude outside.
b He got mad 'cause I wouldn't give him a cigarette.
c Ain't that a bitch?

In essence, the abstract tells us, the audience, what the story is going to be about. Sometimes the abstract leads straight into the *orientation*: otherwise it might act as a discrete unit or be followed by a pause designed to receive 'what happened?' invitations. If the abstract tells us briefly what the story is about, the orientation will establish the time, place, persons and their activity or the situation. Another term for orientation might be 'setting'. The orientation is most commonly found between the abstract and the complicating action, though it may be embedded within the opening clauses of the narrative itself.

Occasionally elements of the orientation are strategically delayed, and introduced at a later stage in the narrative. This, according to Toolan, has the effect of surprising or shocking the audience, and may be employed when salient facts do not become apparent to the speaker until an advanced stage in the sequence of events being described.

Only the *complicating action* is essential to the production of a narrative. This involves the recapitulation of past experiences in sequential order. Events in the complicating action 'take us through' the narrative, so strictly speaking clauses that have no 'temporal juncture', and which could equally be found elsewhere in the order of clauses, do not belong to the complicating action and are termed 'free clauses'. An example given by Labov will illustrate the nature of the free clause:

a I know a boy named Harry.
b Another boy threw a bottle at him right in the head
c and he had to get seven stitches.

(Labov, 1972: 361)

According to Labov, of the three clauses in this narrative only two are 'narrative clauses'. It is true that the speaker knows a boy called Harry at the beginning and at the end of the episode, so the first clause is termed a 'free clause' because 'it is not confined by any temporal juncture' (1972: 361). Likewise, clauses that contain *used to, would* and the *general present* (as in, 'I know a boy called Harry') 'are not narrative clauses and cannot support a narrative' (1972: 362). The choice of term 'complicating action' is in fact revealing since, as Toolan has pointed out (1988: 157) it is the 'what is done' of a narrative that constitutes for Labov the core text, while 'what is said' about these actions is treated as evaluative commentary. However, there need not be a sharp division between what is being described (the actions) and the verbal reactions to them, and Toolan reminds us that 'our use of words in interaction is typically a performing of actions and not merely an asserting of true or false ... statements' (1988: 158). Thus there is not necessarily a clear distinction between the narrative and evaluative facets of a text.

Evaluation is defined as 'the means used by the narrator to indicate the point of the narrative, its *raison d'être:* why it was told, and what the narrator is getting at' (Labov, 1972: 366). Labov goes on to characterize the distribution of evaluative devices in a text as a 'focus of waves that penetrate the narrative'.

> A complete narrative begins with an orientation, proceeds to the complicating action, is suspended at the focus of evaluation before the resolution, concludes with the resolution, and returns the listener to the present time with the coda. The evaluation of the narrative forms a secondary structure which is concentrated in the evaluation section but may be found in various forms throughout the narrative. (ibid.)

Essentially the evaluation will inform us of why the story is worth telling in the mind of the teller. It will allow us to see that the story was 'worth reporting' (1972: 371) and not 'ordinary, plain, humdrum, everyday or run of the mill' (ibid.). There are two main ways in which evaluation occurs: 'external' and 'internal' (see Labov, 1972, or Toolan, 1988 for a fuller discussion of 'evaluation'; see also Gwyn 2000 for a critique of Labov).

Let's consider how this structure might be applied to an illness narrative. The interviewee is an elderly man whom I will call Ben Coates. The opening question of the interview is aimed at eliciting a narrative response. What in fact emerges is a fully formed narrative which might (though this, of course, could be contested) be designated labels according to Labov's terminology as follows:

```
[A=abstract; O=orientation; CA=complicating action]
R=result/resolution; C=coda
01  INT  what is your own experience of ( . ) of illness?
02  BC   uh ( . ) overseas I nearly died ( . ) uh ( . )            A
03  INT  is this during the war?
04  BC   before the war uh I was in India before the war (3.0)     O
05       I got um ( . ) apart from malaria and things like that    O
06       that was the only illness I got out there                 O
07       I got um ( . ) heat stroke uh first I got sand fly fever   CA
08       and doped myself and carried on ( . )                     CA
09       in the end I collapsed with a temperature of              CA/R
10       a hundred and seven point five ( . )                      CA/R
11       they wheeled me off into hospital                         CA
12       there was a nursing sister there ( . ) [clean] under canvas  CA
13       they had nursing sisters there like hospital staff here    O
14       you know ( . ) and um ( . ) she worked at me eight hours   CA
15       ( . ) give up after eight hours covered me with a sheet   CA
16       this is what I was told I wasn't ( . ) compos mentis [laughs]  E
17       uh ( . ) this nursing orderly he you used to get          CA/O
18       nursing orderlies from different battalions of ( . ) infantry  O
19       would supply nursing orderlies for the hospital and the    O
20       Q Q Queen Alexandra's used to supply the sisters and the   O
21       doctors I suppose [mumbles]                                O
22       um (2.0) and he says she lifted up the sheet again and said  CA/R
23       uh bugger's still fighting come on [laughs]                CA/R
24  INT  yeah so they'd given up on you?                           E
25  BC   well ( . ) when you've got a hundred and seven point five  E
```

```
26         you you=
27   INT   =you should be dead                                      E
               [
28   BC                   getting a bit close to it but then you wouldn't   E
29         know about it cos they bury you the same day out there you   E
30         know ( . ) no ( . ) they don't keep you very long ( . ) um     E
31         ( . ) so that's my first *real* illness                        C
```

Ben takes the opening question as a cue to tell his first story of illness in its
entirety. After line 24, he does not return to this episode in the interview,
but goes on to move through his life in a more or less chronological order
to the present day. It is interesting that his opening echoes the kind of short
pithy introductions that Labov records having received in response to his
'danger of death' stories and defines as an abstract:

```
02   BC   uh ( . ) overseas I nearly died ( . ) uh ( . )
```

where 'I nearly died' is the focal event, and is followed by two short pauses
that perhaps invite the interviewer to press for details. The fact that there
has been no previous mention of 'overseas' (a term in British English that
has been absorbed into bureaucratic and military discourses as referring to
anywhere unspecifically not in 'UK') is no deterrent since the predominant
landscape in Ben Coates' interview is to be one of 'wartime' where the par-
ticularities of geography are rendered temporarily redundant. 'The war'
along with 'the army' was, throughout the conversation, Ben's dominant
sustaining fiction. Hence this episode is placed 'before the war' and, specifically, 'in India'.

Locating the narrative in space ('in India'), and time ('before the war')
serves the basic function of orientation according to Labov's definition. The
minimal information on other illnesses can also be seen as orientation, acting to accentuate the importance of the episode about to be described:

```
04   BC   before the war uh I was in India before the war (3.0)
05        I got um ( . ) apart from malaria and things like that
06        that was the only illness
07        I got out there
          I got um ( . ) *heat* stroke
```

The emphasis given to the word 'heat' suggests the arrival of important new
material, material which marks the beginning of the complicating action of
the narrative:

uh first I got sand fly fever and doped myself and carried on (.) (ll. 07–08)

A necessary component of the sick role is to not allow oneself to succumb
to illness if at all possible, one that is found over and again in the literature
(Herzlich, 1973; Blaxter, 1983; Williams, 1990). The *struggle with illness* is
seen in western culture as heroic, a role compounded perhaps by Ben's position as a professional soldier, where the accusation of 'malingering' might
be particularly face-threatening or otherwise problematic.

> in the end I collapsed with a temperature of a hundred and seven point five
> (ll. 09–10)

The prepositional phrase 'in the end' aids the temporal sequencing of the narrative just as Labov suggests that the question 'what happened next?' requires an answer. The crucial event ('I collapsed') is presented alongside its justification, which is precisely articulated as a numeral plus decimal point ('a hundred and seven point five'). This, I would argue, constitutes a 'mini-result' as well as a part of the continuing complicating action. The shared knowledge that Ben assumes with this utterance is that such a temperature is exceedingly high for a human being. This is followed by a pause ('what happened next?') before we are told:

> they wheeled me off into hospital (1.11)

We are not told who 'they' are, but from the context are no doubt expected to infer his fellow-soldiers or the medical orderlies attached to the regiment. Further orientation is then introduced with details about the staffing of the makeshift hospital:

> 12   BC   there was a nursing sister there (.) [clean] under canvas
> 13   they had nursing sisters there like hospital staff here

We have already been assured of the severity of Ben's condition by two pieces of information, first that his temperature was 107.5 degrees Fahrenheit, and secondly that he had to be 'wheeled' into hospital, presumably because he was unconscious, and/or unable to walk. We are now presented with further information that allows the narrative to progress from being a 'near to death' story to being a 'left for dead' story. Again pauses are made in the appropriate 'what happened next?' slots:

> 14   BC   she worked at me eight hours
> 15   (.) give up after eight hours covered me with a sheet

Ben Coates would have been unable to ascertain that the nursing sister had 'worked at' him for eight hours or covered him with a sheet: this is reported narrative relayed to him after the event by a nursing orderly. He evidently needs to explain this detail, thus validating the authenticity of his account (it comes from an identified other, not himself), and while so doing explains the presence of the orderly in the hospital. But the orderly fulfils another criterion of Labov's: by introducing a 'third party' to the narrative, the narrator is able to provide a *neutral evaluation*, which will carry more dramatic force than his own uncorroborated one (1972: 373):

> 16   this is what I was told I wasn't (.) compos mentis [laughs]
> 17   uh (.) this nursing orderly he you used to get
> 18   nursing orderlies from different battalions of (.) infantry
> 19   would supply nursing orderlies for the hospital and the
> 20   Q Q Queen Alexandra's used to supply the sisters and the
> 21   doctors I suppose [mumbles]

This amount of orientation does not assist the forward flow of the narrative, but it contextualizes the presence of the orderly, without whose account Ben might have been denied knowledge of certain crucial details (the nurse 'working eight hours at him', the sheet covering his head). It is therefore given in full, providing an explanatory link between the two stages of the split evaluation.

We are then told:

22   and he says she lifted up the sheet again and said
23   uh bugger's still fighting come on [laughs]

The *result* or resolution of a narrative in Labovian analysis provides an answer to the question 'what finally happened' (Toolan, 1988: 152). Here we are given the result, which paves the way for the second part of the evaluation. In Ben's account the denouement is skilfully presented so that the mildly deprecating language attributed to the nursing sister ('bugger's still fighting') only serves, by covertly praising him, to boost Ben's own heroic status. It is noteworthy too that the nurse's evaluation is presented as reported speech ('he says she ... said') thus fortifying the evaluative locus of the story. Labov emphasizes that this technique (of attributing evaluations to others present) 'is used only by older, highly skilled narrators from traditional working-class backgrounds. Middle-class speakers are less likely to embed their evaluative comments so deeply in the narrative' (1972: 373).

The interviewer's subsequent question: 'so they'd given up on you?' is itself evaluative, and permits Ben to reformulate *his* evaluation.

24 INT   yeah so they'd given up on you?
25 BC   well (.) when you've got a hundred and seven point five
26   you you=
27 INT   =you should be dead
28 BC   [
                getting a bit close to it

Whereas the two previous evaluations are 'external' (reported speech and action), the speaker now provides what Labov terms a *comparator* (1972: 381). Comparators compare the events which did occur to those which might have, could have, but did not in fact occur. Often the effect is to 'spice up' the story. A comparator may be framed as a negative phrase, through modality and modulation, or through futurity (Toolan, 1988: 160), but also through questions, imperatives and comparative or superlative phrases. In this case the comparator is achieved through the speculation that had the nurse not pulled the sheet back and found him 'still fighting' he would have been buried alive:

29 BC   they bury you the same day out there you
30   know (.) no (.) they don't keep you very long

Toolan (1988: 161) writes that the *coda* 'signals the "sealing off" of a narrative, just as the abstract announces the "opening up"'. It renders the asking of 'and then what happened?' absurd. The coda also removes the narrative from another spatiotemporal context and returns us to the present. Ben Coates' coda happily fulfils both these conditions:

31   so that's my first *real* illness

With which statement Ben 'pushes away' and 'seals off' (Labov, 1972: 366) the preceding narrative events.

Apart from fulfilling the criteria of a mini-narrative, the opening of Ben Coates' interview provides the kind of background to his personal history that is often helpful in identifying an individual's explanatory model of illness. We have learned that Ben was a volunteer soldier (since he was in India before World War II), that he perceives his recovery from this bout of fever as being somewhat exceptional (he had been given up for dead), and that he self-presents in a heroic – or mock-heroic – mould ('bugger's still fighting'), ostensibly (or ostentatiously) making light of the alternative outcome of his illness ('they bury you the same day out there you know'). He has told how, despite contracting sand fly fever, he 'doped [him]self and carried on' which insinuates the kind of stoic individualism observable in many accounts by males of his generation and background (R. Williams, 1990; Gwyn, 1997).

'Personal stories', write Rosenwald and Ochberg, 'are not merely a way of telling someone (or oneself) about one's life; they are the means by which identities may be fashioned' (1992: 1). Most significantly, then, in the context of research interviewing, this extract illustrates how the first story that a respondent provides can do much more than simply prefix the interview with a neatly structured narrative; it helps the speaker to establish *who* they are in relation to the *what* of illness. However, ontological concerns such as these are rarely uppermost in a reading of Labov's work on narrative.

EVALUATION IN NARRATIVE AND CO-CONSTRUCTED DISCOURSE

Now, as a classificatory model, Labov's structure works pretty well, but it does not tell us anything about the story that is being recounted, or the interaction within which it takes place. Elsewhere (Gwyn, 2000) I have argued that in Labovian analyses the structural dynamics of storytelling have been emphasized at the expense of interactional aspects and that this has consequences for the validity of the structural analysis. In order to make any sense out of a patient's story, in order for it to become anything other than a sequenced order of clauses, we need to do rather more than carve up the story into categorial chunks. This is especially true of the research interview, which is itself a shared experience, one whose telling devolves not only on the teller but is actively co-constructed with the interviewer (who often also transcribes the resulting audio-recording). Any shirking of reflexive commitment on the part of the interviewer thus becomes ever more transparent in qualitative research of this kind.

Events, as Bakhtin insists, are always *experienced* rather than merely *perceived*, and furthermore are experienced from a particular position (Holquist, 1990: 21). Perhaps the act of evaluation is more thoroughly co-constructed in narrative discourse than has been previously imagined: the evaluations that one sets out to record provoking a complementary and reflexive evaluation of the researcher's own role in the process of recording interviews of this kind.

In a similar vein, Holmes (1997: 207) has argued that a narrative does not necessarily have to have an obvious 'point', that on occasion, 'the evaluative component is deeply embedded in the context within which the story is told'. This seems to be particularly true of illness narratives. The closer we look, the more the context as well as the narrative reconstruction can be viewed as integral to the evaluative process; and to specify clauses within that as specific instances of evaluation is to diminish the dialogic or rhetorical construction of talk, whereby meaning is constructed interactively between speaker and listener. Labov and Waletzky's discrete evaluative function serves only the forward linear drive towards narrative *telos* or endpoint, presupposing that such evaluation is distinguishable from the surrounding descriptive process itself and the context within which it takes place. This shortcoming of Labov and Waletzky's notion of evaluation would be endorsed by Riessman's (1993) argument that only a *particular kind* of narrative is used in Labov and Waletzky's analysis. Suggesting that evaluation provides the only answer to any hypothetical and disruptive 'so what?' question implies that the purpose of narrative is to provide evaluations; a sadly utilitarian and limiting notion. If we propose instead that evaluation is a constant underlying thread in narrative, developed in the interaction of teller and listener, we attribute more life and meaning to the act of narrative reconstruction *for its own sake*, a weave and interplay of storytelling.

A distinct kind of second-order evaluation comes not from another person in the world of recounted experience, nor from the interviewer's interjections or compliance in silence, but from a speaker self-consciously orienting towards an 'outsider' authorial role in order to describe the events as though they are happening in 'the narration of a narrator' (Bakhtin, 1984: 190).

Katz and Shotter (1996) refer to 'threshold moments' in illness narratives which act as openings into the described world of the patient, or keys to 'the inner world of pain and suffering', and which are turning points in the speaker's self-reflexivity. They term this practice 'social poetics', and its aim is to grasp in these threshold moments the emerging 'movement' within diagnostic interviews or conversations. Not only must a social poetics draw attention to events which might otherwise pass unnoticed, 'but it must also provide us with an understanding of their possible relations and connections to the particular circumstances of their occurrence' (1996: 919). It seems likely that such threshold moments also act as types of evaluation in the narrative of speakers, which I have referred to as second-order evaluation (Gwyn, 2000), that is, an evaluation which is intrinsic to the surrounding descriptive process itself.

In the example I will use, Rebecca Knight, a 45-year-old council worker, is reflecting on her father's death after years of suffering from Alzheimer's disease. She is wondering whether or not to donate his brain to science. Her father's brain is reified in the manner of any other body part, by being isolated as an identifiable object apart from the person of its owner, and yet at the same time the speaker manages to personify it, to allow it qualities belonging to her father; those very qualities which stop her from going ahead with her plan. In the telling, a corresponding objectification of experience takes place, a type of 'objective correlative' (Eliot, 1951: 145), which serves to stimulate the reflexive process of evaluation.

Rebecca first presents the brain as a thing of scientific interest, detached from the person of her father:

01   I *had* thought possibly of donating his brain for Alzheimer's research

She passes a sleepless night after her father's death, kept from sleep, she tells us, by the nagging worry about his brain, and troubled by a 'blasting headache':

Extract 1

01   I *had* thought possibly of donating his brain for Alzheimer's research
02   and don't forget I'd just finished with my boyfriend a few hours earlier as well (.)
03   um I mean he was on the phone to me and it was fine you know
04   but all I had was this blasting headache which I suffered from anyway
05   I still *do* and all I could think of was my father's *brain* (.)
06   because my *head* was so bad I thought I can't have anybody tampering with my
07   father's brain (.) I couldn't (.) tolerate it

Reification in such a literal form is rare, since we do not normally have to make decisions governing the destination of individual body parts belonging to family members, but this passage is further exceptional in that it *personalizes* the whole *depersonalizing* process of reification that medical science succeeds in establishing in our view of ourselves and our bodies. Rebecca refuses the offer to reify a part of her father to the extent that a stranger might 'tamper' with his brain (and notable here is the *manner* in which causality is presented: it was '*because* my *head* was so bad I thought I can't have anybody tampering with my father's brain', suggestive of some kind of sympathetic relationship between Rebecca's headache and her father's soon-to-be extracted brain). Instead she reflects upon the objectification of *experience*, and how strange to *her* were her own perceptions of the events surrounding her father's death, as she carried on against a background of everyday life:

Extract 2

01   RK   I remember spending the whole day waiting for things to happen (.)
02   I remember going into a park in Newport
03   waiting for the death certificate from the GP you know
04   and eating some food and walking in this beautiful park

05   and thinking 'my father's just died' and I haven't slept all
       night (.)
06   [laugh] (.) it was really unreal

Apart from functioning as an evaluation, what does 'really unreal' signify in this extract? Is it a disavowal of the experience as frameable within the boundaries of a 'real' reality? And if reality is not real at certain moments (such as this), is that because some kinds of experience transcend the bounds of ordinary ('real') reality?

In a way, Rebecca's apparent *dis*valuation of her own perception answers these questions: the cataloguing of extraordinary events against the backcloth of an ordinary landscape suddenly renders the ordinary landscape extraordinary. Would the 'beauty' of the park be remarkable were it not for the events surrounding the walk in it? Why does the cinematic silence of this sequence (Rebecca seeming to describe the actions of an actor) need to be shattered by a short laugh, enveloped between silences? Is this laugh 'merely' a discourse marker separating the 'evaluation' from the preceding (evaluative) description of events?

What I believe occurs here is the classification of experience into otherness, thereby effecting an objectification of sorts. This objectification of experience performs precisely the function of a narrative evaluation. The 'poetic' nature of this experience is highlighted in the shift between the 'unnatural' (the extraction and investigation of her father's brain) and the natural (a walk in the park). Such narrative description contains all the evaluation that is needed. Descriptions, as Edwards reminds us, are 'intrinsically selective and categorial, and thereby evaluative' (1997). 'Evaluation', as defined by Labov and Waletzky, can therefore be relegated to the redundant role of a technique used to encapsulate what has already been achieved through narrative description. In Rebecca's narrative a subtle metaphorization of experience takes place. Through the act of description, an event is translated conceptually from the here and now of lived experience to another, indistinct, but equally valid domain, viewed through the 'unreal' lens of sleeplessness and a walk in the park. In this way the quality of the speaker's experience is described as 'other' by means of an experiential metaphor.

Despite these problems relating to the role of an evaluative function, and its limited application to the structural analysis of certain *types* of narrative, Labov's model at least lends an analytical rigour to the study of illness narratives, which otherwise risk floundering in rather vague notions of the 'meaning' of illness, and a quest for the 'explanatory model' of illness within a patient's story – a quest for meaning which runs the risk of itself becoming a kind of 'quest narrative' for the *researcher*, a project in which the research activity serves as a mirror for the speaker/patient's own account. Here the subjective and 'experiential' world of the patient/teller is all important (Kleinman, 1988) and the task of the analyst/researcher seems to involve little more than a verbatim retelling of the patient's story, with an emphasis on empathizing with and relating to the teller's experience.

MYTHO-POETIC MODELS OF NARRATIVE AND MYTH

The 'Actantial' Model of Narrative

Another model of narrative that has attracted the attention of analysts since its first appearance in the heyday of structuralism is the *actantial* model of Greimas (1984, 1987), who developed his ideas from the earlier work of Propp (1968) on the analysis of Russian fairytales. Greimas' model has been summarized and applied in relation to literary theory (Hawkes, 1977; Toolan, 1988), advertising strategies (Vestergaard and Schrøder, 1985), as well as teachers' narratives about 'awkward parents' (Cortazzi, 1993: 90), and it seems particularly pertinent to narrative accounts of illness.

'Greimas', writes Hawkes (1977: 91) 'argues for a "grammar" of narrative in which a finite number of elements, disposed in a finite number of ways, will generate the structures that we recognize as stories'. Accordingly, narratives can be analysed in terms of three fundamental pairs, which Greimas termed *actants*, and the relations between them (1984: 207):

subject	–	object
helper	–	opponent
giver	–	receiver

The relations between the *actants* could be summarized as follows: a hero or *subject* seeks some desired goal or *object*. His or her efforts are challenged by an enemy (*opponent*) and aided by allies (*helper*). After great struggle the *sender* or *giver* (someone of supernatural or elevated status) intervenes and presents the object to the *receiver* (who might be the hero or another person or group of people). Actants are thus the abstract roles which in the actual narrative are represented by *actors* (Greimas, 1984: 203–13; Vestergaard and Schrøder, 1985: 27). The actantial model is claimed to possess universal features: clearly, then, the model must be seen to be universally applicable. Greimas (1984: 204) applies it to the Grail legend, Vestergaard and Schrøder (1985: 28) apply it to the Robin Hood story and Sanatogen vitamins, and, as I mentioned above Cortazzi (1993: 90–3) sees the model in operation in the narratives given by teachers about hostile confrontations with parents. Since these examples all involve some kind of quest or conflict that requires resolution, we might test it against any one of them. Figure 6.1 shows Vestergaard and Schrøder's representation of a Sanatogen advertisement.

In this advertisement good health is symbolized by 'The Sanatogen Smile', the desired object, sought by 'you', the 'subject'. In your quest for good health you are aided by the 'helper' (vitamins and minerals). Your 'opponent' is represented by those factors which might be responsible for a diminished vitamin content – a snack lunch, dieting, eating reheated food, etc. Finally, the 'giver' is represented by Sanatogen and the 'receiver' by 'you' – 'Sanatogen Multivitamins *give* you essential vitamins and minerals' (Vestergaard and Schrøder, 1985: 29).

We might recall the story told by Sylvia and Bruce Ryan concerning Bruce's haemorrhage (see pp. 50–7). I would suggest that, in regard to their

The Sanatogen Smile

Vitamins are essential to good health. In theory, you should be able to get all the vitamins you need from a properly balanced diet.

Sometimes, though, if you're particularly busy, you may only have a snack lunch. Which, of course, may only have snack vitamins. If you're on a diet and eating less calories, you could also be eating less vitamins. Reheating food at lunchtime can reduce the vitamin content.

And of course, if you cut out a meal, you cut out everything that goes with it as well. Sanatogen Multivitamins give you essential vitamins and minerals that help to ensure good health. So take one Sanatogen tablet every morning and be sure of getting the vitamins and minerals you need to last you through the day. Have you got the Sanatogen Smile?

Sanatogen Multivitamins. One a day, every day, for positive health.

GIVER---------->	OBJECT	<----------RECEIVER
(Sanatogen)	(Good Health)	(You)
HELPER---------->	SUBJECT	<----------OPPONENT
(Minerals & Vitamins)	(You)	(Poor Diet etc.)

FIGURE 6.1   The 'Sanatogen Smile': an actantial model
(Vestergaard and Schrøder, 1985: 28)

GIVER---------->	OBJECT	<----------RECEIVER
Saint Cadi's Infirmary	*correct diagnosis and removal of cancerous kidney*	*Bruce*
HELPER(S)---------->	SUBJECT	<----------OPPONENT(S)
Sylvia	*Bruce*	*Illness (haemorrhage)*
the 'good' doctor		*the 'bad' doctor*

FIGURE 6.2   Bruce Ryan's haemorrhage: an actantial model

narrative, the actant roles be represented as follows: Bruce, the *subject* and *receiver*, realizes he is ill: his illness, made apparent by the haemorrhage he suffers, is the overt *opponent*. Sylvia's attempts to help him place her in the role of *helper*. Her efforts however are thwarted by the actions of the locum, or 'bad' doctor, who, by acting in collusion with the illness (misdiagnosing the complaint and prescribing the wrong medicine, thereby potentially harming Bruce still further), is cast in the role of *opponent* also. Bruce is aided by the 'good' doctor at the infirmary who as an individual is designated as *helper*, in contrast to the institution, which, due to the elevated terms in which Bruce and Sylvia speak of it, and its role as a local provider of services, is the perceived *giver, sender* or *superhelper*. (See Figure 6.2)

As I suggested above, the 'binary patterning of logical opposition' (Hawkes, 1977: 88) behind Greimas' model is specifically evidenced by the symmetry of the 'good doctor' throwing away the bad medicine that the locum so irresponsibly prescribes with the comment 'don't give him *these*'. It is possible to go further, and use the actantial model as a tool in the sense-making process central to the analysis of illness narratives. Bruce and Sylvia's explanatory model of Bruce's illness experiences *as a whole*, and not just of this incident, might well be fitted into the same broad structural terms, and this would suggest adherence to a personal mythology of events, or a sustaining fiction, that opposes the individual and the illness within the mythic frame of the heroic quest.

The 'Quest' Narrative in Medical Sociology

Frank (1995) considers three dominant narrative strategies in the accounting of illness. The first of these is the *restitution* narrative, in which health is regarded as the normal condition to which any sick person will be restored. The basic plot of this narrative runs as follows: 'Yesterday I was healthy, today I'm sick, but tomorrow I'll be healthy again.' The restitution narrative is the one that other people want to hear and which provides the medical care system with its *raison d'être*. The second of Frank's stories is the *chaos* narrative, and this is dispreferred in Western society, since it contravenes the principles of restitution. Its plot imagines no return to wellness. Chaotic stories reflect the chaotic trajectory of the illness, lacking causality or sense. Chaos negates the expectation that in life 'one event is expected to lead to another'. In short, chaos narratives are unbearable.

Thirdly, and most significantly for Frank, is the *quest* narrative. On this topic he is indebted to the work of Joseph Campbell, an enigmatic scholar whose work has largely been overlooked in the academic tradition. Campbell, who was in turn heavily influenced by the findings of the psychoanalyst Carl Jung, developed the notion of the monomyth, based on his analysis of hundreds of myths worldwide (1993). The monomyth, essentially, describes the actions of a hero who suffers, achieves self-knowledge, and then makes that knowledge known. The central metaphor of the myth is that of a journey, or quest, and involves the stages of *departure, initiation* and *return*.

The departure begins with a call. This might be the symptom, the lump, dizziness, a cough. In the celebrated account of his cancer given by the late John Diamond (1998) it is a phone call from his wife telling him that the oncologist has discovered cancer cells in his biopsy – all this while he is watching *EastEnders* on TV, a key moment in which the familiar world is transformed. After crossing the threshold into the world of the sick, the hero begins a second-stage initiation. According to Frank, tellers of quest stories use the metaphor of initiation implicitly and explicitly. Explicitly patients might involve themselves in a patient support group or on-line discussion group, but the implicit initiation is surely the initiation into the vast marquee of technomedicine with all its obscure ritual and symbolism, which demands full subservience to its own rites of initiation. Campbell refers to initiation as the road of trials – which in the illness story includes all the sufferings, physical and emotional, that the patient endures. So, for example, Diamond, in the TV adaptation of his cancer narrative (first shown on *Inside Story*, BBC 1: 15.06.98; updated 16.06.99), plays around with the grotesque plastic mask he must wear for radiotherapy sessions, likening it to a prop in a sado-masochism movie, but one which he must put over his own face in order to get better. This initiation period is the plot of the illness narrative, the 'complicating action' in terms of Labov's narrative structure. In the quest narrative the hero undergoes transformation, which is crucial to the hero's attaining of responsibility. Quest stories of illness, according to Frank, 'imply that the teller has been given something by the experience, usually some insight that must be passed on to others' (1995: 118).

Thirdly and finally we come to the return. The storyteller returns as one who is no longer ill but who is marked by illness. The marked person lives in this world but is also denizen of another world: in Campbell's words 'master of two worlds'. Those familiar with Sontag's work will recall the introduction to her *Illness as Metaphor* (1991: 3): 'Illness is the night-side of life, a more onerous citizenship. Everyone who is born holds dual citizenship, in the kingdom of the well and in the kingdom of the sick.'

Whatever the routes through illness and suffering the principal role of the storyteller in these narratives is that of witness. As such it fits well with Frank's notion of the communicative body (see page 16): 'the communicative body seeks to share the boon that it has gained upon its own return. Others need this boon for the journeys they necessarily will undertake.'

There are clear links between the quest narrative and Greimas' actantial model (there are also connections with the 'restitution' model of illness narrative, but these tend to be enveloped within the grander 'quest' schedule). This should not be surprising since both Campbell and Greimas were (like Propp before them), in their different ways trying to synthesize all myth and fairy story within one explanatory format. Attractive as these models might be within a structural or purely 'psychological' dimension, there is little in them which adds to a discursive perspective on narrative. Moreover, postmodern trends in the humanities and in social studies have questioned the whole basis of narrative that reflects life in uncomplicated structural terms. Postmodernists argue that the episodic nature of much storytelling invokes different conceptualizations of what a narrative might be. It is relevant, in passing, to note that White (1993) considers the attraction of models of narrative which claim 'complete authority' or universal application as being itself culturally determined. White claims that such universal models typically occur in societies 'isolated from significant linguistic diversity' and 'underpinned by a unified, homogeneous, and therefore "absolute" language'. This authority, according to White, is based in myth and is essentially transcendental. In societies characterized by polyglossia (the simultaneous presence of two or more languages within a single cultural system) such transcendentalism would be impossible. This is because 'certain traditional genres such as myth, epic, and tragedy are the products of a centralizing tendency in language, a monoglossic absolutism. This is why structuralism works so well for these genres: sealed off from heteroglossia, they are immune from an intertextual interference' (White, 1993: 142–3). That said, it is worth being aware of such models, if only to illustrate how even a brief narrative, such as the one described by the Ryans in Chapter 2, can be seen to predicate seemingly universal applications of mythic elements within the narrative structure.

NARRATIVE AS A RESOURCE FOR HEALTH CARE PRACTITIONERS

What is important from a health care practitioner's point of view is not the same (necessarily) as the concerns of the researcher into language and communication. The medical carer will be concerned, primarily, with the patient's story as a resource for therapy. In other words, the doctor, by listening to the patient's story, is able to formulate ways to manage that patient's sickness. Greenhalgh and Hurwitz list the main benefits to the doctor in studying patient narrative under the separate headings of (1) the diagnostic encounter; (2) the therapeutic process; (3) the education of patients and professionals, and (4) research.

Why Study Narratives?

In the *diagnostic encounter*, narratives:

- are the phenomenal form in which patients experience ill health;
- encourage empathy and promote understanding between clinician and patient;
- allow construction of meaning;
- may supply useful analytical clues and categories.

In the *therapeutic process*, narratives:

- encourage a holistic approach to management;
- are themselves intrinsically therapeutic or palliative;
- may suggest or precipitate additional therapeutic options.

In the *education* of patients and professionals, narratives:

- are often memorable;
- are grounded in experience;
- enforce reflection.

In *research*, narratives:

- set a patient-centred agenda;
- challenge received wisdom;
- generate new hypotheses.

(Greenhalgh and Hurwitz, 1999: 7)

The business of narrative is perceived by Greenhalgh and Hurwitz as having potentially far-reaching consequences for the practice of their profession:

even in the most autocratic and conservative recesses of medical practice, professors are known to instruct their students to 'Listen to the patient: s/he's telling you the diagnosis' (1999: 6). Inevitably, they remind us, when a doctor takes a medical history, the roles of ethnographer, historian and biographer should be added to that of scientist in order to reach a proper understanding of the patient's condition, and for this the ability to listen to and contextualize the patient's story within the overall picture of their illness experience is essential. They call for a change in the way in which medicine is taught, practised and accredited, drawing on research into the analysis and therapeutic use of narrative in a holistic and nonetheless evidence-based medicine (1999: 14).

In order to investigate how the analysis of narrative can help engender a reflexive approach, and thus feed back into the provision of training for GPs, we shall consider a study (Elwyn and Gwyn, 1998) in which the account given by a patient abruptly changes the focus of a consultation, allowing the doctor a degree of insight into the patient's condition which might not otherwise have been gained.

NARRATIVE ANALYSIS IN CLINICAL PRACTICE

The patient is a woman, aged 52, visiting an inner-city practice. Because she has an urgent problem she has been unable to see her 'usual' doctor and has to consult with, for her, a new practitioner. She begins with a torrent of symptoms: puffy eyes and legs; burning urine; going backwards and forwards to the toilet; pain in the back and a sore throat. Whilst her story emerges the doctor examines the urine sample she has given to him. He diagnoses a 'water infection' (she gets recurrent urine infections) and asks the patient if she is allergic to any antibiotics. She responds with a sigh and the words: 'I feel *terrible*'. In the English of South Wales the term 'terrible' is employed, as one clinician has helpfully remarked, as a standard descriptive term for almost any condition (Gwyn, 1997). At this point the consultation might well have terminated with a prescription. But then the patient lets out a discreet cough. We are 2 minutes 30 seconds into a consultation which lasts nearly 7 minutes in total. The extract which follows lasts two minutes:

[P=Patient
D=Doctor]

```
047   D   ... I'm going to give you something called Augmentin
048       it's a little white bullet ( . )
049       if you take them three times a day ( . )
                              [
050   P                      mhm
051   D   and we'll see if it helps you
052   P   okay that's lovely [coughs briefly]
053   D   anything else?
054       (2.0)
055   P   uh ( . ) dya dya oh is it Dyazide? (1.0)
```

```
056        the ( . ) water tablets I'm on?
057   D    you take those regularly?
058   P    yeah every day ( . )
059        now I always take them in the morning but (1.0)
060        would it be all right to take them in the night? ( . )
061        you know because oh [sighing]
062        it drives me mad you know
063        cos I ( . ) pass water so much=
064   D    =course you do=
065   P    =and as I say if I'm on holiday I think well
066        I don't want to be running into the toilet all the time
067   D    why are you taking ( . ) water tablets?
068   P    because I'm on HRT?
069   D    o yeah=
070   P    =um ( . ) clif clif cilafin is it? well I've got enough of those ( . )
                [
071   D              mmm:    mm
072   P    but I wanted the er Seroxat
073        the antidepressant tablets please
074   D    you take those do you?
075   P    yeah
076   D    how long have you been taking those?
077   P    ( . ) uh: well my son was killed (2.0) five years ago (2.0)
078        just after that then ( . ) three months after ( . )
079        my ( . ) granddaughter
080        three month old twin granddaughter died of meningitis (1.0)
081        then in the January ( . ) my son in law got uh
082        died of a heart complaint
083        twenty two so I refused to take anything you know
084        but then ( . ) Doctor Y insisted ( . )
085        and I have found them and I started work
086        after thirty years I'm a receptionist at the um
087        [names famous Welsh institution] ( . )
088        and I have really found that that has ( . )
089        been more of a help to me (2.0) [breathes heavily]
090        but Doctor Y said she still wanted me to take those antidepressants
091        but I was thinking ( . ) would I be able to take one one day
092        leave one off the next day
093        to try and (1.0) would you know
094        would that be all right do you think or?
095   D    do you want to do that?
```

When the doctor completes prescribing (ll. 47–51), the patient responds with 'okay that's lovely' (l. 52), and what might best be described as a discreet cough. The cough, in these circumstances, functions as a discourse marker signalling the speaker's wish *not* to terminate the interaction. The doctor's next utterance 'anything else?' is characteristic of doctors' pre-closing moves in medical interactions (Silverman, 1997) and suggests that the consultation might be closed here, but leaves such closure to the patient. The patient is in a position to enable the doctor to proceed to closing, or herself to shift to a new topic. She opts to respond (l. 55), after a false start, first with a pause, then a request for 'water tablets'. The pause here indicates that there is to be a new topic, but it precludes any accusation of indecent haste, suggesting that the patient does not wish to be perceived simply as itemizing a shopping list. The ritual of correct timing maintains the necessary gravity accorded to the ceremony of consultation and prescription. Although the pause in line 54 lasts barely two seconds, its significance should not be underestimated.

While seeming to struggle with the brand name, the patient effectively foregrounds the new topic of her 'water tablets', phrasing the statement/question with a high-rising tone: 'is it Dyazide? (.) the (.) water tablets I'm on?' (ll. 55–6). A high rising tone is a vernacular feature that involves a rising intonation pattern on utterances which *function* as statements. It often serves as a facilitative device, inviting confirmation by the listener (Crystal, 2000). The doctor's response is one of apparent puzzlement: 'you take those regularly?' (l. 57), in which the word 'regularly' acts as a qualifier which begs the more relevant question of why the patient takes them at all. Once the patient has completed her explanation (ll. 65–6), the doctor asks the question 'why are you taking (.) water tablets?' (l. 67), to which the answer ('because I'm on HRT?') is again delivered with a high rising tone, which seems either to indicate uncertainty as to the correctness of this response or else questions the relevance of the doctor's question. As an answer to the doctor's question, however, it is of no help, since it does not provide a satisfactory biomedical reason. The doctor hedges the explanation ('o yeah') *without* however committing himself in any way to an acceptance of the patient's explanation (cf. J. Coupland et al., 1994). But already, the patient is moving on to the next topic. She dismisses the water tablet topic while the doctor is still mulling it over – a prolonged 'mmm:' (l. 71) – and proceeds (l. 72–3): 'I wanted the er Seroxat the antidepressant tablets please'.

The use of the past tense ('I wanted') for a present-tense request serves as a means by which the speaker removes herself from the here and now, a common feature of 'negative politeness' (Coulthard and Ashby, 1976). This is consistent with a reluctance to be perceived as too pushy or demanding, and consolidated by the 'please' at the end of the utterance. The doctor's response this time indicates a less restrained surprise: 'you *take* those do you?' Having just queried (l. 67) the patient on her use of diuretics, and apparently unconvinced by her explanation, the doctor might be reluctant to ask her bluntly about the source of her depression, but at the same time the seemingly unrelated sequence of her taking water tablets, HRT, and her call for antidepressants demands rather more substantiation. Moreover, perhaps, the doctor needs to assert his professional role as custodian of the drugs cabinet. The patient replies to the question ('you *take* those do you?', the slight but unexpected emphasis on 'take' indicating the doctor's momentary confoundedness) with a simple 'yeah' (l. 75), and the doctor follows up with a question formulated out of professional concern and framed in linear time: 'how long have you been taking those?'

There is a pause, a false start again (uh:), and then the patient chooses to respond not in *linear* time, but in *event* time: 'well my son was killed' (l. 77) – the event which for her began the sequence of events which culminated in her being prescribed antidepressants on a regular basis. These opening phrases are interspersed by lengthy pauses:

(.) uh: well my son was killed (2.0) five years ago (2.0)

Linear time (five years) is relevant only in relation to event time (her son's death). On this subject, Mishler (1984) has made the famous distinction between the 'voice of medicine' and the 'voice of the lifeworld'. Let's remind ourselves of the relevant detail from the extract discussed in Chapter 3 (see pp. 70–1), where Mishler cites a consultation between a general practitioner and a young woman who is abusing alcohol:

D: . . . .
   . . . . How long have you been drinking that heavily?
P: . . . . Since I've been married.
D: . . . . .
   . . . . How long is that?
P: (giggle) Four years. (giggle)

Mishler argues that the practitioner, by insisting on a 'real' time scale (four years) over a more meaningful, personal one, subordinates the voice of the lifeworld to the voice of medicine, dismissing the importance of a biomedical time frame for medical judgements. The comparison with our example is clear, but the doctor in our case does *not* interrupt the patient, allows her time to pause, to tell her story. A first pause leaves the doctor discursive space to come in if he wishes, but he does not. By not interfering the doctor allows the voice of the lifeworld to take precedence (i.e. life-meaning comes before time-meaning) *but by so doing* he gives his patient the opportunity to fill in the kinds of linear detail which she thinks might be relevant, and which she immediately does anyway ('five years ago').

More important to our argument is the means by which this introduction of biographical detail helps establish a narrative basis to the patient's depression and thus legitimizes her continued use of antidepressants. The account, with its litany of deaths, provides the general practitioner with an idea of this patient's 'sustaining fiction', to use Hillman's expression. As proposed at the beginning of this chapter, we are all continuously involved in adding new stories to the sustaining fictions of our own biographies, of accounting for 'how things are'. The whole biographical process is a narrative-making endeavour. Stories are renewed, reconstructed or abandoned, but are always central to the individual's presentation of self and sense of personal identity. So when we examine this fragment's precise formulation we find (l. 77) that this woman's son did not simply 'die'. Rather, the doctor is being asked to take in that her son was 'killed', that is, suffered death as the victim of a particular agent or set of circumstances. Implicit in the pauses here is the opportunity for the doctor to request *how* her son came to be killed, an opportunity that he chooses not to take. However, the pauses do act as a rhetorical device, allowing for the gravity of her loss to sink in, and accounting for the prescribed drugs. But that is not all. Seeing that the doctor does not request further information about the circumstances of her son's death (a request which, in any case, might be highly threatening to both parties), the patient then lists two other losses in her family: the death of a baby granddaughter from meningitis, and the loss of a son-in-law from a heart complaint. The fact that the causes of death and the ages of the dead are enumerated in both these other cases only draws attention back to the lack of explanation regarding the killing of her son.

By emphasizing the extent of her losses within a short space of time, the patient is avoiding the possibility of being categorized as somebody requesting antidepressants without good cause. Hanging over every patient is the potential accusation of malingering, resulting in the obligation to prove that the malady is not contrived and to express a wish to get well, a position reinforced by this patient's immediate assurance that she 'refused to take anything' (l. 83) (i.e. any drugs). Indeed, as she recounts, it was only at her doctor's instigation (Doctor Y *insisted*) that she began taking antidepressants at all. Having done so, she 'started work after thirty years', again justifying the sick role by a demonstrable commitment to society and the work ethic. She names the well-known institution where she works with a degree of pride. Moreover, she insists that it was her doctor who 'wanted her' to take the tablets (reinforcing her own passivity in this decision, despite their effectiveness) – and then (as if further evidence of her good intentions were needed) she states her wish to reduce the doses, thus maintaining her contractual responsibilities to recovery. This wish to lower the dosage is shown as *her* choice, unaided (indeed hindered by) her practitioner ('Doctor Y said she *still* wanted me to take those antidepressants'), strengthening the representation of herself as a responsible member of society, one who understands and respects the dangers of prescribed drugs.

The patient is now searching for a strategy to reduce or stop her use of antidepressants, and has asked the doctor outright whether it is all right to take her tablets every other day. For the doctor, the narrative has appeared out of the blue. He has recorded:

> One second I had been prescribing Dyazide and oestrogens, the next I'm following the death processions of her son, granddaughter and son-in-law. Added to which she neatly telescopes a declaration that she's ready now to move on. Would that be all right? To withdraw from medication. To effectively contradict my partner. To participate in a shared decision about the end of grief, about a symbolic farewell to a son, killed five years ago. I hadn't expected this. I attempted to give her autonomy over her decision, yet hoping not to abandon her, offering a firm steer that firstly it would be safe to withdraw and secondly that she was going about it in the correct way. This wasn't enough it seemed. She wanted to know what I thought about the decision. How could I tell her that I didn't know. That if I had lost a son I can't imagine surviving at all, never mind coming off tablets. I suppose my hunch was that she wanted to try it out, so I went along with that, using posture more than words. (Elwyn and Gwyn, 1998: 173)

There is good evidence from workshops with medical practitioners to suggest that discourse and narrative analysis provide insight into various dimensions of the medical consultation that would otherwise have been overlooked. As such, analysis of this kind provides an incisive tool for research and, in certain cases, for training, in many areas of clinical practice. Specifically, by being aware of certain discourse strategies such as signalling practices and discourse markers in the patient's talk, general practitioners might be able to *listen more constructively* to their patients' stories (Katz and Shotter, 1996; Margalith and Shapiro, 1997).

CONCLUSION

The universal activity of telling stories has always been the principal method by which people attach meaning to their lives, and construct for themselves a valid social identity. Experiences are first lived, then related, and it is in the relating of them that some kind of progressive order is attributed to an otherwise inchoate existence. In the area of illness experience telling stories of the self has particular importance, since the process of adjusting to illness, or remaking a life after a period of illness, necessitates a more intense degree of self-disclosure and of sense-making than might normally be encountered in other everyday activities.

Nor is it only patients who make such use of stories: doctors too use narrative as an invaluable tool in communicating with each other and with students in the clinical and teaching environment. Moreover, a 'storied' approach to both the experiencing and the management of illness has gained support from medical researchers in recent years, launching the movement known as 'narrative-based medicine', and encouraging health care professionals to apply a narrative awareness to the diagnostic encounter, the therapeutic process, the education of patients and health care workers, as well as in their own research.

While it is possible to study narrative on a purely structural level, analysing features of discourse within a rigid patterning of orientation, complicating action and resolution, problems arise when the reader attempts to burrow beneath the surface structure of the text and examine evaluation as though it were an element somehow distinct from the process of narration itself; or elsewhere, to view narrative evaluation as other than a co-constructed feature, highly dependent on the context in which the narrative has been elicited.

Other, mytho-poetic models, in which the progress of the narrative is seen to conform to archetypal patterns, while being of considerable interest, do little to furnish a discursive perspective on health and illness. However, there is considerable potential for pursuing the kind of approach to illness narrative devised by Frank, in which patient stories are seen to conform to one of three generic types: the restitution narrative, the chaos narrative and the quest narrative. Frank does not seek to diminish the uniqueness of any individual illness story by limiting the choice to these three types of narrative, but suggests, rather, that these types be used as *listening devices* (1995: 76) by those whose job it is to hear what the sick have to say. By the same token, these devices might serve as a broad template for those whose task it is to analyse texts, but not to the extent that they are granted meta-status, which obscures or diminishes the importance of narrative action or the co-construction of spoken discourse.

NOTE

1 It is, in passing, interesting to speculate that the six phases of the doctor–patient consultation as described by Byrne and Long (see page 62) can be mapped onto Labov's model: phases 1 and 2 (in which the doctor establishes a relationship with the patient and attempts to discover their reason for the visit) corresponding to 'orientation'; phase 3 (in which the doctor carries out an examination of the patient) corresponding with the 'complicating action'; phase 4 (in which the doctor – or the doctor and patient – considers the condition) matching 'evaluation'; phase 5 (in which the doctor details treatment or further investigation) mapping onto the 'result', and phase 6 (the termination of consultation, and departure of patient into the world beyond the clinic) matching Labov's 'coda'.

Conclusion

In recent years discourses on the body have saturated public consciousness. As I write, an advertising billboard featuring the image of a naked woman, supine in a simulation of erotic excitement, dominates the main road near my house. This currently controversial image promoting a well-known perfume suggests a body project of sorts, in which sexuality and desire are 'projected' towards a population of consumers. In my newspaper I read that the model's body shape was photographically 'treated' to make her appear slimmer. Thus a body image is manipulated *post hoc* to sell a perfume which is also the name of a narcotic drug, just as other bodies are projected as ways of developing fitness and conserving one's health, and pressures are exerted on teenagers and children to conform to a particular body shape. All such body projects might be seen as metonymic of a pervasive 'normative' consciousness, from which deviance is marginalized in ever more subtle and insidious ways.

Simultaneously, the phenomenon known as information overload (result: 'the saturated self') has as one of its consequences a proliferation of proto- or quasi-medical conditions, syndromes and illnesses which progressively demand pathologizing and legitimizing. Only legitimized illnesses can be treated through the proper channels and provide individuals with the sick role needed for exemption from an over-onerous 'membership' of society. This process of legitimization has to be carried out through the rhetoric of medicalization. Illness continues to be reified, notably through the 'exogenous' attribution of illness to an invasive element ('germs'; 'bacteria'; a 'virus') which 'comes in' and 'takes over' the body (a corollary of 'spirit invasion' in indigenous cultures). In David Lan's play *Desire* and Boas' account of the shaman Quesalid, we learn that there is not a substantial divide between 'physical' and 'affective' (or spiritual) disorders: but we do not need to examine 'exotic' cultures to discover this. The Cartesian dichotomy has emphasized the mind/body split in the practice of Western medicine over the past 200 years, but it is a distinction which is currently being challenged by the practices of complementary therapies and an increasing consumer preference for holistic and Oriental medicines such as homeopathy, herbalism and acupuncture. Surgeries and clinics are employing complementary therapists as well as counsellors to administer the 'talking cure' while it is increasingly recognized that a GP might not be the best person for these listening and counselling tasks. He once was, perhaps (and the use of the masculine pronoun is deliberate), in the idealized community of the 'country doctor' which furnishes collective memory, but we wonder if he really was even then, or if that was not a conventionalized pastoral service complementing the spiritual ministry of the priesthood.

The culture of medicine has permeated the lives of people in previously unencountered ways. The advent of telemedicine, 'direct' forms of health care provision such as 'NHS Direct' appears, superficially, to be obscuring the traditional roles of doctor and patient. The introduction of nurse practitioners offers the promise of widening the remit of the power/knowledge basis that for years characterized the 'doctor-knows-best' school of thought, while within medical circles an apparent concern with 'patient centredness' and more specifically with 'shared decision making' has indicated that power imbalance and asymmetry are regarded (perhaps naïvely) by progressive medical thinkers as unfortunate relics from the bad old days, which need to be discarded. They look forward to a future in which health care providers and patients share common goals, forming a democratic alliance against disease and working together to provide the best choices for the patient, negotiated through a humanistic and caring medical system.

Meanwhile, the media have a perennial interest in all things medical. Television programmes relating to medicine, health care and specific illness conditions purport to reflect (or else themselves help generate) a pervasive obsession with health. The relationships between doctors, nurses and their patients are the staple fare of television soaps, while 'docusoaps' and documentaries plunder every permutation of medical discourse from the invasive camera in the bedroom of the volunteer dying (TV deaths are increasingly in vogue) to camera journeys around the recesses of the human body. Overwhelmingly, television explores illness issues in such a way as to emphasize the scare element with periodic examinations of apocalypse and plague, phenomena in which cinema too takes an interest. But medical authority is still an intrinsic part of the picture, as if, when all else is uncertain, in a world without God, there is at least the certainty of 'the doctor'. This certainty and faith has been undermined in recent years by reports of medical negligence, of doctors performing operations which they were not competent to do, of high levels of drug and alcohol addiction among doctors and of doctors murdering their patients. And yet such is the kudos and *mana* attached to the white coat and the stethoscope that many otherwise confident and assertive people become powerless and childlike the moment they walk into the doctor's surgery.

The role of discourse in all these subjects is paramount. Whether or not we take the view that nothing precedes discourse, or that 'nothing is knowable outside of language', there is no denying the role of language and discourse in helping to determine our perception of the world we live in and in turn describe. Our self-presentation takes place through our bodies – in spite of the proclaimed advent of the cyborg, or human-machine mutant, there is, after all, nothing else to 'self-present' *with*. Our bodies describe the story of our lives for better or for worse. But never before has embodiment been such a public affair. In direct proportion to calls for greater gender and age equality and tolerance of marked or marginalized bodies, has arisen an implicit standardization of body shape and health regimes, personified by glowing models of humanity on our billboards and television screens. At the same time, an increasingly medicalized point of view has become anchored in everyday talk about the body, health and illness. For instance, people generally have a far greater awareness of their own dietary requirements than they did a generation ago, whatever they choose to *do* about it. Internet access allows a knowledge base for further self-education on all aspects of health care. As indicated in the film *Lorenzo's Oil*, anyone with enough determination and resourcefulness can become an expert in the field of their own (or someone else's) illness, despite specialist knowledge becoming ever more specialized.

The ways in which discourses of the body, illness and medicine have arisen and continue to perpetuate themselves have, within the context of this book, been conducted through the study of metaphor and narrative. Metaphor sorts the conceptual categories through which the world is perceived, and narrative 'storifies' it for us. Metaphor likens every experience to another one, and, following Sontag's allegory that illness is another country, we learn to speak its language, and become all of us bilinguals in the language of health and the language of sickness. Both languages thrive on metaphor, but the world of the sick is inundated in it: and as we cast around for likenesses and similes through which to tell our stories, we restructure our illness experience from the perspective of the present. Only our unfolding lives take place in the present tense, and even they are subject to storification the moment that the present moment has passed. Everything known lies in the past, and everything is potential narrative. The use of narrative in examining the discourses of illness and of medicine is therefore crucial and reciprocal: the healthcare worker or doctor hears the patient's story and the patient gains insights into his or her own experience through the telling of that story. Whether or not the doctor listens has important consequences, and may determine whether or not that patient receives the care they need or some other kind of care and therapy.

We act out our lives through the discourses we make, language being first and foremost a species of action. Our descriptions of the world, of our place in it, and of our experiences, help determine our relationship to ourselves and to others. The study of these discourses, in relation to our bodies, our illnesses and our medical carers, provides us with a clearer understanding of who we are, and who we might become.

References

Agar, M., and Hobbs, J. (1982) 'Interpreting discourse: coherence and the analysis of ethnographic interviews', *Discourse Processes* 5: 1–32.

Ainsworth-Vaughn, N. (1998) *Claiming Power in Doctor–Patient Talk*. Oxford: Oxford University Press.

Aitkenhead, D. (1998) 'Before they say goodbye', *The Modern Review* 4 February 1998: 32–7

Andersen, C. E. (1994) 'The Case: another side of cancer', *Second Opinion* 19: 27–31.

Armstrong, D. (1983) *The Political Anatomy of the Body*. Cambridge: Cambridge University Press.

Armstrong, D. (1987) 'Bodies of knowledge: Foucault and the problems of human anatomy', in G. Scambler (ed.), *Sociological Theory and Medical Sociology*. London: Tavistock.

Arney, W. and Bergen, B. (1983) 'The anomaly, the chronic patient and the play of medical power', *Sociology of Health & Illness* 5 (1): 1–24.

Atkinson, P. (1981) *The Clinical Experience*. Farnborough: Gower.

Atkinson, P. (1995) *Medical Talk, Medical Work*. London: Sage.

Austin, J. (1962) *How to do things with words*. Cambridge, Mass: Harvard University Press.

Bakhtin, M. (1984) *Problems of Dostoevsky's Poetics*. Manchester: Manchester University Press.

Bal, M. (1985) *Narratology: Introduction to the Theory of Narrative*. Toronto: University of Toronto Press.

Baron, R. (1985) 'An introduction to medical phenomenology: "I can't hear you while I'm listening"', *Annals of Internal Medicine* 105: 606–11.

Barthes, R. (1972) *Mythologies*. London: Paladin.

Barthes, R. (1982) 'Introduction to the structural analysis of narratives', in S. Sontag (ed.), *A Barthes Reader*. London: Jonathan Cape.

Barthes, R. (1988) 'Introduction to the Structural Analysis of Narratives', in S. Sontag (ed.), *A Barthes Reader*. London: Cape.

Baudrillard, J. (1983) *Simulations*. New York: Semiotext(e).

Baudrillard, J. (1988) *Selected Writings*, (ed.) M. Poster. Stanford: Stanford University Press.

Bauman, R. and Sherzer, J. (1989) *Explorations in the Ethnography of Speaking*. 2nd edition. Cambridge: Cambridge University Press.

Bauman, Z. (1992) *Mortality, Immortality, and Other Life Strategies*. Stanford: Stanford University Press.

Beckman, H. and Frankel, R. (1984) 'The effect of physician behavior on the collection of data', *Annals of Internal Medicine* 101: 692–6.

Bell, A. (1991) *The Language of News in the Media*. Oxford: Blackwell.

Berger, A. A. (1997) *Narratives in Popular Culture, Media and Everyday Life.* Thousand Oaks, CA: Sage.

Berger, P. and Luckmann, T. (1967) *The Social Construction of Reality.* Harmondsworth: Penguin.

Billig, M. (1988) 'Social representation, objectification and anchoring: a rhetorical analysis', *Social Behaviour* 3: 1–16.

Billig, M. (1991) *Ideology and Opinions: Studies in Rhetorical Psychology.* London: Sage.

Billig, M. (1999a) 'Whose terms? Whose ordinariness? Rhetoric and ideology in conversation analysis', *Discourse and Society* 10: 543–58.

Billig, M. (1999b) 'Conversation analysis and the claims of naivety', *Discourse and Society* 10: 572–6.

Black, M. (1962) 'Metaphor', in M. Black (ed.), *Models and Metaphors.* Ithaca, NY: Cornell University Press.

Blaxter, M. (1983) 'The causes of disease: women talking', *Social Science & Medicine* 17 (2): 56–69.

Blaxter, M. (1990) *Health and Lifestyles.* London: Routledge.

Blaxter, M. (1993) 'Why do the victims blame themselves?' in A. Radley (ed.) *Worlds of Illness.* London: Routledge.

Blaxter, M. and Paterson, E. (1982) *Mothers and Daughters: A Three-Generational Study of Health Attitudes and Behaviour.* London: Heinemann.

Boas, F. (1930) 'The religion of the Kwakiutl', in *Columbia University Contributions to Anthropology*, Vol. 10, part II, pp. 1–41. New York: Columbia University Press.

Bourdieu, P. (1977) *Outline of a Theory of Practice.* Cambridge: Cambridge University Press.

Bourdieu, P. (1984) *Distinction: a Social Critique of the Judgement of Taste.* London: Routledge and Kegan Paul.

Brown, P. and Levinson, S. (1987) *Politeness: Some Universals in Language Usage.* Cambridge: Cambridge University Press.

Brown, G. and Yule, G. (1983) *Discourse Analysis.* Cambridge: Cambridge University Press.

Broyard, A. (1992) *Intoxicated by my Illness, and Other Writings on Life and Death.* New York: Clarkson N. Potter.

Bruner, J. (1990) *Acts of Meaning.* Cambridge, MA: Harvard University Press.

Byrne, P. and Long, B. (1976) *Doctors Talking to Patients.* London: DHSS.

Cameron, D., Frazer, E., Harvey, P., Rampton, B. and Richardson, K. (1992) *Researching Language: Issues of Power and Method.* London: Routledge.

Campbell, J. (1993) [1949] *The Hero with a Thousand Faces.* London: Fontana.

Cassell, E. (1976) 'Disease as an "it": concepts of disease revealed by patients' presentations of symptoms', *Social Science & Medicine* 10: 143–6.

Cassell, E. (1978) *The Healer's Art.* Harmondsworth: Penguin.

Charles, C., Gafni, A. and Whelan, T. (1997) 'Shared decision-making in the medical encounter: what does it mean? (Or it takes at least two to tango)', *Social Science & Medicine* 44: 681–92.

Charles, C., Redko, C., Whelan, T., Gafni, A. and Reyno, L. (1998) 'Doing nothing is no choice: lay constructions of treatment decision-making among women with early stage breast cancer', *Sociology of Health & Illness* 20 (1): 71–95.

Churchill, L. and Churchill, S. (1982) 'Storytelling in medical arenas: the art of self-determination', *Literature and Medicine* 1: 73–9.

Clifford, J. (1988) *The Predicament of Culture.* Cambridge, MA: Harvard University Press.

Clifford, J. (1997) *Routes: Travel and Translation in the Late Twentieth Century.* Cambridge, MA: Harvard University Press.

Cockx, L. (1989) 'Van placenta tot placebo: een medisch-antropologische verkenning', *Medische Antropologie* 1 (1): 4–20.

Cornwell, J. (1984) *Hard-Earned Lives.* London: Tavistock.

Cortazzi, M. (1993) *Narrative Analysis.* London: Falmer Press.

Coulthard, R. and Ashby, A. (1976) 'A linguistic description of doctor–patient interviews', in M. Wadsworth and D. Robinson (eds) *Studies in Everyday Medical Life.* London: Martin Robinson.

Coupland, J., Robinson, J. and Coupland, N. (1994) 'Frame negotiation in doctor–elderly patient consultations', *Discourse and Society* 5 (1): 89–124.

Coupland, N., Coupland, J. and Giles, H. (1991) *Language, Society and the Elderly.* Oxford: Blackwell.

Cowie, B. (1976) 'The cardiac patient's perception of his heart attack', *Social Science & Medicine* 10: 87–96.

Crawford, D. (2000) *The Invisible Enemy: the Natural History of Viruses.* Oxford: Oxford University Press.

Crystal, D. (2000) Letter to *The Independent*, 23 October 2000.

Debord, G. (1994) [1967] *Society of the Spectacle.* New York: Zone Books.

Diamond, J. (1998) *C: Because Cowards get Cancer Too....* London: Vermillion.

Diekema, D. (1989) 'Metaphors in the physician–patient relationship', *Soundings* 72 (1).

DiGiacomo, S. (1992) 'Metaphor as illness: postmodern dilemmas in the representation of body, mind and disorder', *Medical Anthropology* 14: 109–37.

Douglas, M. (1984) *Purity and Danger.* London: Ark.

Dreuihle, E. (1988) *Mortal Embrace: Living with AIDS.* New York: Hill and Wang.

Dreyfus, H. and Rabinow, P. (1982) *Michel Foucault: beyond Structuralism and Hermeneutics.* Brighton: Harvester.

Duranti, A. and Goodwin, C. (1992) (eds) *Rethinking Context: Language as an International Phenomenon.* Cambridge: Cambridge University Press.

Eco, U. (1990) *Travels in Hyperreality: Essays.* San Diego: Harcourt Brace Jovanovich.

Edwards, D. (1997) *Discourse and Cognition.* London: Sage.

Edwards, D. and Potter, J. (1992) *Discursive Psychology.* London: Sage.

Eisenberg, L. (1977) 'Disease and illness: distinctions between professional and popular ideas of sickness', *Culture, Medicine and Psychiatry* 1: 9–23.

Eliot, T. S. (1951) *Selected Essays.* London: Faber and Faber.

Elwyn, G. and Gwyn, R. (1998) 'Stories we hear and stories we tell: analysing talk in clinical practice', in T. Greenhalgh and B. Hurwitz (eds) *Narrative Based Medicine*, pp. 165–75. London: BMA.

Elwyn, G., Gwyn, R., Edwards, A. and Grol, R. (1999) 'Is shared decision making feasible in a consultation for a viral upper respiratory tract infection? Assessing the influence of patient expectations for antibiotics, using discourse analysis', *Health Expectations* 2 (2): 105–17.

Fairclough, N. (1989) *Language and Power.* London: Longman.

Fairclough, N. (1992) *Discourse and Social Change.* Cambridge: Polity Press.

Fairclough, N. (1995) *Media Discourse.* London: Arnold.

Featherstone, M. (1991) 'The body in consumer culture', in M. Featherstone, M. Hepworth and B. Turner (eds) *The Body: Social Process and Cultural Theory.* London: Sage.

Featherstone, M. and Hepworth, M. (1991) 'The mask of ageing and the postmodern life course,' in M. Featherstone, M. Hepworth and B. Turner (eds) *The Body: Social Process and Cultural Theory.* London: Sage.

Fernandez, J. (1974) 'The mission of metaphor in expressive culture', *Current Anthropology* 15 (2): 119–45.

Fisher, S. (1995) *Nursing Wounds: Nurse Practitioners, Doctors, Women Patients and the Negotiation of Meaning.* New Brunswick, NJ: Rutgers University Press.

Fisher, S. and Todd, A. D. (1983) *The Social Organization of Doctor–Patient Communication.* Washington, DC: Center for Applied Linguistics.

Foucault, M. (1972) *The Archaeology of Knowledge.* London: Tavistock.

Foucault, M. (1973) *The Birth of the Clinic.* London: Tavistock.

Foucault, M. (1977) *Discipline and Punish.* London: Allen Lane.

Fowler, R., Hodge, R., Kress, G. and Trew, A. (eds) (1979) *Language and Control.* London: Routledge and Kegan Paul.

Fox, N. (1993) *Postmodernism, Sociology and Health.* Buckingham: Open University Press.

Frank, A. (1991) 'For a sociology of the body: an analytical review', in M. Featherstone, M. Hepworth and B. Turner (eds) *The Body: Social Process and Cultural Theory.* London: Sage.

Frank, A. (1995) *The Wounded Storyteller.* Chicago: University of Chicago Press.

Frank, A. (1996) 'Reconciliatory alchemy: bodies, narratives and power', *Body & Society* 2 (3): 53–71.

Frankel, R. (1983) 'The laying of hand: aspects of gaze, touch and talk in medical encounter', in S. Fisher and A. Todd (eds) *The Social Organization of Doctor–Patient Communication.* Washington, DC: Center for Applied Linguistics.

French, M. (1998) *A Season in Hell.* London: Virago.

Friedson, E. (1970) *Professional Dominance: the Social Structure of Medical Care.* Chicago: Aldine.

Galtung, J. and Ruge, M. (1965) 'The structure of foreign news', *Journal of Peace Research* 2 (1): 64–91.

Geertz, C. (1983) *Local Knowledge: Further Essays in Interpretive Anthropology.* London: Fontana.

Geertz, C. (1988) *Works and Lives: the Anthropologist as Author.* Stanford, CA: Stanford University Press.

Gentner, D. and Jeziorski, M. (1993) [1979] 'The shift from metaphor to analogy in Western science', in A. Ortony (ed.), *Metaphor and Thought.* Cambridge: Cambridge University Press.

Gibbs, R. (1994) *The Poetics of Mind.* Cambridge: Cambridge University Press.

Goffman, E. (1959) *The Presentation of Self in Everyday Life.* Harmondsworth: Penguin.

Goffman, E. (1967) *Interaction Ritual: Essays in Face-to-face Behaviour.* London: Allen Lane.

Goffman, E. (1968) *Stigma: Notes on the Management of Spoiled Identity.* Harmondsworth: Penguin.

Goffman, E. (1974) *Frame Analysis.* New York: Harper and Row.

Goffman, E. (1983) 'The interaction order', *American Sociological Review* 48: 1–17.

Good, B. (1994) *Medicine, Rationality and Experience: an Anthropological Perspective.* Cambridge: Cambridge University Press.

Goodenough Report (1944) *Report of the Inter-Departmental Committee on Medical Schools.* London: HMSO.

Greenhalgh, P. and Hurwitz, B. (1999) 'Why study narrative?' in T. Greenhalgh and B. Hurwitz (eds) *Narrative Based Medicine.* London: BMA.

Greimas, A.-J. (1984) *Structural Semantics.* Lincoln: University of Nebraska Press.

Greimas, A.-J. (1987) *On Meaning: Selected Writings in Semiotic Theory.* London: Frances Pinter.

Groddeck, G. (1950) *The Book of the It.* London: Vision.

Guggenbühl-Craig, A. (1980) *Eros on Crutches: On the Nature of the Psychopath.* Dallas: Spring Publications.

Gumperz, J. and Hymes, D. (1972) (eds) *Directions in Sociolinguistics: the Ethnography of Communication*. New York: Holt, Rinehart and Winston.

Gwyn, R. (1997) 'The voicing of illness: narrative and metaphor in accounts of illness experience'. Unpublished PhD thesis, Cardiff University.

Gwyn, R. (1999a) '"Captain of my own ship": metaphor and the discourse of chronic illness', in L. Cameron and G. Low (eds) *Researching and Applying Metaphor*. Cambridge: Cambridge University Press.

Gwyn, R. (1999b) '"Killer bugs", "silly buggers" and "politically correct pals": competing discourses in health scare reporting', *Health* 3 (3): 335–45.

Gwyn, R. (2000) '"Really unreal": narrative evaluation and the objectification of experience', *Narrative Inquiry* 10 (2): 313–40.

Gwyn, R. and Elwyn, G. J. (1999) 'When is a shared decision not (quite) a shared decision? Negotiating preferences in general practice discourse', *Social Science & Medicine* 49: 437–47.

Habermas, J. (1972) *Knowledge and Human Interest*. London: Heinemann.

Hak, T. (1999) '"Text" and "con-text": talk bias in studies of health care work', in S. Sarangi and C. Roberts (eds) *Talk, Work and Institutional Order*. Berlin: Mouton de Gruyter.

Halliday, M. (1978) *Language as Social Semiotic*. London: Edward Arnold.

Halliday, M. (1985) *An Introduction to Functional Grammar*. London: Edward Arnold.

Hawkes, T. (1972) *Metaphor*. London: Methuen.

Hawkes, T. (1977) *Structuralism and Semiotics*. London: Methuen.

Heath, C. (1992) 'The delivery and reception of diagnosis in the general-practice consultation', in P. Drew and J. Heritage (eds) *Talk at Work: Interaction in Institutional Settings*. Cambridge: Cambridge University Press.

Helman, C. (1978) '"Feed a cold, starve a fever": folk models of infection in an English suburban community, and their relation to medical treatment', *Culture, Medicine and Psychiatry* 2: 107–37.

Helman, C. (1981) 'Disease versus illness in general practice', *Journal of the Royal College of General Practitioners* 31: 548.

Helman, C. (1984) *Culture, Health and Illness*. Oxford: Butterworth-Heinemann.

Helman, C. (1987) 'Heart disease and the cultural construction of time: the Type A behaviour pattern as a Western culture-bound syndrome', *Social Science & Medicine* 25 (9): 969–79.

Herzlich, C. (1973) *Health and Illness*. London: Academic Press.

Herzlich, C. and Pierret, J. (1985) 'The social construction of the patient: patients and illnesses in other ages', *Social Science & Medicine* 20 (2): 145–51.

Herzlich, C. and Pierret, J. (1987) *Illness and Self in Society*. Baltimore, MD: Johns Hopkins University Press.

Hillman, J. (1983) *Healing Fiction*. Woodstock, CT: Spring Publications.

Hodge, R. and Kress, G. (1993) *Language as Ideology*. 2nd edition. London: Routledge.

Hodgetts, D. and Chamberlain, K. (1999) 'Medicalization and the depiction of lay people in television health documentary', *Health* 3 (3): 317–34.

Holmes, J. (1997) 'Women language and identity', *Journal of Sociolinguistics* 1 (2): 195–223.

Holquist, M. (1990) *Dialogism: Bakhtin and his World*. London: Routledge.

Hunter, K. (1991) *Doctors' Stories: the Narrative Structure of Medical Knowledge*. Princeton, NJ: Princeton University Press.

Ibba, M. (1991) 'Metaphors we are healed by: on the use of metaphors in medical language', in *Georgetown University Round Table on Languages and Linguistics*. Washington, DC: Georgetown University Press.

Ikeda, D. (1988) *Unlocking the Mysteries of Birth and Death: Buddhism in the Contemporary World*. London: Macdonald.

Illich, I. (1976) *Limits to Medicine: Medical Nemesis: the Expropriation of Health*. London: Marion Boyars.

Jameson, F. (1987) 'Foreword' to A.-J. Greimas, *On Meaning: Selected Writings in Semiotic Theory*. London: Frances Pinter.

Johnson, M. (1987) *The Body in the Mind*. Chicago: University of Chicago Press.

Jones, R. (1997) 'Marketing the damaged self: the construction of identity in advertisements directed towards people with HIV/AIDS', *Journal of Sociolinguistics* 1 (3): 393–418.

Josselson, R. and Lieblich, A. (eds) (1993) *The Narrative Study of Lives*, Vol. 1. London: Sage.

Jung, C. G. (1983) [1961] *Memories, Dreams, Reflections*. London: Fontana.

Katz, A. and Shotter, J. (1996) 'Hearing the patient's voice: towards a social poetics in diagnostic interviews', *Social Science & Medicine* 43: 919–31.

Kerby, A. (1991) *Narrative and the Self*. Bloomington: Indiana University Press.

Kierkegaard, S. (1987) *Either/Or Part II*. Princeton, NJ: Princeton University Press.

Kleinman, A. (1988) *The Illness Narratives*. New York: Basic Books.

Knudsen, S. (1999) *From Metaphor to Fact*. Copenhagen: Samfundslitteratur.

Kress, G. (1989) *Linguistic Processes in Sociocultural Practice*. Oxford: Oxford University Press.

Kress, G. and Fowler, R. (1979) 'Interviews', in R. Fowler, R. Hodge, G. Kress and A. Trew (eds) *Language and Control*. London: Routledge and Kegan Paul.

Kuhn, T. (1993) [1979] 'Metaphor in science', in A. Ortony (ed.), *Metaphor and Thought*. Cambridge: Cambridge University Press.

Labov, W. (1972) *Language in the Inner City*. Oxford: Blackwell.

Labov, W. and Waletsky, J. (1967) 'Narrative analysis: oral versions of personal experience', in J. Helms (ed.), *Essays on the Verbal and Visual Arts*. Seattle: University of Washington Press.

Lakoff, G. (1987) *Women, Fire and Dangerous Things*. Chicago: University of Chicago Press.

Lakoff, G. (1993) 'The contemporary theory of metaphor', in A. Ortony (ed.), *Metaphor and Thought*. Cambridge: Cambridge University Press.

Lakoff, G. and Johnson, M. (1980) *Metaphors We Live By*. Chicago: University of Chicago Press.

Lan, D. (1990) *Desire and Other Plays*. London: Faber and Faber.

Lasch, C. (1991) *The Culture of Narcissism*. New York: Norton.

Lerner, G. (1991) 'On the syntax of sentences-in-progress', *Language in Society* 20: 441–58.

LeShan, L. (1977) *You Can Fight for Your Life: Emotional Factors in the Causation of Cancer*. New York: M. Evans.

Lévi-Strauss, C. (1967) *Structural Anthropology*. Harmondsworth: Penguin.

Lupton, D. (1994a) *Medicine as Culture*. London: Sage.

Lupton, D. (1994b) *Moral Threats and Dangerous Desires*. London: Taylor and Francis.

Lupton, D. (1997) 'Consumerism, reflexivity and the medical encounter', *Social Science & Medicine* 45: 373–81.

Lyotard, J.-F. (1984) *The Postmodern Condition: a Report on Knowledge*. Manchester: Manchester University Press.

Macleod, M. (1993) 'On knowing the patient: experiences of nurses undertaking care', in A. Radley (ed.), *Worlds of Illness*. London: Routledge.

Mair, M. (1976) 'Metaphors for living', *Nebraska Symposium on Motivation*. Lincoln: University of Nebraska Press.

Margalith, I. and Shapiro, A. (1997) 'Anxiety and patient participation in clinical decision-making: the case of patients with ureteral calculi', *Social Science & Medicine* 45: 419–27.

Maynard, D. W. (1992) 'On clinicians co-implicating recipients' perspective in the delivery of diagnostic news', in P. Drew and J. Heritage (eds) *Talk at Work: Interaction in Institutional Settings*. Cambridge: Cambridge University Press.

Meek, J. (2001) 'They reproduce, but they don't eat, breathe or excrete', *London Review of Books* 23 (6): 17–18.

Mills, S. (1997) *Discourse*. London: Routledge.

Mishler, E. (1984) *The Discourse of Medicine: Dialectics of Medical Interviews*. Norwood, NJ: Ablex.

Mishler, E. (1986) *Research Interviewing*. Cambridge, MA: Harvard University Press.

Montgomery, S. L. (1991) 'Codes and combat in biomedical discourse', *Science as Culture* 2 (3): 341–91.

Moscovici, S. (1984) 'The phenomenon of social representations', in R. Farr and S. Moscovici (eds) *Social Representations*. Cambridge: Cambridge University Press.

Moscovici, S. and Hewstone, M. (1983) 'Social representations and social explanations: from the "naive" to the "amateur" scientist', in M. Hewstone (ed.), *Attribution Theory: Social and Functional Extensions*. Oxford: Blackwell.

Mulkay, M. (1991) *Sociology of Science: a Sociological Pilgrimage*. Milton Keynes: Open University Press.

Paget, M. A. (1983) 'On the work of talk: studies in misunderstandings', in S. Fisher and A. Todd (eds) *The Social Organization of Doctor–Patient Communication*. Washington, DC: Center for Applied Linguistics.

Paget, M. A. (1995) 'Performing the text', in J. van Maanen (ed.), *Representation in Ethnography*. Thousand Oaks, CA: Sage.

Parsons, E. and Atkinson, P. (1992) 'Lay constructions of genetic risk', *Sociology of Health and Illness* 14: 437–55.

Parsons, T. (1951) *The Social System*. Glencoe: The Free Press.

Parsons, T. (1958) 'Definitions of health and illness in the light of American values and social structure', in E. Jaco (ed.), *Patients, Physicians and Illness*. Glencoe: The Free Press.

Peräkylä, A. (1995) *AIDS Counselling: Institutional Interaction and Clinical Practice*. Cambridge: Cambridge University Press.

Pill, R. and Stott, N. (1982) 'Concepts of illness causation and responsibility: some preliminary data from a sample of working-class mothers', *Social Science & Medicine* 16: 43–52.

Pill, R. and Stott, N. (1985) 'Preventive procedures and practices among working class women: new data and fresh insights', *Social Science & Medicine* 21: 975–83.

Pill, R., Jones-Elwyn, G. and Stott, N. (1989) 'Opportunistic health promotion: quantity or quality?' *Journal of the Royal College of General Practitioners* 39: 196–200.

Porter, R. (1997) *The Greatest Benefit to Mankind*. London: HarperCollins.

Potter, J. (1996) *Representing Reality*. London: Sage.

Potter, J. and Wetherell, M. (1987) *Discourse and Social Psychology*. London: Sage.

Propp, V. (1968) [1928] *Morphology of the Folktale*. Austin: University of Texas Press.

Radley, A. (1993a) 'The role of metaphor in adjustment to chronic illness', in A. Radley (ed.), *Worlds of Illness*. London: Routledge.

Radley, A. (1993b) *Worlds of Illness*. London: Routledge.

Radley, A. (1994) *Making Sense of Illness.* London: Sage.

Radley, A. and Billig, M. (1996) 'Accounts of health and illness: dilemmas and representations', *Sociology of Health & Illness* 18: 220–40.

Rhodes, T. and Shaughnessy R. (1990) 'Compulsory screening: advertising AIDS in Britain, 1986–89', *Policy and Politics* 18 (1): 55–61.

Richards, I. A. (1936) *The Philosophy of Rhetoric.* London: Oxford University Press.

Ricoeur, P. (1980) 'Narrative time', *Critical Inquiry* 7 (1): 169–90.

Riessman, C. (1993) *Narrative Analysis.* Newbury Park, CA: Sage.

Rogers, W. S. (1991) *Explaining Health and Illness: an Exploration of Diversity.* Hemel Hempstead: Harvester Wheatsheaf.

Rosenwald, G. C. and Ochberg, R. L. (1992) 'Introduction: life stories, cultural politics, and self-understanding', in G. C. Rosenwald and R. L. Ochberg (eds) *Storied Lives: the Cultural Politics of Self-understanding.* New Haven, CT: Yale University Press.

Sackett, D., Scott Richardson, W., Rosenberg, W. and Haynes, R. (1997) *Evidence Based Medicine: How to Practice and Teach EBM.* New York: Churchill Livingstone.

Sacks, H. (1992) *Lectures on Conversation.* 2 volumes, ed. G. Jefferson. Oxford: Blackwell.

Sacks, H., Schegloff, E. and Jefferson, G. (1974) 'A simplest systematics for the analysis of turn-taking in conversation', *Language* 50: 696–735.

Sacks, O. (1985) *The Man Who Mistook His Wife for a Hat.* London: Duckworth.

Sarangi, S. and Coulthard, M. (eds) (2000) *Discourse and Social Life.* Harlow: Longman.

Sarangi, S. and Roberts, C. (eds) (1999a) *Talk, Work and Institutional Order.* Berlin: Mouton de Gruyter.

Sarangi, S. and Roberts, C. (1999b) 'The dynamics of interactional and institutional orders in work-related settings', in S. Sarangi and C. Roberts (eds) *Talk, Work and Institutional Order.* Berlin: Mouton de Gruyter.

Schegloff, E. (1997) 'Whose text? Whose context?' *Discourse and Society* 8: 165–87.

Schegloff, E. (1998) 'Reply to Wetherell', *Discourse and Society* 9: 413–16.

Schegloff, E. (1999a) 'Schegloff's texts' as "Billig's data": a critical reply', *Discourse and Society* 10: 558–72.

Schegloff, E. (1999b) 'Naivete vs sophistication or discipline vs self-indulgence: a rejoinder to Billig', *Discourse and Society* 10: 577–82.

Schegloff, E. and Sacks, H. (1973) 'Opening up closings', *Semiotica* 8: 165–87.

Scheper-Hughes, N. (1984) 'Infant mortality and infant care: cultural and economic constraints on nurturing in northeast Brazil', *Social Science & Medicine* 19 (5): 533–46.

Scheper-Hughes, N. and Lock, M. (1986) 'Speaking "truth" to illness: metaphors, reification, and a pedagogy for patients', *Medical Anthropology Quarterly* 17 (5): 137–40.

Scheper-Hughes, N. and Lock, M. (1987) 'The mindful body: a prolegomenon to future work in medical anthropology', *Medical Anthropology Quarterly* 18 (1): 6–41.

Scholes, R. and Kellogg, R. (1966) *The Nature of Narrative.* New York: Oxford University Press.

Schutz, A. (1962) *Collected Papers I: the Problem of Social Reality.* The Hague: Martinus Nijhoff.

Schweitzer, A. (1990) [1933] *Out of My Life and Thought: an Autobiography.* New York: Henry Holt.

Scollon, R. (2000) 'Methodological interdiscursivity: an ethnographic understanding of unfinalisability', in S. Sarangi and M. Coulthard (eds) *Discourse and Social Life.* Harlow: Longman.

Shilling, C. (1993) *The Body and Social Theory*. London: Sage.

Showalter, E. (1997) *Hystories: Hysterical Epidemics and Modern Culture*. London: Picador.

Silverman, D. (1987) *Communication and Medical Practice*. London: Sage.

Silverman, D. (1997) *Discourses of Counselling: HIV Counselling as Social Interaction*. London: Sage.

Silverman, D. (1998) *Harvey Sacks: Social Science and Conversation Analysis*. New York: Oxford University Press.

Smith, A. (ed.) (1990) *The British Medical Association Complete Family Health Encyclopedia*. London: Dorling Kindersley.

Sontag, S. (1991) *Illness as Metaphor/AIDS and its Metaphors*. Harmondsworth: Penguin.

Steen, G. (1994) *Understanding Metaphor in Literature*. London: Longman.

Stein, H. F. (1990) *American Medicine as Culture*. Boulder, CO: Westview.

Stewart, M., Brown, J., Weston, W., McWhinney, I., McWilliam, C. and Freeman, T. (1995) *Patient Centred Medicine: Transforming the Clinical Method*. Thousand Oaks, CA: Sage.

Stibbe, A. (1996) 'The metaphorical construction of illness in Chinese culture',*Journal of Asian Pacific Communication* 7 (3/4): 177–88.

Stott, N. (1983) *Primary Health Care: Bridging the Gap between Theory and Practice*. Berlin: Springer-Verlag.

Strong, P. (1979) *The Ceremonial Order of the Clinic*. London: Routledge.

Strong, P. (1990) 'Epidemic psychology: a model', *Sociology of Health & Illness* 13 (3): 249–59.

Stubbs, M. (1983) *Discourse Analysis: the Sociolinguistic Analysis of Natural Language*. Oxford: Blackwell.

Ten Have, P. (1989) 'The consultation as a genre', in B. Torode (ed.), *Text and Talk as Social Practice*. Dordrecht and Providence, RI: Foris Publications.

Toolan, M. J. (1988) *Narrative: a Critical Linguistic Introduction*. New York: Routledge.

Treichler, P., Frankel, R., Kramarae, C., Zoppi, K. and Beckman, H. (1984) 'Problem and problems: power relationships in a medical encounter', in C. Kramarae, M. Shultz and W. M. O'Barr (eds) *Language and Power*. London: Sage.

Tulloch, J. and Lupton, D. (1997) *Television, AIDS and Risk: a Cultural Studies Approach to Health Communication*. St Leonards, NSW: Allen and Unwin.

Turner, B. (1984) *The Body and Society*. Oxford: Blackwell.

Turner, B. (1987) *Medical Power and Social Knowledge*. London: Sage.

Valabrega, J. P. (1962) *La Relation Thérapeutique: Malade et Médecin*. Paris: Flammarion.

Van der Geest, S. and Whyte, S. (1989) 'The charm of medicines: metaphors and metonyms,' *Medical Anthropology Quarterly* 3 (4): 345–67.

Van Dijk, T. A. (1987) *Communicating Racism: Ethnic Prejudice in Thought and Talk*. London: Sage.

Vestergaard, T. and Schrøder, K. (1985) *The Language of Advertising*. Oxford: Blackwell.

Vico, G. (1968) [1744] *The New Science*, trans. T. G. Bergin and M. H. Fisch. Ithaca, NY: Cornell University Press.

Vidal, G. (2000) 'Discourses of the unsayable: Health care professionals' representations of death and dying.' Unpublished PhD thesis, Cardiff University.

West, C. and Frankel, R. (1991) 'Miscommunication in medicine', in N. Coupland, H. Giles and J. Wiemann (eds) *'Miscommunication' and Problematic Talk*. Newbury Park, CA: Sage.

Wetherell, M. (1998) 'Positioning and interpretative repertoires: conversation analysis and post-structuralism in dialogue', *Discourse and Society* 9 (3): 387–412.

Wetherell, M. and Potter, J. (1992) *Mapping the language of racism*. London: Harvester Wheatsheaf.

White, A. (1993) *Carnival, Hysteria and Writing: Collected Essays and Autobiography*. Oxford: Clarendon Press.

Wilkinson, S and Kitzinger, C. (2000) 'Thinking differently about thinking positive: a discursive approach to cancer patients' talk', *Social Science & Medicine* 50: 797–811.

Williams, G. (Gareth) (1984) 'The genesis of chronic illness: narrative reconstruction', *Sociology of Health & Illness* 6 (2): 175–200.

Williams, G. (Glyn) (1999) *French Discourse Analysis; the Method of Post-structuralism*. London: Routledge.

Williams, R. (1990) *A Protestant Legacy: Attitudes to Death and Illness among Older Aberdonians*. Oxford: Oxford University Press.

Williams, S. and Calnan, M. (1996) *Modern Medicine: Lay Perspectives and Experiences*. London: UCL Press.

Williamson, J. (1989) 'Every virus tells a story', in E. Carter and S. Watney (eds) *Taking liberties: AIDS and Cultural Politics*. London: Serpent's Tail.

Wolfson, N. (1976) 'Speech events and natural speech: some implications for socio-linguistic methodology', *Language in Society* 5: 189–209.

Young, K. (1987) *Taleworlds and Storyrealms: The Phenomenology of Narrative*. Dordrecht: Martinus Nijhoff.

Young, K. (1989) 'Narrative embodiments: enclaves of the self in the realm of medicine', in J. Shotter and K. Gergen (eds) *Texts of Identity*. London: Sage.

Zheng Wei-da (1994) *Zhong yi zhi liao zhong liu jing yan* [The Experience of Curing Cancer with Chinese Medicine]. Beijing: Zhong Guo Yi Yue Ke Ji Publishing.

Zola, I. K. (1972) 'Medicine as an institution of social control', *Sociological Review* 20 (4): 487–504.

Zulaika, J. (1988) *Basque Violence: Metaphor and Sacrament*. Reno and Las Vegas: University of Nevada Press.

Index